"An outstanding contribution to the history of the Bible's reception. This book is a rich resource of writings from women who were an integral part of the tapestry of nineteenth-century biblical interpretation. Joshua and Judges harbor some of the Bible's more troubling texts, and it makes for fascinating reading to follow the varieties of responses that these interpreters offer to readers of their own times. Skillfully constructed and lucidly presented, *Women of War, Women of Woe* succeeds in both informing and provoking inquiry regarding the nature and practice of biblical interpretation."

— David M. Gunn
Texas Christian University

"No 'archetypal woman interpreter' here — this collection highlights the diversity in nineteenth-century women's biblical interpretation. Edited with respect and love, its recovery work invites readers into conversation with interpretive foremothers and often difficult biblical texts. Insightful editorial commentary and study questions further the discussion, challenging assumed norms and inspiring a new generation to the ongoing interpretive task."

— Lissa M. Wray Beal
*Providence University College
and Theological Seminary*

Women of War, Women of Woe

Joshua and Judges through the Eyes
of Nineteenth-Century Female Biblical Interpreters

Edited by

Marion Ann Taylor and Christiana de Groot

WILLIAM B. EERDMANS PUBLISHING COMPANY
GRAND RAPIDS, MICHIGAN

© 2016 Marion Ann Taylor and Christiana de Groot
All rights reserved

Published 2016 by
Wm. B. Eerdmans Publishing Co.
2140 Oak Industrial Drive N.E., Grand Rapids, Michigan
49505

Library of Congress Cataloging-in-Publication Data

Names: Taylor, Marion Ann, editor.
Title: Women of war, women of woe : Joshua and Judges through the eyes of nineteenth-century female biblical interpreters / edited by Marion Ann Taylor and Christiana de Groot.
Description: Grand Rapids, Michigan : Eerdmans Publishing Company, 2016.
Identifiers: LCCN 2015050542 | ISBN 9780802873026 (pbk. : alk. paper)
Subjects: LCSH: Bible. Joshua — Feminist criticism — History — 19th century. |
Bible. Judges — Feminist criticism — History — 19th century.
Classification: LCC BS1295.52 .W66 2016 | DDC 222/.20608209034 — dc23
LC record available at http://lccn.loc.gov/2015050542

www.eerdmans.com

Contents

Preface	ix
Introduction: Women and War	1

1. Rahab   19

Sarah Ewing Hall: *A Sanitized Rahab*	21
Susanna Haswell Rowson: *Is Lying Always Wrong?*	25
Sarah Hale: *Redeeming Rahab*	30
Cecil Frances (Fanny) Alexander: *From Scarlet Thread to Blood Drops*	33
Charlotte Maria Tucker: *The Sign of the Cord*	36
Etty Woosnam: *True Conversion*	41
Leigh Norval: *Daring to Be Different*	44
Josephine Elizabeth Butler: *The Saving Shelter of the Home*	47
Elizabeth Cady Stanton: *The Question of Motives*	51

2. Achsah, Caleb's Daughter   55

Lydia: *Achsah Spiritually Considered*	57
Grace Aguilar: *Achsah and the Age of Chivalry*	62
Charlotte Maria Tucker: *The Hebrew Daughter's Prayer*	67
Elizabeth Cady Stanton: *Assertiveness Training*	68
Marianne Farningham: *Giving Good Gifts*	70

3. Deborah — 75

- Grace Aguilar: *Superwoman* — 77
- Clara Balfour: *Redefining Femininity* — 85
- Barbara Kellison: *Helpmeet and Head* — 91
- Julia McNair Wright: *Knowledge Is Power* — 93
- Harriet Beecher Stowe: *An Inspired Poet* — 101
- Elizabeth Baxter: *An Imperfect, But Useful Woman* — 105
- Clara B. Neyman: *Genius Knows No Sex* — 111

4. Jael — 114

- Sarah Ewing Hall: *Jael's Masculine Resolution and Cruelty* — 116
- Mary Cornwallis: *Using the Only Means in Her Power* — 119
- Eliza R. Stansbury Steele: *A Mother's Love* — 121
- Eliza Smith: *The Worst Woman Ever* — 129
- Emily Owen: *Jael: A Heroine?* — 132
- Constance de Rothschild and Annie de Rothschild: *A True Hebrew Woman at Heart* — 135
- Harriet Beecher Stowe: *The Tiger, Tracked, Snared, and Caught* — 138
- Elizabeth Jane Whately: *God's Executioner* — 141
- Etty Woosnam: *Unsexing Jael and Fighting Demon Drink* — 143
- Anne Mercier: *Deborah Was Wrong about Jael* — 147
- M.G.: *Nailing Sin to the Cross* — 149
- Elizabeth Cady Stanton: *Cold-Blooded Fiend* — 152

5. Jephthah's Daughter — 155

- Caroline Howard Gilman: *Obedient unto Death* — 157
- Sarah Ewing Hall: *A Child Protests: A Mother Listens* — 162
- Mary Anne Schimmelpenninck: *It's All about Translation* — 164
- Susanna Rowson: *The American Dream Sacrificed* — 166
- Eliza R. Stansbury Steele: *Maid of Gilead, Fare Thee Well* — 168
- Adelia C. Graves: *Her Life Bought Our Freedom* — 174

Contents

Rose Terry Cooke: *Cursed Above All Women*	191
Cecil Frances Alexander: *Saintly Sacrifice*	194
Leigh Norval: *Like Father, Like Daughter*	197
Elizabeth Cady Stanton: *A Woman in the "No-Name Series"*	198
Louisa Southworth: *Only a Girl*	200

6. Manoah's Wife — 203

Grace Aguilar: *Concealing Your Superiority*	205
Mary Elizabeth Beck: *Drink Milk Not Beer*	211
Edith M. Dewhurst: *Nameless But Known*	216
M.G.: *Saintly Mothers*	219
Clara B. Neyman: *Demythologizing the Angel*	225
Elizabeth Cady Stanton: *Mrs. Manoah Doe*	228

7. Delilah — 231

Mary Cornwallis: *A Cautionary Tale*	232
Sarah Hale: *Samson the Traitor*	234
Harriet Beecher Stowe: *Delilah the Destroyer*	236
Ella Wheeler Wilcox: *The Road to Sweet Hell*	240
Clara B. Neyman: *The Double Standard*	242

8. The Levite's Concubine — 244

Mary Cornwallis: *Abused to Death*	246
Josephine Butler: *The Weak and Prostrate Figure Lying at Our Door*	248
Josephine Butler: *Cold Dead Hands upon Our Threshold*	253

Bibliography	259
Index of Names and Subjects	268
Index of Scripture	276

Preface

This book is part of a larger project that seeks to fill the painful lacuna of missing female voices in the history of biblical interpretation. The initial collection of nineteenth-century women's writings on the female figures in Joshua and Judges was to be included in a book on nineteenth-century women's writings on the women in the Bible. However, when it was discovered that the numbers of nineteenth-century women who published on women in the Bible are in the hundreds, the scope of the original book was limited to the book of Genesis. In 2006, Baylor University Press published *Let Her Speak for Herself*, a collection of nineteenth-century women writing on women in Genesis.

This current book features the writings of nineteenth-century women on the female figures in Joshua and Judges. Marion Taylor and Christiana de Groot compiled this collection of writings. Each summer and during our respective sabbaticals for the past six years, we read nineteenth-century interpretations of the stories of the women found in the books of Joshua and Judges. The Taylor cottage on Eagle Lake in Northern Ontario, with the sounds of loons and bullfrogs in the background, provided an inspiring venue for visiting with our foremothers.

We are profoundly grateful for the tangible and intangible support of family, friends, colleagues and institutions. The commitment to supporting scholarship at the institutions where we teach, Wycliffe College at the University of Toronto and Calvin College in Grand Rapids, is greatly appreciated. Our students have heard us talk about nineteenth-century women and their interpretations in our various classes, and their thoughtful responses on selections from this book have been a valuable resource and encouragement. We want to especially thank Christine Smaller, Heather Weir, Brian German, Miriam Diephouse MacMillan, and Sophia Chen for their helpful feedback and practical work of scanning, editing and compiling a bibliography. The students in Marion Taylor's class, "Women Interpreters," and Christiana de Groot's class, "When Women Read the Old Testament," test drove early drafts of many of the chapters and deserve special recognition. Dr. Thomas Power, the theological librarian at the Graham Library, is to be applauded for his generous support and practical help during the research and writing stages of this book.

The Canadian Society of Biblical Studies and the Society of Biblical Literature have provided excellent venues for presenting papers on nineteenth-century writings on the women in Joshua and Judges. Our colleagues' comments provided insight and clarity, and our volume is stronger because of their contributions.

We are especially thankful for a generous grant from the Reid Trust and for several earlier Lilly theological grants that funded research on the recovery of forgotten nineteenth-century interpreters of the Bible.

Our most profound gratitude we reserve for our foremothers; those many nineteenth-century women whose writings challenged, inspired, and encouraged us. Our lives are richer because of their commitment to put their thoughts on paper, and we trust that your lives will also be enriched as you read this volume.[1]

---

1. Added biblical citations in footnotes are placed in square brackets.

INTRODUCTION

Women and War: Nineteenth-Century Women Interpreters of the Women in Joshua and Judges

"They Being Dead, Yet Speak"

In 1890 Edith Dewhurst authored a book as a resource for women who taught other women, and titled it *They Being Dead, Yet Speak.*[1] She believed that women in Scripture had much to teach contemporary women. Dewhurst considered women apt interpreters, teachers, and students of the Bible and felt that she herself had insight into the meaning of Scripture that was worth passing on. Dewhurst's convictions about women's ability to learn, interpret, teach, and proclaim Scripture have been contested over the years, but we are among those who applaud the accomplishments of women who wrote, taught, and learned in resistance to the norms of society. We too have found that in spite of the cultural and historical distance between us and the women in Scripture and in the nineteenth century, our common humanity shines through. Their hopes and struggles resonate with our own. This is not to suggest that there is always solidarity between their interpretations and our own. Sometimes their particular agendas and assumptions result in readings that are extraordinary. "Wow!" one reader of nineteenth-century women writers exclaimed, "Nineteenth-century women thought this!"[2]

Reading the biblical texts with nineteenth-century women is a very rich experience. It illuminates the biblical texts, sheds light on the lives of the authors, recovers a neglected chapter of reception history, and helps us under-

---

1. Edith M. Dewhurst, *"They Being Dead, Yet Speak": Outlines for Mothers' Meetings and Women's Bible Classes,* second series of "Women of the Old Testament" (London: Marshall Bros., 1890).

2. Christine Smaller, a student in Marion Taylor's class, Women Interpreters of Scripture, 2012. Used with permission.

stand and apply Scripture in our present context. Reading what nineteenth-century interpreters say about women, war, and violence in the books of Joshua and Judges is especially significant today as we engage these same issues today. Jimmy Carter's recent book, *A Call to Action: Women, Religion, Violence, and Power*,[3] surveys the worldwide phenomenon of women's oppression and religion's role in perpetuating or eradicating it. The conquest and settlement narratives were relevant in the nineteenth century and continue to address our time.

The convictions driving our book are shared by many scholars today who are turning to the past for help with the task of reading Scripture. This realization is reflected in the decision of the editorial committee of the *Women's Bible Commentary: Twentieth-Anniversary Edition* to expand what constitutes the meaning of biblical texts. "The meaning of the Bible is not just 'what it meant' when it was composed, if ever we could fully reconstruct that. Nor is it simply 'what it means' now, as our contemporary societies engage the Bible. What the Bible means and the effects it has had include the entire history of its reception and engagement."[4] So in addition to commentaries on individual books of the Bible, this latest edition of the *Women's Bible Commentary* includes essays on the history of interpretation of such women as Eve, Miriam, Jael, Judith, and Mary. The importance of recovering forgotten female voices in the history of the Bible's reception is also reflected in a growing number of publications on individual books of the Bible,[5] specific subjects,[6] and the women interpreters of the Bible themselves.[7] We too are

---

3. New York: Simon & Schuster, 2014.

4. Carol A. Newsom, Sharon H. Ringe, and Jacqueline E. Lapsley, eds., *Women's Bible Commentary: Twentieth-Anniversary Edition* (Louisville: Westminster John Knox Press, 2012), xxiii.

5. See, for example, David Gunn's commentary on Judges, which focuses on the book's reception history and includes a sampling of interpretations by both male and female writers (*Judges* [Oxford: Blackwell, 2005]), and the collection of nineteenth-century women's writings in Marion Ann Taylor and Heather E. Weir, *Let Her Speak for Herself: Nineteenth-Century Women Writing on Women in Genesis* (Waco, Tex.: Baylor University Press, 2006).

6. Joy A. Schroeder has included the voices of women in her important works, *Deborah's Daughters: Gender, Politics, and Biblical Interpretation* (New York: Oxford University Press, 2014); and *Dinah's Lament: The Biblical Legacy of Sexual Violence in Christian Interpretation* (Minneapolis: Fortress, 2007). *Strangely Familiar: Protofeminist Interpretations of Patriarchal Biblical Texts*, ed. Nancy Calvert-Koyzis and Heather E. Weir (Atlanta: Society of Biblical Literature, 2009), showcases essays featuring women's interpretive work on biblical texts. See also Marion Ann Taylor, "The Psalms outside the Pulpit: Applications of the Psalms by Women of the Nineteenth Century," in *Interpreting the Psalms for Teaching and Preaching*, ed. Herbert W. Bateman IV and D. Brent Sandy (St. Louis, Mo.: Chalice, 2010), 219-32, 284-86.

7. Marion Ann Taylor and Agnes Choi, eds., *Handbook of Women Biblical Interpreters: A*

Introduction

convinced that reading Scripture through the eyes of past interpreters helps us in our quest for meaning today.[8]

Dead Women Who Speak: Why Women's Voices?

Until recently, accounts of the history of the interpretation of the Bible in the nineteenth century have focused almost entirely on the lives and writings of male scholars writing for the academy and the church, especially those who followed the Enlightenment dictum "Read the Bible like any other book."[9] Missing from such studies is any mention of the women who embraced, practiced, popularized, or criticized this new approach to the study of the Bible.[10] Also missing is the so-called popular voice, which constituted the

---

Historical and Biographical Guide (Grand Rapids: Baker, 2012); *Recovering Nineteenth-Century Women Interpreters of the Bible*, ed. Christiana de Groot and Marion Ann Taylor (Atlanta: Society of Biblical Literature, 2007). Women are highlighted in the multivolume *The Bible and Women: An Encyclopedia of Exegesis and Cultural History*. See the website bibleandwomen.org. for the current status of publication.

8. Similarly, scholars such as John Thompson and John Goldingay agree that one generation's blindness to the meaning of a text can be corrected by reading through the eyes of interpreters from another generation or context. As Thompson states, "We don't fully know what the Bible means until we know something about what the Bible has meant" (*Reading the Bible with the Dead: What You Can Learn from the History of Exegesis That You Can't Learn from Exegesis Alone* [Grand Rapids: Eerdmans, 2007], 11). Similarly, Goldingay, *Theological Diversity and the Authority of the Old Testament* (Grand Rapids: Eerdmans, 1987), 41–42: "There are certain aspects of this written witness [canon of Scripture] which one generation can 'hear' in the way that another cannot, so that interpreters who want to appropriate the text's significance as fully as possible are willing to look at it through the eyes of other generations' exegesis as well as of their own, which are inevitably blinkered in certain respects."

9. Benjamin Jowett, "On the Interpretation of Scripture," in *Essays and Reviews*, ed. Frederick Temple (London: Parker & Sons, 1860), 377; John Rogerson, *Old Testament Criticism in the Nineteenth Century* (London: SPCK, 1984); W. B. Glover, *Evangelical Nonconformists and Higher Criticism in the Nineteenth Century* (London: Independent Press, 1954); Donald K. McKim, ed., *Historical Handbook of Major Biblical Interpreters* (Downers Grove, Ill.: InterVarsity, 1998); and Gerald Bray, *Biblical Interpretation: Past and Present* (Downers Grove, Ill.: InterVarsity, 1996).

10. Timothy Larsen, *A People of One Book: The Bible and the Victorians* (Oxford: University Press, 2011), 6–7. For an examination of nineteenth-century women's engagement with criticism in Britain, see Marion Ann Taylor, "Women and Biblical Criticism in Nineteenth-Century England," *The Bible and Women: An Encyclopaedia of Exegesis and Cultural History*, ed. Ruth Albrecht and Michaela Sohn-Kronthaler (Atlanta: Society of Biblical Literature, forthcoming), vol. 8.2.

majority of the religious participants in Britain and North America.[11] The need for recovering these neglected voices is ongoing, and this work contributes to filling this gap in the history of interpretation.

An exception to this convention is Timothy Larsen's recent groundbreaking work on the Bible and the Victorians. Larsen committed to making at least half of the figures in his case studies women. "Choosing women subjects," he concluded, "has provided a deeper and richer connection to the lived experience of faith and doubt in the Victorian era and generated stimulating results that recast some set piece assumptions and generalizations about various traditions in fruitful ways."[12] Our study has also chosen women as subjects, focusing on the writings of the forgotten popular female voices of the nineteenth century who commented on female figures in Joshua and Judges. This agenda allows the forgotten majority voices to speak again.

Scholars in the humanities who have been recovering women's writings have long assumed that gender is "the essential factor in understanding the status and coherence" of women's writings.[13] The editors of *Major Women Writers of Seventeenth-Century England,* for example, explain to their readers that their work rests upon "an implicit foundation . . . that the sex of the author is the crucial factor in the interpretive process."[14] In our research, we have found that women often read with a distinctive female lens, but not exclusively. Other factors, including class, nationality, culture, literary genre, and audience, influence a woman's interpretive process. For example, gender identity is not a major factor in the Rothschilds' history of Israel, but it defines Josephine Butler's reading strategy. The Rothschilds do not attend to the application of biblical texts in their book for young people of both sexes, and their gender identity is not apparent. However, Josephine Butler addresses a broad audience with the intention of applying the biblical message to contemporary issues such as human trafficking and violence against women and writes self-consciously as a woman, even identifying her

---

11. "It is regrettable that accounts of religious history traditionally have so often focused overwhelmingly on men — and particularly so for studies of the Victorian age when we know that at most religious services a majority of those in attendance were women"; Larsen, *One Book,* 7.

12. Ibid.

13. Jo Carruthers, "'Neither Maide, Wife or Widow': Ester Sowernam and the Book of Esther," *Prose Studies* 26.3 (December 2003): 325.

14. Carruthers, "'Neither Maide, Wife or Widow,'" 325, citing James Fitzmaurice, Josephine Roberts, Carol L. Barash, Eugene R. Cunnar, Nancy A. Gutierrez, eds., *Major Women Writers of Seventeenth-Century England* (Ann Arbor, Mich.: University of Michigan Press, 1997), 14.

Introduction

approach as a "motherly" reading.[15] In her writing, gender is clearly crucial, and feminist concerns abound. Studying writings like those of Butler can help us learn to engage the Bible in our own gendered world.[16]

Why Focus on Women in Joshua and Judges?

The books of Joshua and Judges recount the conquest and settlement of the Israelites. This history includes human sacrifice, sexual assault, betrayal, tribal rivalries, and warfare. Not surprisingly, these narratives have posed interpretive challenges for readers in communities of faith throughout history.[17] They questioned God's mandate to exterminate the Canaanites, and they asked how the murderous Jael could be called "most blessed of women" (Judges 5:24). More basically, they asked how to apply moral standards and find spiritual meaning in texts separated by time and culture, and yet address the contemporary issue of warfare. The nineteenth century witnessed much violence and conflict, including the American Civil War, the War of 1812 (1812–15), the Crimean War (1854–56), and rebellions in the English colonies in Canada, India, South Africa, Nepal, and Ireland. Women interpreters of Scripture differed on how to apply Joshua and Judges to these situations. Quaker prison reformer Elizabeth Fry (1780–1845) was one of the many women who struggled with the stories of violence and war in the Old Testament, finding them difficult to reconcile with the Christian dispensation. Commenting on the story of the Levite's concubine and its gruesome consequences specifically, Fry opined: "Too different to the Christian dispensation is where war is permitted."[18] Discerning the message of the stories about the conquest and settlement of Israel is challenging, to be sure.

Many nineteenth-century women shared Fry's discomfort with the narratives in Joshua and Judges. At the same time they were especially drawn to the stories of the women in these texts. It was in conversation with these and other biblical texts that they wrestled with the public and private, spiritual

---

15. Josephine Butler, "The Bar Sinister," in *The Lady of Shunem* (London: H. Marshall, 1894), 70–92, as cited in *Let Her Speak for Herself*, 237.

16. Here we adapt the title of the festschrift for Katharine Doob Sakenfeld: *Engaging the Bible in a Gendered World: An Introduction to Modern Feminist Biblical Interpretation*, ed. Linda Day and Carolyn Pressler (Louisville: Westminster John Knox, 2006).

17. David Gunn's commentary on Judges focuses on the book's reception history; *Judges* (Oxford: Blackwell, 2005).

18. As quoted in Larsen, *One Book*, 190.

and practical issues of their day.[19] Were the women in Joshua and Judges allies or foes? Should Deborah be a role model for women entering public life? Or was she an exception? Is Rahab's deception in order to protect the spies excusable? Their stories along with those of other women in the conquest narratives became lightning rods for reflection on a surprising number of issues related to their political, social, and private lives. For example, Josephine Butler applied the concubine's tragic tale to the laws regulating prostitution and made connections between war and injustice clear. She writes: "Admitting to the full horror and sin of war, yet I ask myself, can peace be near where injustice triumphs, or where unrecognized and unredressed human woes and wrongs continue to fester in the heart of a nation?"[20] Nineteenth-century women's engagement with hermeneutical issues, ethical dilemmas, political conflict, and personal morality is intriguing and instructive for us today.

What Were Nineteenth-Century Assumptions and Debates about Gender?

During the nineteenth century gender expectations were under negotiation. The traditional view concerning men's and women's essential nature and gender roles is often referred to as "the cult of domesticity" or the "cult of true womanhood."[21] The king in Alfred Tennyson's mid-nineteenth-century seriocomic narrative poem *The Princess* articulates this traditional view well:

> Man for the field and woman for the hearth:
> Man for the sword and for the needle she:
> Man with the head and woman with the heart:
> Man to command and woman to obey;
> All else confusion. — *Pt. V, lines 427-31*

In both Britain and America, men and women ideally inhabited separate spheres. Although this ideal was never fully realized for the middle and

---

19. Ibid.
20. This quotation is from Butler's essay "A Typical Tragedy: Dead Hands upon the Threshold," excerpted in the chapter on the Levite's concubine.
21. For a discussion of these terms see Barbara Welter, "The Cult of True Womanhood: 1820-1860," *American Quarterly* 18 (1966): 151-74. See also Welter, *Dimity Convictions: The American Woman in the Nineteenth Century* (Columbus: Ohio State University Press, 1976).

Introduction

lower classes, it was held as the model. Women's lives centered on family and home, where they reigned with considerable power as "angels," priests, or moral beacons of the home.[22] While women exercised considerable power within the private sphere, their clearly defined roles restricted their power. Although they comprised the majority of church members, for example, women were generally discouraged from exercising leadership in the church. Husbands participated in public life and provided for their wives and children, who were their dependents. Men could vote, sign contracts, earn and keep money, receive inheritances, and own property, while women's rights mostly disappeared when they married. Laws differed slightly in different contexts, but by and large, women could not vote, have independent access to money, sign contracts, or keep a significant portion of their earnings. Sexual expectations also varied greatly as men and women were held to different standards of sexual conduct. Men could avail themselves of prostitutes with impunity, while prostitutes were outcasts of society. Differences between the sexes, as Tennyson's king figure suggests, extended to "nature." Women were expected to display the qualities of piety, purity, submissiveness, self-sacrifice, and domesticity.[23]

As the century progressed, however, traditional attitudes about woman's power and place in the home and in society were challenged. The label "the Woman Question" summarizes the many facets of the ongoing transformation in gender relations. Women slowly gained economic and legal rights, rights within marriage, the possibility of advanced education, and (in the twentieth century) the right to vote. The Bible was often used as a conversation partner in the ongoing debates. Even debates in Parliament over women's suffrage invoked Scripture. Thus the argument of the MP for Huddersfield, Mr. Leatham, that "the experience of ages, sanctioned by [Christian] Revelation, has assigned a distinct sphere to man and woman which clearly meant that God had not intended women to vote," was countered in 1876 by feminist Anglican Lydia Becker, who claimed that Christianity was in "favour" of women's rights.[24]

---

22. Callum G. Brown, *The Death of Christian Britain: Understanding Secularization, 1800–2000* (London: Routledge, 2001), 35; Barbara Welter, "The Feminization of American Religion: 1800–1860," in *Clio's Consciousness Raised: New Perspectives on the History of Women*, ed. Mary S. Hartman and Lois Banner (New York: Harper & Row, 1974), 137–57; Darrel M. Robertson, "The Feminization of American Religion: An Examination of Recent Interpretations of Women and Religion in Victorian America," *Christian Scholar's Review* 8.3 (1978): 238–46.

23. Welter, *Dimity Convictions*, 21.

24. Laura Schwartz, "The Bible and the Cause: Freethinking Feminists vs. Christianity, En-

Many of the women excerpted in this book used the stories of the women in Joshua and Judges to engage ongoing debates about "The Woman Question." Could nineteenth-century women like Achsah negotiate or possibly own property? What about women's intelligence? Could a Victorian woman use her head as well as her heart to negotiate like Rahab to save her own life as well as the lives of her family? What about education and women's roles in the public sphere? Could the seemingly well-educated public figure Deborah be a role model? Or perhaps Jephthah's daughter more correctly modeled a woman's life as she meekly submitted to the will of her heroic sword-wielding father. Was a woman's sacrifice to be celebrated or mourned? Or does the wicked, manipulative Delilah show where a woman's true power lies or what happens when a man submits to a woman's power? Does the story of the Levite's concubine speak to the issue about sexual double standards and the rights of prostitutes? Nineteenth-century women used the Bible as a powerful tool as they negotiated changes in political, economic, and professional roles of women.

The women excerpted in this book were not all on the same page in the complex debates about woman's nature, power, and place in the home and society. Often they exhibited feminist agendas as well as traditional views. In fascinating ways, these authors, such as Grace Aguilar, advocated feminist positions regarding girls' rights for religious education and at the same time espoused that women should stay at home and submit to their husbands. Elizabeth Wordsworth, founder of Lady Margaret Hall at Oxford, a college for female students, strongly supported education for women yet opposed giving women the right to vote.[25] They, like other women, transgressed societal norms in some areas at the same time that they championed conventional norms in others. These women interpreters are an illuminating case study in how feminist ideals of women's equal worth, roles, and opportunities developed by fits and starts in the nineteenth century.

---

gland 1870–1900," *Women: A Cultural Review* 21.3 (2010): 267. See also E. Lyttleton, "Women's Suffrage and the Teaching of St. Paul," *Contemporary Review* 69 (1896): 680–91.

25. For more information on Wordsworth, see Rebecca G. S. Idestrom, "Wordsworth, Elizabeth (1840–1932)," in *Handbook of Women Biblical Interpreters: A Historical and Biographical Guide*, ed. Marion A. Taylor and Agnes Choi (Grand Rapids: Baker, 2012), 540–42.

Introduction

What Genres Did Nineteenth-Century Women Use to Interpret Scripture?

The definition of what constitutes biblical interpretation in this collection is broad. On the one hand, it includes examples of genres traditionally restricted to theologically educated scholars and clergy. Some women who interpreted Scripture used the traditional genres of biblical commentary and sermon and thereby implicitly challenged cultural and ecclesial norms that restricted women from authoring commentaries or preaching. Sarah Trimmer, Mary Cornwallis, and Gracilla Boddington boldly embraced the traditional genre of commentary, building on the earlier work of eighteenth-century commentator Juliana Yonge.[26] Similarly, Quaker women regularly preached,[27] and Anglican women such as M.G. published "addresses" that were really sermons given to women. Harriet Beecher Stowe and others preached with their pens,[28] and some women, such as Florence Nightingale and Esther Hewlett Copley, wrote sermons preached by men.[29]

On the other hand, this collection of women's interpretations of Scripture showcases nontraditional interpretive genres, including poetry, catechetical writing, drama, historical fiction, devotional essay, published notes, and female biography. Nineteenth-century women, like women throughout history, produced a variety of written responses to Scripture. Many used nontraditional genres, which generated less censure and more readily lent themselves to their intended popular audiences. Some popular interpre-

---

26. Excerpts from Trimmer's and Cornwallis's commentaries are found in this book. Boddington wrote commentaries on every book of the New Testament. See Agnes Choi, "Boddington, Gracilla (1801–87)," in *Handbook of Women Biblical Interpreters*, ed. Taylor and Choi, 82–85. See I. (Juliana) Yonge, *Practical and Explanatory Commentary on the Holy Bible: Taking the Whole in One Point of View from the Creation to the End of the World* (London: R. Faulder, 1787).

27. Elizabeth Isichei claims that "in the early Victorian period, woman ministers greatly outnumbered men"; *Victorian Quakers* (Oxford: University Press, 1970), 94, as cited in Larsen, *One Book*, 169.

28. Marion Ann Taylor, "Harriet Beecher Stowe and the Mingling of Two Worlds: The Kitchen and the Study," in *Recovering Nineteenth-Century Women Interpreters of the Bible*, ed. de Groot and Taylor, 99–115.

29. Three of Nightingale's sermons and an introductory essay are included in vol. 2 of *The Collected Works of Florence Nightingale: Florence Nightingale's Spiritual Journey: Biblical Annotations, Sermons, and Notes* (Waterloo: Wilfred Laurier University Press, 2001), 325–61. For an analysis of her use of Scripture, see the essay by Christiana de Groot, "Florence Nightingale: A Mother to Many," in *Recovering Nineteenth-Century Women Interpreters of the Bible*, ed. de Groot and Taylor, 117–33.

tive genres, such as poetry and drama, encouraged imaginative writing and allowed women freedom to experiment with gendered exegesis. All these women, employing a diversity of genres, were commentators on Scripture.

Many women who commented specifically on the female figures in Scripture adapted the popular eighteenth- and nineteenth-century literary tradition of female biography to include the women in Scripture. This genre's original purpose, "to demonstrate the utility and constructive nature of women's literary activities; and to provide didactic examples of women who combined domestic affections and domestic duty with their unorthodox pursuits," was reshaped by women writing on biblical figures to supply moral and spiritual exemplars.[30] In 1811, Frances Elizabeth King adapted this genre in *Female Scripture Characters: Exemplifying Female Virtues*.[31] In her encyclopedic work *Woman's Record; or, Sketches of All Distinguished Women from the Creation to A.D. 1854*, Sarah Hale embraced the genre of female biography but also extended it to biographies of women in Scripture. Hale's intentions were clearly didactic, as she sought to prove "that WOMAN is God's appointed agent of *morality*, the teacher and inspirer of those feelings and sentiments which are termed the virtues of humanity."[32] Writing biographies of biblical women for the purpose of teaching morals was not only popular but also lucrative. Harriet Beecher Stowe, for example, supported her family by publishing her impressive coffee-table book *Woman in Sacred History*, among other of her writings. Other women writing in this genre and excerpted in this volume include Grace Aguilar, Clara Lucas Balfour, Etty Woosnam, and Elizabeth Baxter. This genre appealed to nineteenth-century women writers and readers especially well.[33] Other popular interpretive genres, including catechetical writings, historical fiction, poetry, and drama, are also included in this volume.[34] Whereas this volume cites poems in their entirety, we could

---

30. Elizabeth Fay, "Grace Aguilar: Rewriting Scott Rewriting History," in *British Romanticism and the Jews: History, Culture, Literature*, ed. Sheila A. Spector (New York: Palgrave Macmillan, 2002), 219–20.

31. King's book was a response to Thomas Robinson's 1793 publication *Scripture Characters; or, A Practical Improvement of the Principal Histories in the Old and New Testament*, which considered only men as models. For a fuller discussion of the development of the genre of Scripture biography, see Christiana de Groot, "Contextualizing *The Woman's Bible*," *Studies in Religion* 41.4 (2012): 566–67.

32. Sarah Hale, *Woman's Record; or, Sketches of All Distinguished Women from the Creation to A.D. 1854* (New York: Harper & Bros., 1855), xxxv.

33. See the article by Rebecca Styler, "A Scripture of Their Own: Nineteenth-Century Bible Biography and Feminist Bible Criticism," in *Christianity and Literature* 57.1 (2007): 65–85.

34. Shira Wolosky's article, "Women's Bibles: Biblical Interpretation in Nineteenth-Century

Introduction

include only selections from Adelia Graves's full-length five-act drama on Jephthah's daughter and Steele's lengthy fictionalized biographies of Deborah and Jael.

How Did Women Interpret?

The authors featured in this book lived in a culture that was "Scripture saturated."[35] They also lived during a period of great change with respect to views on the Bible's history, its nature, and methods of interpretation. They were more or less aware of scholarly and ecclesial debates about Scripture and had formulated their own views on Scripture and methods of interpretation. Not surprisingly, their views on Scripture and theology covered a wide spectrum: most valued Scripture as sacred, some viewed it as the last great enemy, and some read it idiosyncratically.

Most women excerpted in this book valued the literal/historical sense of Scripture and used the scholarly resources that they could access to shed light on its meaning. Harriet Beecher Stowe was interested in questions of history, but was also critical of modern scholarship. She imposed a type of salvation-historical grid on the stories in Scripture and traced the development of the "sacred stock" from its early beginnings to its fulfillment in the New Testament. While Stowe relied on the scholarly expertise of her husband for historical, geographical, and cultural data, other women drew on information gleaned from commentaries, histories, dictionaries, travel diaries, and even archeological finds housed in the British Museum. Many women were interested in questions of chronology and assigned dates to particular stories, frequently using Bishop James Ussher's chronology to date the conquest and settlement.[36]

Women interpreters often used extrabiblical sources to explain the background assumed in the stories regarding everyday life and culture. They drew word pictures to describe ancient houses and walled cities and even described the kind of tent peg that killed Sisera. They explained "oriental"

American Women's Poetry," *Feminist Studies* 28.1.2 (2002): 191–211, surveys how women used poetry to interpret Scripture.

35. Larsen, *One Book*, 6. Larsen uses this term to describe Victorian England, but the case could also be made that a similar ethos was present in nineteenth-century America.

36. Bishop James Ussher's (1581–1656) chronology, which dated creation at 4004 B.C. and the visit of the spies to Jericho at 1451 B.C., was widely used in the nineteenth century. It was often printed in the margins of King James study Bibles.

customs of hospitality to shed light on enigmas in the story of Jael and "oriental" sleeping postures to explain Samson's position in the lap of Delilah.

Women who knew biblical languages read the stories in the Hebrew original and in the early Greek and Latin translations in order to illumine difficult verses.[37] The well-educated Mary Anne Schimmelpenninck, for example, applied her linguistic skills to the interpretive crux in the story of Jephthah's daughter and defended a change in translation to resolve the moral problem of a father killing his daughter.

Although many interpreters were influenced by the growing sense of the importance of historicism and the value of the Enlightenment dictum "Read the Bible like any other book," they still read the Bible as Scripture, expecting it to continue to speak into their lives. Yet, when they read Joshua and Judges, they entered into a world that was very different than their own. Their increased historical sensibilities made the differences between the world of the text and their own even more pronounced. They encountered differences in culture and religious and moral beliefs: Rahab was a lying harlot and Jael was a ruthless killer. One response to such differences was rejection of a text's value for teaching morality. For example, Florence Nightingale judged many Old Testament stories as unworthy of passing on to children:

> The story of Achilles and his horses is far more fit for children than that of Balaam and his ass, which is only fit to be told to asses. The stories of Samson and of Jephthah are only fit to be told to bulldogs and the story of Bathsheba to be told to Bathshebas. Yet we give all these stories to children as "Holy Writ." There are some things in Homer we might better call "holy" writ, many in Sophocles and Aeschylus. The stories about Andromache and Antigone are worth all the women in the Old Testament put together, nay, almost all the women in the Bible.[38]

Contributors to the late-nineteenth-century *The Woman's Bible* concluded that although the Bible contained some profound wisdom, for the most part it contributed to women's oppression. Its editor, Elizabeth Cady Stanton, discerned patriarchal bias in many biblical texts and called women to resist

---

37. Charlotte Elizabeth Tonna (1790–1846) was one of many women who believed that English women should study the Bible in its original languages. To this end, she included a series of basic lessons on how to read Hebrew in *The Christian Lady's Magazine*, which she edited from 1834 to 1846.

38. Lynn McDonald, ed., *Florence Nightingale's Theology: Essays, Letters and Journal Notes* (Waterloo: Wilfred Laurier University, 2002), 3: 550.

Introduction

the subordinate role that some passages advocated. She viewed Jephthah's daughter not as a young woman to emulate, but rather to judge for submitting to her father's vow.

While Nightingale and Stanton rejected "difficult" portions of Scripture, women who viewed Scripture as authoritative found alternative ways of reckoning with the difficulties and differences presented in the conquest stories. Most behavioral and moral differences were evaluated as either wrong or exceptional and not generative. Interpreters judged Jael's killing of Sisera as wrong; Deborah's praise of Jael as the most blessed of women was also wrong. Elizabeth Baxter understood Deborah's engagement in the public sphere to be an exception and inferred that her household duties suffered due to her public involvement. To explain these differences in what was considered moral, a number of women either drew on the notion of progressive revelation or invoked evolutionary biology, arguing that the ancients were primitive, but their own culture was enlightened. However, some women viewed differences as generative or prophetic. Grace Aguilar used Old Testament history to shed light on the present in order to change it for the better. She recognized that Deborah had more rights and freedoms than Victorian Jewish women. Adelia Graves protested the treatment of Jephthah's daughter by her father and her community and memorialized her through a five-act play.

Another typical response of nineteenth-century interpreters to the differences between the world of the reader and the world of the text was to emphasize what readers had in common with the ancient peoples of the Old Testament; specifically, many women assumed they shared a common humanity, including needs, feelings, and faith, with the figures who inhabited the world of the text. They looked for and at times "fictionalized" points of connection with biblical women. The Anglo-Catholic teacher of women, M.G., assumed that biblical characters acted "exactly as we ourselves would be likely to act under the same circumstances."[39] Aguilar encouraged Jewish women to be proud of their foremothers, who were a "true and perfect mirror of themselves."[40] This exemplary hermeneutic worked well for biblical characters such as Manoah's wife and Jephthah's daughter, whose lives could be interpreted as modeling such scripted values as piety, purity, submission, and domesticity. Eliza Steele's assumption of sameness in a woman's nature allowed her to provide Jael with a "reasonable" motive for murder, believing

---

39. M.G., *Women Like Ourselves: Short Addresses for Mothers' Meetings, Bible Classes, etc.* (London: Society for the Promotion of Christian Knowledge, 1893), iv.

40. Grace Aguilar, *The Women of Israel* (New York: D. Appleton & Co., 1872), 2.

that any woman would kill the man who endangered the lives of women, including her own daughter.[41] The young poet Caroline Gilman empathized with Jephthah's daughter's plight, likening it to that of all women; she felt her pain, judging her a victim.[42] The notion of shared or common natures authorized women to fill in the blanks of the text with dialogue, description, and evaluative comments and directive. So Rose Terry Cooke gave voice to Jephthah's daughter's losses: "No soft baby fingers tinged like an ocean shell, No light baby footsteps within my tent shall dwell."[43]

A number of nineteenth-century women also stressed the common relational connections they shared with women in Scripture. Like them they were daughters, wives, and mothers. The actions of Caleb's daughter provoked much discussion about father-daughter relations and property rights. Manoah's wife was an ideal mother, concerned for the health and well-being of her unborn child. Interpreters often remade biblical figures into "women like themselves." Deborah's activities as wife and mother in the private sphere were greatly embellished to offset her "public" heroic roles of judge and warrior. Perceived "sameness" extended to women who were like others they knew in nineteenth-century society. Sameness allowed Josephine Butler to enter into the narrative of the Levite's concubine and feel empathy for the victim, who was like so many female victims in Victorian society. Butler extended the idea of common humanity to the men and women of England who, like the men inside the house in Gibeah, were ignoring the plight of the women outside "our" doors.[44]

The sense of solidarity with figures in Scripture allowed interpreters to fill in the blanks in the stories with what they knew to be true about life. This hermeneutical approach opened up stories that otherwise might be locked into the past. Connecting with the female self especially allowed women to interpret biblical stories through the lens of their experiences. It is in these places that the gender identity and feminist consciousness of the interpreters are most evident. It is also in these spaces that women often give voice to

---

41. This quotation is from Eliza R. Stansbury Steele, excerpted in the Jael chapter. C. S. Jessopp, similarly went to great lengths to justify Jael's motives in her thirty-eight-page epic poem "Jael," *Two Dreams: I. Jael, II. Bathsheba* (Norwich: A. H. Goose & Co., 1882).

42. See Caroline Howard Gilman, "Obedient unto Death," in the chapter on Jephthah's daughter.

43. See Rose Terry Cooke's poem "Jephtha's Daughter," in the chapter on Jephthah's daughter.

44. See Butler's essay "A Typical Tragedy: Dead Hands upon the Threshold," excerpted in the chapter on the Levite's concubine.

Introduction

their concerns and challenge assumptions in the world of the text, such as a double standard for men and women, the namelessness of women, or the authority exercised by a father over a daughter.

Other common strategies used to find meaning when the stories presented difficulties or seemed to be moored in the distant past were typology and allegory. Typology allowed interpreters to discern the hidden or spiritual meaning coded in persons, places, and events. For example, Charlotte Tucker identified Rahab's scarlet cord, that "singular device for saving herself and her family," as that "forcible type of the redeeming blood of Christ." Jephthah's daughter's sacrifice was regarded as a type of Christ's sacrifice by Graves and Alexander. The classic interpretive methods of typology and allegory were, however, under review during the nineteenth century. Typology was despised by many who felt it was antiquated,[45] but strongly encouraged by Anglo-Catholics, such as Rossetti and Alexander, who felt that church tradition legitimated typology. Lydia defends the use of typology from Scripture in her essay on Achsah.

Closely linked to typology is allegory, which also seeks to find moral or spiritual meanings hidden in the details of the text. Etty Woosnam's figuration of the story of Jael is typical of an allegorical approach: King Jabin is a type of sin, his officers symbolize worldliness, Sisera is the antitype and archenemy of the church, and Woosnam calls every young woman to be "a spiritual Jael and nail down to the ground her Sisera."[46] Allegory opened up more interpretive possibilities, especially for dealing with problematic passages.

Which Dead Women Speak; or, Who Is Included in This Book?

This book features nineteenth-century British and American women's reflections on eight female figures in Joshua and Judges: Rahab, Achsah, Deborah, Jael, Manoah's wife, Jephthah's daughter, Delilah, and the Levite's concubine. Each figure merits a chapter, and they are treated in the order they occur

---

45. In the preface to her commentary on the Ten Commandments, which features typology, Christina Rossetti anticipates that some might find her approach quaint: "Old fashioned it certainly is to search the Scriptures (see Acts xvii.10–12) for our examples and warnings; but surely the dread of appearing old fashioned is one form of the Disinclination in which already we have thought to discern a breach of the First Commandment!" Christina Rossetti, *Letter and Spirit: Notes on the Commandments* (London: SPCK, 1883), 43–44.

46. See the excerpt by Etty Woosnam in the Jael chapter.

in Joshua and Judges. The selections are ordered according to their publication date. With the possible exception of the excerpts taken from Aguilar's *Women of Israel* and Stanton's *The Woman's Bible*, the selections are from forgotten, unread, or "under-read texts."[47]

The chapters are uneven in terms of length. Writings on certain figures, such as Delilah and the Levite's concubine, are scarce,[48] whereas writings on Deborah, Jael, and Jephthah's daughter are abundant. We decided to include a broad spectrum of commentaries, including those of well-known writers such as Stowe, as well as forgotten authors such as Lydia. We chose selections whose content is engaging and often surprising on the one hand and representative or typical selections on the other hand. We tried to highlight the variety of women's writings in terms of literary genre, intended audience, ideology, and interpretive approach or hermeneutics. Finally, we included a diversity of voices — British and American, Jewish and Christian, and others. Unfortunately, our search for women's commentaries did not locate substantive writings on the women in Joshua and Judges by Catholic, Canadian, African American women, and other racialized minorities.[49]

While more than seventy nineteenth-century women interpreters are quoted or mentioned in this book, the writings of thirty-five are formally excerpted. Eighteen are British, one is Irish, one is Scottish, fourteen are American, and one, Susanna Rowson, is remembered as a British-American author. Brief biographies of the authors preface their excerpted writings. What is remembered about individual authors varies significantly. We have full biographies written about women such as Stowe, Baxter, and Stanton, while the identities of pseudonymous authors such as Lydia and M.G. are lost, and very little is remembered about a number of other authors, including Julia Wright and Clara Neyman. Most authors in the book would self-identify as Christian; some affiliated with one denomination throughout their lives, while others changed their theological views and denominations several times. While most English authors were Anglican and shared liturgy and tradition, they differed in styles of worship, theology, and biblical hermeneutics. Aguilar and the Rothschilds were Jewish at the time they published the works included in the collection. Stanton, Southworth, and Neyman were

---

47. See the discussion of the problem of "under-read texts" of women's literature in Nancy K. Miller, *Subject to Change: Reading Feminist Writing* (New York: Columbia University Press, 1988), 83–84, 129–30.

48. Women were reticent about discussing sexuality and violence in public and in print.

49. Examples of women's writings on other subjects are found in Taylor and Weir, eds., *Let Her Speak for Herself: Nineteenth-Century Women Writing on Women in Genesis*.

post-Christian in the 1890s. Most women were well educated; a surprising number knew Greek and Hebrew and had access to fine theological libraries. Many, such as Baxter, Stowe, and Graves, had connections to men in the academy, the church, and the world of publishing. The economic status of authors varied, although most were middle and upper class. A number of authors such as Hale, Stowe, and Balfour, supported themselves, while others, such as Charlotte Tucker and Cornwallis, supported specific missions or charities through their literary endeavors.

Why Read with the Dead about Women in Joshua and Judges?

Brevard Childs suggests that examples of biblical interpreters from the past who have "truly immersed themselves in a specific concrete historical context, such as Luther in Saxony, retain the greatest value as models for the future actualization of the biblical text in a completely different world."[50] We also suggest that the biblical interpreters included in this book, immersed as they are in specific historical contexts, retain great value for us today as we interpret Scripture in our contemporary world. For example, knowing how Butler interpreted Judges 19 to ground her opposition to the Contagious Diseases Acts opens up Scripture in a powerful way. Her advocacy work for prostitutes equipped her to actualize the troubling narrative of the Levite's concubine for her generation.

In addition to making us better readers and interpreters of Scripture, nineteenth-century interpreters teach us about the past. We learn about their history and culture. Because they viewed Scripture as a mirror of themselves, they reveal much of their own lives to their readers. Their efforts to right the wrongs they perceived in their culture, notably their struggles for the rights of women, children, and the marginalized, their advocacy for education for girls as well as boys, and their concern for the health of mothers and their unborn children, educate us.

This collection is also important because it forefronts the importance of forgotten and under-read women interpreters whose lives and work can inspire. When we look into the mirror of their lives, we see women who are in some ways like us, but who are also very unlike us. Their courage to comment on Scripture and to preach with their pens is commendable. Some

---

50. Brevard S. Childs, *Biblical Theology of the Old and New Testaments: Theological Reflection on the Christian Bible* (Minneapolis: Fortress, 1992), 88.

interpreters carried forward and popularized the opinions of great interpreters and scholars from the past; others popularized the cutting-edge work of their contemporaries. Some challenged both the authority of Scripture and the traditions of its interpretation and often rejected its message. Many were loyal to the text, understanding it as the Word of God, and defending its message. In dealing with difficult texts on war and violence, they dared to hear the Scriptures in new ways. Some of their interpretations seem quite innovative even today. Their writings allow us to witness the development of approaches that more recently have been identified as feminist, such as the hermeneutics of sympathy, the hermeneutics of suspicion, the hermeneutics of experience, and the hermeneutics of informed trust.[51] Like some nineteenth-century women interpreters, many contemporary voices recognize weaknesses in the historical-critical method of interpretation that garnered strength over the course of the nineteenth and twentieth centuries. At the same time, a number of contemporary voices are embracing figural approaches such as typology.[52] We can see more clearly in nineteenth-century writings how theology and ideology shape interpretation, and we can build on these insights to examine our own ideas. We can learn to question the assumptions that we bring to the text, and we can explore our own blind spots.

The believers and unbelievers included in this book were not of one mind about most things, but they were united in looking to the Bible as their conversation partner. Their diverse interpretations give witness to the missing popular voices of the women interpreters of the nineteenth century. As they engaged the stories of agents and victims, the good and the bad, the named and the unnamed women of the conquest narratives, they were entertained, disturbed, provoked, and inspired, and they called for spiritual and moral change at personal and societal levels. Their writings are inspiring and instructive for us. It is our view that these dead can and should continue to speak.

---

51. Ahida E. Pilarski, "The Past and Future of Feminist Biblical Hermeneutics," *Biblical Theology Bulletin: A Journal of Bible and Theology* 41 (2011): 16–23.

52. See, for example, the Brazos Theological Commentary on the Bible.

1

Rahab

The intriguing story about Rahab and her collaboration with the Israelite spies in Joshua 2 begins with Joshua sending out two spies to investigate Jericho. When these men spend the night in her home, the king of Jericho is informed and orders Rahab to hand them over. Instead of complying, Rahab hides the spies under flax on her roof and claims that they have recently departed and the king's men should be able to overtake them if they pursue in haste. Rahab then declares her allegiance to the God of Israel, asking the spies that she and her family be spared when the inevitable defeat of Jericho occurs. The spies agree, promising to save her family, providing that Rahab remains silent about the planned attack. After she helps them escape by lowering them from the outer wall of the city in a basket, the spies leave her with final instructions: Rahab must hang a crimson cord from her window and gather her family in her house or they will not be spared. Joshua 6 describes the attack on Jericho, where the Israelites march around the city repeatedly blowing trumpets and shouting, and eventually the walls fall down. All the inhabitants are slaughtered except for Rahab and her family.

The story of Rahab begins the conquest narrative, and commentators have a diversity of responses to the battle of Jericho. Women like Sarah Hale, whose focus is biographical, do not engage the problem of war head on; however, most women in this chapter do reveal their theology of war either explicitly or implicitly. Most justify the "massacre" and emphasize the sin of the Canaanites, which requires divine retributive justice. The most vivid language of war is found in Cecil Alexander's poetic reflection and Charlotte Tucker's description of the war: "The swords of Israel were bathed in blood." Josephine Butler justifies the battle by speaking of the "divine government, and the presence and favour of God granted to the invading people," language that is consistent with Article 37 of the Thirty-Nine Articles of the Anglican Church.

Nineteenth-century commentators reflected on Rahab's character and actions. Her endeavors raised many questions about the ethics of lying, the nature of conversion, and salvation. Interpreters considered the meaning of key words, engaging the historical debate about whether the Hebrew word *zonah* is properly translated "innkeeper" rather than "prostitute." The historicity of the narrative was discussed, and opinions ranged from a commitment to its accuracy to the conclusion that it was a myth. The question of how "a merciful Creator would have commanded Joshua and his companions to put all the inhabitants of Canaan to the sword"[1] looms in the shadows of many treatments of this story.

Some commentators read Joshua's account through the lens of the three New Testament passages that mention Rahab: Matthew 1:5 lists Rahab as the mother of Boaz, and hence she is in the lineage of Jesus; Hebrews 11:31 praises Rahab, the prostitute, for her faith; and James 2:25 cites Rahab as an example of a believer who is justified by her works when she welcomed the spies and sent them off by another route. This intertextual dialogue led interpreters to consider Rahab's actions in the context of the history of salvation and in turn supported typological interpretations.

Because women dialogued with the text in light of their concerns, their own contexts are illuminated as much as Rahab's story. Sarah Hall notes that Rahab's family moved to the suburbs. Josephine Butler, an Anglican, notices that Rahab's entire family, rather than the individual Rahab alone, is saved. Elizabeth Cady Stanton speaks openly about her hope that her comments about biblical women such as Rahab would "rid" women of "some of their superstitions" about the Bible — "the very book which is responsible for their civil and social degradation."

Most commentators did not dwell at length on Rahab's identity as a prostitute; issues related to sexuality were generally not discussed in Victorian society. Susanna Haswell Rowson raised the question of treason and whether Rahab should be considered a traitor who betrayed her own people. Stanton thought it possible that Rahab was a turncoat, aligning herself with the

---

1. In her treatment of the apparent moral difficulties in the Old Testament history, Anglican apologist Elizabeth Whately discusses the contentious issue of the extermination of the Canaanites. She defends God's justice, arguing that the Canaanites were idolatrous criminals deserving punishment, and goes so far as to claim that it was an act of mercy to kill infants since they then were "cut off before they were conscious of evil." On the other hand, Whately notes that God showed his mercy to the "heathens" Rahab and Ruth; see "Objections to the Old Testament," in *How to Answer Objections to Revealed Religions* (London: Religious Tract Society, 1875), 38.

victors. However, British and American interpreters generally followed the lead of the biblical narrator, identifying with the Israelites and applauding Rahab's loyalty to the God of Israel and justifying the destruction of the inhabitants of Jericho.

The authors excerpted in this chapter wrote for a variety of audiences using various genres, and, except for Stanton, all revered the Bible as divinely inspired. They intentionally listened to its "message" in order to apply its moral and theological teaching to their own lives and hoped readers would do the same.

Sarah Ewing Hall

A Sanitized Rahab

Sarah Hall (1761–1830) was born and raised in Philadelphia, where her father, the Reverend John Ewing, was minister of the First Presbyterian Church and provost of the University of Pennsylvania.[2] Much of Hall's informal education came indirectly through her father and the many learned guests who passed through their home. In addition she learned by proxy, listening in on lessons in such subjects as Greek, Latin, and literature intended for her brothers. Hall loved classical literature, history, and astronomy, often studying late into the night. Later in life Hall learned Hebrew. She married John Hall, the son of a Maryland planter, in 1782 and moved to Maryland. Later she returned to Philadelphia, where she published essays in the prominent literary periodical *The Port Folio* on various social issues, including dueling, female education, and religious subjects. Her major publication, *Conversations on the Bible* (1818), published under the pseudonym A Lady of Philadelphia, retells the stories of the Old Testament in the form of a conversation between a mother and her three children (Catherine, Fanny, and Charles). Hall cleverly used the questions of the children to raise interpretive issues, and her answers filled in

---

2. For a fuller discussion of Hall, see Bernon Lee, "Hall, Sarah (Ewing) (1761–1830)," in *Handbook of Women Biblical Interpreters: A Historical and Biographical Guide*, ed. Marion A. Taylor and Agnes Choi (Grand Rapids: Baker, 2012), 240–42. See also Bernon Lee, "Conversations on the Bible with a Lady of Philadelphia," in *Recovering Nineteenth-Century Women Interpreters of the Bible*, ed. Christiana de Groot and Marion Ann Taylor (Atlanta: Society of Biblical Literature, 2007), 45–62.

the gaps in the stories with information drawn from other parts of Scripture, history, geography, and academic commentaries. She used her writing as a platform for her views on such issues as the equal rights of women.

The following selection from Hall's *Conversations* begins with a straightforward description by Mother on the activities of the spies. In response to a question from Charles about how the spies could be hidden on the roof, Mother describes the architecture of houses in the ancient world. In addition to situating the text in its cultural context, Mother explains that the laws in the Pentateuch on house building were intended to keep Israelites safe and limit the violent effects of war on the household. Hall depicts the God of Israel as a benevolent deity concerned about daily life, as well as a God of justice who employs Israel's warriors as "ministers of divine justice." She interprets the fall of Jericho as a just response to the resistance of the king of Jericho. Interestingly, the children raise the question of what happened to Rahab and her family, and Mother assures them that the Israelite spies remembered their promise, and that Rahab and her family were spared and "conducted with . . . all their moveable property to the suburbs," an echo of moving day in nineteenth-century Philadelphia. Mother also asserts that Rahab and her family needed to be purified before they could be fully included in Israel, showing an awareness of purity laws. Further drawing on Matthew's genealogy, Mother declares that Rahab became a proselyte, married Salmon, a prince, and became part of the lineage of David.

Mother sanitizes the narrative in order to make it appropriate for her young readers. Hall glosses over problematic issues of Rahab's profession and conduct and briefly defends exterminating the residents of Jericho because of their unwillingness to repent of "their multiplied offences."

MOTHER. Whilst Joshua was busied in these dispositions for a removal, his messengers had made their way into the city of Jericho, though not without the peril of their lives. The victorious march of Israel had spread dismay among the Canaanites — their army but a few miles distant, the presence of two strangers in the city would naturally create suspicion; accordingly they were carefully watched and at length traced to the house of Rahab, a woman who lived on the eastern wall of the town, and a mandate from the king of Jericho required her instantly to deliver them up. But their hostess aware of their danger, had humanely concealed them on the top of her house, beneath

Rahab

a quantity of flax which had been spread there to dry, so that they escaped the search of the king's messengers. She acknowledged, indeed, that they had lodged in her house, whence they had but lately departed, and affected to assist in their arrest, by directing the messengers towards the river, the fords of which she said the spies could not yet have reached. Having thus rid herself of the unwelcome intruders, she repaired to her guests, and hastened them away, confessing that she had been prompted to this act of kindness, by the universal terror of her countrymen, and her own perfect conviction that the whole land was given to the Israelites by *their* God. She believed, he was the *true* God, and that his purposes could not be frustrated; she therefore entreated, that she and her relatives might be protected when Jericho should be taken. This just return for the favour she had shown to them they readily promised, on the condition, that her family and friends, should be gathered into her house, and there remain: but for the safety of an individual who should venture into the streets, they would not be responsible.

CHARLES. How could the young men be concealed on the top of a house?

MOTHER. The roofs of houses are not in every country inclined like ours. In Palestine, and in other eastern climates, they were then flat, and still continue so — for customs with them, do not fluctuate as they do with us. The inhabitants walk, sit, and sometimes in hot weather, even sleep on them. The Mosaical law embracing a great variety of particulars, affecting the safety, or the comfort of its subjects, provided that they should make "battlements for their roof, that they might not bring blood upon their house, if any man should fall from thence."[3] Their houses were also low, — not more than one, or at most, two stories high. That of Rahab, being at the extremity of the city, the escape of the spies was facilitated by letting them down by a cord from the top, to the outside of the wall — after it had been agreed by the parties, that the same cord (which being of scarlet would be conspicuous) should be exhibited in a window in front as a signal to the Israelites, and ensure the inviolability of the mansion. Pursuing her advice, the young men hastened to the neighbouring mountains, and lay in their recesses, until their pursuers, despairing of success had returned to the city. On the evening of the third day, they arrived safely at the Hebrew camp, and encouraged their brethren to go boldly forward — for the disheartened Canaanites would be an easy conquest. . . .

This last miracle [crossing the Jordan] added to all that had gone before, operated powerfully in favour of the progress of the Israelites. The inhabitants of Canaan trembled before the omnipotence of the God of Israel —

3. [Deuteronomy 22:8.]

but they did not repent of their sins, and endeavour to avert his anger. The king of Jericho did not, like his subject, Rahab, submit to the appointed conqueror, and make terms for himself and his people, but foolishly determined on resistance. His "city was straitly shut up, none went out, and none came in"; they trusted in the strength of their bulwarks: nor was the singular mode of warfare adopted by the Hebrew general at all calculated to weaken their confidence. No preparation adapted to a siege could be discerned from the wall of Jericho — nothing could be seen, but the formidable invaders armed indeed in warlike array with their standards waving and bearing their sacred shrine, encircling the city, day after day, and returning peaceably at night to their camp. No rude noise — not a voice assailed the ear — the solemn march was alone interrupted by the sound of trumpets, continually blown by the priests who carried the Ark. In these mysterious circuits, the superstitious heathens must imagine some preparatory ceremony like their own futile incantations to propitiate their deities: but while no step more decidedly hostile was taken, they would still rely on their barriers for security. Six days, their flattering hopes deceived them — on the seventh instead of retiring as usual after a single circuit, the strangers encompassed the city seven times; at the conclusion of the seventh, a long, and louder blast was heard, — the tremendous shout of victory ascended to heaven, and the walls of Jericho fell prostrate before the Ark of the Covenant. The ministers of divine justice poured in on every side and the astonished inhabitants received the punishment decreed, to their multiplied offences!

FANNY. I hope the promise made to Rahab, was now remembered?

MOTHER. It was faithfully observed. She was conducted with all her relatives, and all their moveable property to the suburbs of the Hebrew camp.

CATHERINE. Why to the suburbs — why not into the part of the camp, where she would be most secure from the resentment of her countrymen?

MOTHER. Because aliens might not enter the camp of Israel until they were at least legally purified, which could not be done in this moment of confusion. They were effectually protected, however; Rahab herself, became afterwards a proselyte to the Hebrew religion, and married Salmon, a prince of the tribe of Judah, and the ancestor in a direct line, of the celebrated David king of Israel.[4]

Source: Sarah Ewing Hall (A Lady of Philadelphia), *Conversations on the Bible,* 4th edition (Philadelphia: Harrison Hall, 1827 [originally 1818]), 136–37, 140–42.

---

4. [See Matthew 1:5–6.]

Rahab

SUSANNA HASWELL ROWSON

Is Lying Always Wrong?

The early years of Susanna Rowson (1762–1824) were very difficult.[5] Her mother died shortly after her birth in Portsmouth, England, and her father, a Royal Navy Lieutenant stationed in Boston, remarried and returned to England to bring his daughter back to Massachusetts. The family survived shipwreck in the Boston Harbor in 1765. With the outbreak of the American Revolution in 1775, Rowson's father was placed under house arrest, his property confiscated, and the family moved inland and then to England in a prisoner exchange in 1778.

In 1786, she married William Rowson, a hardware merchant and horse-guard trumpeter, and published her first novel, *Victoria*. Five years later she published her best-selling moralizing novel *Charlotte Temple*, and in 1793 both Susanna and her husband became actors and moved to America as members of a theater company. In 1797 Rowson founded a prestigious academy for young women to supplement her income from writing. She published a wide variety of books, including social commentary, poetry, and textbooks, in addition to editing the *Boston Weekly Magazine* (1802–5). She was best known as an English and American novelist, though she thought of herself primarily as an educator.[6]

Rowson wrote a lengthy two-volume textbook on the Bible (volume 1 was 416 pages; volume 2, 395). *Biblical Dialogues* includes stories from the Old and New Testaments and key events in church and secular history until the time of the Reformation. She employs a family setting to explain the Bible — the father is the primary teacher; the mother, Mrs. Alworth, functions as a coach; and a son, Horatio, asks the hard questions. Echoing Hall's presentation, the parents attempt to whitewash the troubling features of the narrative, beginning with Rahab's identity. The father's opening speech identifies Rahab as a "widow" who provides lodging for the spies. The expansion of the text

---

5. James W. Vining and Ben A. Smith, "Susanna Rowson: Early American Geography Educator," *Social Studies* 98 (1998): 263-70.

6. Susanna Rowson described her passion for teaching in the preface to *Biblical Dialogues*: "My whole soul was engaged in my duties, my pupils became to me as my children, and few things were of consequence to me that did not contribute to their improvement, their present and eternal happiness"; see *Biblical Dialogues between a Father and His Family, Comprising Sacred History from the Creation to the Death of our Saviour Christ* (Boston: Richardson and Lord, 1822), 1.iv.

locates it in familiar territory for nineteenth-century urbanites and confers socially acceptable status to a woman who is not listed as a man's dependant. This sanitizing of Rahab does not go far enough for the mother, however, and she coaches the father to clarify Rahab's occupation. The father then explains that, in Hebrew, the same word indicates "hostess" or "innkeeper" and "a woman of ill-fame," but he does not cite evidence for these claims, and so Horatio must take them on trust. The father emphasizes his point by claiming that in Joshua the word certainly means innkeeper, citing Rahab's marriage into the tribe of Judah (Matthew 1:5) as proof she could not have been a prostitute.

Horatio pursues other facets of Rahab's character and actions and questions whether she did the right thing in hiding enemies of the state, lying to the king, and betraying her country. The father draws out the implied chronology of the narrative in order to answer Horatio's query and submits that it is important to understand that before the potentially treacherous acts occur, Rahab has already heard of the God of Israel and has come to believe and trust this God instead of the gods of her neighbors. Due to her loyalty to the God of Israel, she considered it her duty to protect the spies and side with the Israelites. Horatio accepts this explanation while persisting to question the appropriateness of Rahab's lying to the king's officials. The father's answer is complex. He first suggests that when she hid them, she had already committed herself to lying; otherwise, what was the point in hiding them? Furthermore, if she told the truth, and the spies were discovered and killed, Rahab would be guilty of their death since she was complicit. The argument is quite sophisticated, claiming that those who are complicit in a crime are as guilty as those who actually perpetrate the crime. The father's answer satisfies the son, who then concludes that Rahab was not a criminal.

FATHER. The exact period it would be difficult to ascertain; but it was not long after Joshua undertook the momentous charge of conducting them [the Israelites]. This great general was sensible that his situation was a very arduous one; he saw himself indeed at the head of six hundred thousand fighting men, but then the nations he had to subdue, were a warlike and gigantic people, who had taken every method of defence, and confederated their forces against him; but God was pleased to assure him of his continued aid and protection, that he would be constantly with him as he had been with his servant Moses, provided he was obedient to his laws as he had been; thus encouraged, Joshua proceeded boldly nothing doubting, and the city of Jericho being directly opposite the place where the Israelites were to pass the Jordan, he resolved there to make his first attack; but previous to the commencement of the siege, he thought it advisable to send two spies into the city, to reconnoitre the strength of the place, and observe the several avenues to see where it would be easiest of [sic] assault. When the spies were despatched, he sent officers throughout the camp to give the people notice that within three days they were to cross the Jordan; they were therefore ordered to provide themselves with victuals for their march. I must here observe to you my children, that though the chief of their food during their sojourn in the wilderness, was manna, yet as they approached the promised land, and could procure provisions in an ordinary way, the miraculous bread gradually decreased, and at length was totally withdrawn;[7] they were now in the country of Og and Sihon, whom they had conquered; and the victuals they were commanded to supply themselves with, were such as their conquests afforded; in the mean time the spies who were sent upon the hazardous expedition, got safe into the city, and took up their lodging at a public house, that was kept by a widow woman named Rahab.

MRS. ALWORTH. Do, my dear, explain to the children that the appellation given to Rahab in the scriptures was not always understood as a term of reproach and infamy, as it is now.

FATHER. You are kind to remind me of this necessary explanation. In the Hebrew language, my children, there is but one word to express a hostess, or woman who keeps a house of entertainment for travellers, and a woman of ill-fame; but we have not the smallest reason to suppose that it is applied to Rahab in the latter sense; for, after the taking of Jericho, she married into the tribe of Judah; her husband's name was Salmon, he was of a noble family, himself a prince. Boaz was the offspring of this union; Boaz was the father of Obed; from Obed descended Jesse, and from Jesse king David. This Canaanitish woman is also mentioned by St. Paul as an example to future generations, of faith and good works.[8] While the spies were in Rahab's house, by some means intelligence of them was carried to

---

7. [Joshua 5:12.]

8. Like many other nineteenth-century authors, Rowson assumed that the book of Hebrews, which mentions Rahab as an example of faith (11:31), was authored by the Apostle Paul. Writing later in the century, Woosnam correctly refers to "the author of chapter xi.31 of the Hebrews." Rahab is held forth as an example of justification by works in James 2:25.

the king of the place, who immediately ordered the gates to be shut, and strict search to be made for the men; but Rahab, having some notice given her of the danger they were in, hid them under some hempen stalks which lay drying on the roof of her house. When the king's officers came to search, she told them that two strangers had indeed been there, and they had departed but a short time since, they might be easily overtaken. Having thus sent the officers upon a fruitless pursuit, she went to the spies, and having requested a promise, that when the army should enter the city, orders might be given to spare her, and whoever might be in the house with her, which they solemnly promised should be done; she then let them down from her house (which was built upon the city wall,) by a scarlet cord, which they directed her to hang from her window in the day when the city should be taken, and it should be a signal for the safety of her, and her household; they then made the best of their way to the neighbouring mountains, where they lay concealed, till those who went in pursuit of them might be supposed to have returned to the city; when they hastened to the camp, and arrived there in safety.

HORATIO. Surely sir, we can by no means justify the conduct of Rahab, for thus concealing the foes of the state, uttering absolute falsehoods to the king's officers; and in a manner, betraying her country into the hands of its most cruel enemies.

FATHER. Her conduct has, I must confess at first view, that appearance; but if we reflect a little, and read the account given by Joshua with attention, we shall change our opinion. It is natural to suppose by the declaration Rahab makes to the spies, that the inhabitants of not only Jericho, but all the land of Canaan, had heard of the mighty nation who had travelled through the wilderness to take possession of their country; that this mighty nation was under the immediate protection of a great and powerful Being whom they worshipped, and whom they declared to be the only living and true God; and that this God had promised to deliver the land of Canaan into their hand; this Rahab might have heard in common with others; she might also have heard of what happened to the king of Egypt and his host, when they pursued Israel; of what had taken place on the eastern side of the Jordan; how the Amalekites, Amorites, and Og, king of Bashan, had been discomfited, their territories taken from them, and themselves and subjects put to the sword, of this she could not be supposed ignorant. It is natural to imagine that, in reflecting on these things, she began to doubt the power of those gods she had been taught to worship, and to wish to come to a knowledge of the true God, for you find her addressing the spies in this manner, "I know that the Lord hath given you the land, and that your terror is fallen upon us, and that all the inhabitants of the land faint because of you; for the Lord your God, he is God in heaven above, and in the earth beneath." Here Rahab acknowledges that the maker and ruler of the universe had a right to dispose of all kingdoms and countries at his good pleasure; as she believed in the power, so she had faith in the goodness of this Almighty Ruler; and was willing to give herself, and all belonging to her into his hand, nothing doubting, that he would deliver her from the sword in the day of peril; considering also the two spies as servants of the Most High, she conceived it a duty to protect and deliver them, that her good works might be a proof of her faith.

HORATIO. But she certainly told a falsehood to the king's officers.

FATHER. To save innocent blood is always commendable; if it could have been done without prevarication, it would have been better; but we will suppose a man in the heat of intoxication, and mad with passion pursued another with a drawn sword, with an intent to kill him, suppose the one so pursued, rushed into your house and demanded protection, you would naturally conceal him; but of what use would your concealment be, if, when the infuriated enemy pursued and demanded his victim, you instantly led him to his place of concealment, and gave him into his hands? Rahab might thus argue with herself, "These men came to me in full confidence that they should be safe, and procure for themselves such accommodations as travellers want; shall I suffer them to be murdered in the very place where they sought an asylum? No, I will conceal them, and mislead their pursuers: should I betray them, I should be as guilty of their death, as those who actually shed their blood." Thus thinking, and thus arguing, how could Rahab have conducted herself more conformably to what she conceived to be the will of God, than by joining those who were so visibly supported by his almighty arm, and separating herself from a people, who were devoted by this divine power to destruction.

HORATIO. Her conduct certainly does not appear criminal when viewed in this manner.

FATHER. Besides Horatio if you read the tenth, eleventh and twelfth verses of the twentieth chapter of Deuteronomy, you will find that the Israelites were obliged to offer peaceable terms to every city before they besieged it; if the terms were accepted, the prince and his people became tributary to the Hebrews; if they were rejected, they were liable to all the consequences of siege, conquest, and the rapine and slaughter which usually follow; this being the case, certainly any of the inhabitants who chose to accept the terms offered, might throw themselves upon the mercy of the conqueror, and crave protection from him without offending against either loyalty or patriotism.

Source: Susanna Rowson, *Biblical Dialogues between a Father and His Family Comprising Sacred History from the Creation to the Death of Our Saviour Christ* (Boston: Richardson & Lord, 1822), 1.239–43 [this section follows a discussion of Moses's death and Joshua's succession].

Sarah Hale

Redeeming Rahab

Sarah Hale (1788–1879) was born in Newport, New Hampshire, the daughter of Captain Gordon Buell, a revolutionary soldier, and Martha Whittlesey.[9] Hale's mother educated her at home, and her brother, a student at Dartmouth, taught her Latin and philosophy. She worked as a school teacher before marrying David Hale in 1813, but his death in 1822 meant that she had to find work to support herself and her five children. She soon launched her successful career as a writer and editor. She became editor of the *Ladies' Magazine* in 1828 and nine years later was appointed editor of *Godey's Ladies Book*. Hale authored thirty-six books and many articles in the magazines she edited, most of which were intended for female audiences. Hale was also involved in a number of organizations, including societies that sent women overseas to work in medicine and missions.

Hale often elevated women in her writings, believing that they were morally and spiritually superior to men.[10] This ideology is reflected in her most ambitious publishing project, a biographical dictionary of women beginning with Eve and continuing through history to include Hale's contemporaries, entitled *Woman's Record; or, Sketches of All Distinguished Women, from*

---

9. For a fuller discussion of Hale, see Heather Macumber, "Hale, Sarah (1788–1879)," in *Handbook of Women Biblical Interpreters: A Historical and Biographical Guide*, ed. Marion A. Taylor and Agnes Choi (Grand Rapids: Baker, 2012), 238–40. Also see Hale's comments in the chapters on Delilah and Deborah.

10. For a fuller discussion of nineteenth-century assumptions about women's nature, see the introduction.

the Beginning till A.D. 1850.[11] Her dictionary was one of many attempts by nineteenth-century women to recover the history of women, who had been overshadowed or forgotten in histories written by men.

Hale's entry on Rahab fits the genre of her book, and in contrast to Rowson, she feels no need to whitewash Rahab's occupation or engage the ethics of war. The only hint of judgment occurs in her choice of "massacre" to describe the battle of Jericho. After a straightforward recounting of the biblical narrative, she argues that, while several commentators translate the Hebrew word *zonah* as "innkeeper," it clearly means "harlot" and no exception should be made with this text. She further supports her conclusion by citing historical evidence indicating that there were no inns in the time and place in which the story is located. She then adds a theological argument to her linguistic and historical argument when she writes that the Bible does not gloss over characters. What a person was before conversion is not significant if, once converted, one's life is changed for the good. She concludes that Rahab must have converted and become a good person because she married a prince of Israel. Rather than deprecating Rahab's character, Hale describes her as a woman of "fidelity, discretion, and a believer in the God of Israel." She completes her entry by dating the event to 1451 B.C., following Bishop James Ussher's chronology.[12]

Rahab

A WOMAN of Jericho. When Joshua, the leader of the Israelitish host, sent out two spies, saying, "Go view the land, even Jericho," it is recorded "that they went, and came into an harlot's house, named Rahab, and lodged there." The king of Jericho hearing of their visit, sent to Rahab, requiring her to bring the men forth; but instead of complying, she deceived the king, by telling him that they went out of the city about the time of the shutting of the gate, and whither they went, she knew not, but doubtless if the king pursued after them they would be overtaken. In the mean time, while the messengers thus

---

11. This work went through several editions. The edition excerpted here has the year 1854 in the title.

12. Bishop James Ussher's (1581–1656) chronology was widely used in the nineteenth century, and its dates were often printed in the margins of the King James Version. Hall also used Ussher's chronology to date the conquest of Jericho.

put upon the false track pursued after them to the fords of Jordan, Rahab took the two men up to the roof of the house, which, after the custom of eastern cities, was flat, and hid them under the stalks of flax which she had spread out there to dry.

This strange conduct, in defence of two strangers, she explained to the spies, by telling them, after they reached the roof, that "she knew that the Lord had given the children of Israel the land, for they had heard of their doings from the time that they came out of Egypt, so that all the inhabitants of the land faint because of you."

In return for her care, she made them swear unto her that they would save alive herself and all her family, — father, mother, brothers, sisters, and all that they had. Having thus secured herself from threatened destruction, she let them down by a cord through a window, for her house was upon the town wall, and they escaped to the mountains, whence, after three days, they returned to the camp of Joshua.

For the important service rendered to these spies, herself and kindred were saved from the general massacre which followed the capture of Jericho, her house being designated by a scarlet cord let down from the window out of which the spies escaped.

Several commentators, anxious to relieve the character of a woman so renowned from the imputation cast upon her by the opprobrious epithet usually affixed to her name, would translate the Hebrew word *Zonah*, which our version renders "harlot," by the term "hostess" or "innkeeper." But the same Hebrew word in every other place means what the old English version says, and we see no reason to make its use here an exception; besides, there were no inns in those days and countries; and when, subsequently, something answerable to our ideas of them were introduced, in the shape of caravanseri, they were never kept by women.

It is a remarkable feature of the Bible, that it glosses over no characters, but freely mentions failings and defects, as well as goodness and virtue; and hence, when errors of life are spoken of as connected with any individual, it is not incumbent on us to defend all the life of that individual, if the character is good from the time that it professes to be good; the evil living which went before, may freely be named without compromising or reflecting upon subsequent goodness.

Her remarks to the spies evince her belief in the God of the Hebrews, and her marriage, at a later period, with Salmon, one of the princes of Israel, proves her conversion to Judaism.

The Jewish writers abound in praises of Rahab; and even those who do not deny that she was a harlot, admit that she eventually became the wife of a prince of Israel, and that many great persons of their nation sprang from this union.

According to the Bible, Rahab was a woman of fidelity, discretion, and a believer in the God of Israel; and the only individual, among all the nations which Joshua was commissioned to destroy, who aided the Israelites, and who was received and dwelt among the people of God as one with them. St. Paul quotes her as one of his examples of eminent faith.[13] These events occurred B.C. 1451.

Source: Sarah Hale, *Woman's Record; or, Sketches of All Distinguished Women, from the Creation to A.D. 1854* (New York: Harper & Bros., 1855), 54.

CECIL FRANCES (FANNY) ALEXANDER

From Scarlet Thread to Blood Drops

Fanny Alexander (1818–95) was born in Dublin, the second daughter of Major John Humphreys and Elizabeth Frances Reed.[14] Alexander's talent for writing was apparent early on, and she was encouraged in her writing by her father and such eminent clergy as Anglican Walter Hook. In 1833 the family moved to County Tyrone, where Alexander wrote some of her best-known poetry and hymns. Some of her hymns were included in Irish hymnbooks when she was in her twenties, and her reputation as a great hymn writer grew over time. The influence of the Oxford Movement can be seen in many of her writings, including her 1846 publication, *Verses for Holy Seasons,* and her most popular work, *Hymns for Little Children* (1848). In 1850 Alexander married the Anglo-Catholic poet and priest William Alexander. She became very involved in the life of his parish and continued to write and publish poetry when health and other responsibilities allowed. Alexander's collection entitled *Poems on Subjects in the Old Testament* (1854) showcases her gifts as

---

13. [Hebrews 11:31.]

14. For a fuller discussion of Alexander, see Leon Litvack, "Alexander, Cecil Frances," in *The Oxford Dictionary of National Biography,* ed. H. C. G. Matthew and Brian Harrison (Oxford: Oxford University Press, 2004), 1:661–62.

an interpreter of the Old Testament texts. In 1867, William Alexander became bishop of Derry and Raphoe, and the family moved to the bishop's palace in Londonderry. Christians still sing a number of her more than four hundred hymns, including "All Things Bright and Beautiful," "There Is a Green Hill Far Away," and "Once in Royal David's City." The collection of her poetry published a year after her death contains her poem on Rahab.

The first half of Alexander's poem "Rahab" outlines the story, focusing on Rahab's heroic faith memorialized in Hebrews 11:31. The second half of the poem shifts to the present and explores the story's spiritual relevance. Alexander spiritualizes the spies who knocked on Rahab's door, likening them to "thoughts," which are "God's angels" sent to inspire believers to do "some deed of Christian worth." Her description of Christians' reception of these angelic thoughts is intriguing: "And we tremble at their presence, / And we blush to let them forth, / In some word of tender feeling, / Or some deed of Christian worth." This is not a description of a robust Christian faith engaged in courageous and heroic acts, such as Rahab's actions in hiding the spies, but is a picture of a modest faith confined to private feelings and acts of charity. Alexander also connects the "scarlet thread" hung out of Rahab's window with the "blood drops" of atonement — both of which secure safety in battle. As Rahab's faith saved her from the death of Israel's foes, the faith of Christians saves them from temptation when they are youths, and on the final battle day, the day of death, it will likewise deliver them.

Rahab

"By faith Rahab perished not with them that believed not, when she had received the spies with peace."

Heb. xi.31.

Rise up, rise up, O Rahab;
And bind the scarlet thread
On the casement of thy chamber,
When the battle waxeth red.

From the double feast of Gilgal,
From Jordan's cloven wave,

Rahab

They come with sound of trumpet
With banner and with glaive.

Death to the foes of Israel!
But joy to thee, and thine,
To her who saved the spies of God,
Who shows the scarlet line!

'Twas in the time of harvest,
When the corn lay on the earth,
That first she bound the signal
And bade the spies go forth.

For a cry came to her spirit
From the far Egyptian coasts,
And a dread was in her bosom
Of the Mighty Lord of Hosts.

And the faith of saints and martyrs
Lay brave at her heart's core,
As some inward pulse were throbbing
Of the kingly line she bore.

As there comes a sudden fragrance
In the last long winter's day,
From the paly silken primrose
Or the violet by the way.

And we pause, and look around us,
And we feel through every vein
That the tender spring is coming
And the summer's rosy reign.

In the twilight of our childhood,
When youth's shadows lie before,
There come thoughts into our bosoms
Like the spies to Rahab's door.

And we scarcely know their value;
Or their power for good or ill,

But we feel they are God's angels,
And they seek us at His will.

And we tremble at their presence,
And we blush to let them forth,
In some word of tender feeling,
Or some deed of Christian worth.

Yet those guests perchance may witness
In that awful battle day,
When the foe is on the threshold,
And the gates of life give way:

When the soul that seeks for safety,
Shall behold but one red sign
But the blood drops of Atonement
On the cross of Love Divine!

Source: Cecil Frances Alexander, *Poems,* edited with a preface by William Alexander, Archbishop of Armagh and Primate of All Ireland (London: Macmillan & Co. Ltd., 1896), 85–87.

Charlotte Maria Tucker (A.L.O.E.)

The Sign of the Cord

Charlotte Maria Tucker (1821–93), the sixth child of Henry St. George Tucker and his wife, Jane Boswell, was born in Barnet, Hertfordshire, and lived in London until her mother's death in 1869.[15] Henry Tucker's appointment as chair of the East India Company in 1826 brought with it increased wealth and social connections. He disapproved of girls' schools but educated his five daughters at home, allowing them to follow their interests. Charlotte's

---

15. For a fuller discussion of Tucker, see Heather Weir, "Tucker, Charlotte, Maria (A.L.O.E.) (1821–93)," in *Handbook of Women Biblical Interpreters: A Historical and Biographical Guide,* ed. Marion A. Taylor and Agnes Choi (Grand Rapids: Baker, 2012), 511–14.

interests gravitated toward music, dance, drawing, and teaching, and she entertained her younger siblings through the plays that she wrote. Her father also did not approve of women working so Charlotte had to wait until after his death in 1851 to begin her career as an author. She published her first book, *Claremont Tales*, under the pseudonym A.L.O.E. (A Lady of England) and continued to publish between two and seven books a year between 1852 and 1875. Her primary audience was children, and her intention was to instruct them in Scripture and the evangelical Anglican tradition. Following the death of her mother and sister in 1869, Tucker moved to India, where she worked as a missionary and teacher until her death eighteen years later. A plaque commemorating her life and work is on the wall of the Anglican cathedral in Lahore, Pakistan.

One of Tucker's most creative educational books, *House Beautiful; or, The Bible Museum* (1868), was inspired by the House Beautiful in *Pilgrim's Progress* and Tucker's love of the great objects housed in the British Museum. In the preface to her book, she explained that she was going to write about objects in the Bible, drawing the analogy between her book and a museum. She intended the book to help the Christian reader engage in "holy musings on the past."[16] *House Beautiful* contains forty-one meditations on biblical objects, with the concluding meditation focusing instead on the names of the twelve tribes listed in Revelation 7. This book was addressed to a general audience, including but not restricted to children.

Tucker's lesson on Rahab begins with an object lesson on the scarlet cord. Tucker, like Susanna Rowson and Sarah Hall, identifies the cord that let down the spies in the basket with the cord that Rahab hung from her window. Justice is achieved when the cord that saved the spies also saved Rahab and her family. Tucker suggests that the scarlet cord would have been preserved and become a family relic. In her retelling of the story, Tucker edits the dialogue between Rahab and the spies, pictures events from Rahab's point of view by describing the procession of the Israelites as it would have appeared from Rahab's position on the wall, and fills in the emotional responses of Rahab and her family to the attack. However, unlike Rowson, Tucker does not question the justice of God's actions. She avers that the Israelites' conquest of Jericho succeeded in "executing the sentence passed by a righteous God upon His guilty creatures."

Like Cecil Frances Alexander, Tucker uses typology to unpack the story's spiritual significance for her readers. Like Rahab, those in Christ's church

---

16. A.L.O.E. [Charlotte Maria Tucker], *House Beautiful* (London: T. Nelson & Sons, 1868), vi.

have nothing to fear as they wait the final battle. She draws two further lessons about the life of faith from her reading of Christ as "our scarlet cord" and James 2:25; namely, a believer's faith should be active and visible.

In the end, Tucker has only positive characterizations of Rahab. Perhaps because she includes children in her audience, her rendition of the story pits good against evil in a simple way and effectively glosses over the moral complexities of the narrative.

Rahab's Scarlet Cord

No fragile cord this, the "scarlet thread" which Rahab fastened in her window. Its firm twist has borne the weight of the two Israelite spies whom this woman of a doomed race, strong in faith, saved from the pursuit of their enemies. It was a moment of deep anxiety when Rahab led the spies to the casement in the darkness of night, and ere they descended by that scarlet cord, earnestly pleaded with them for the family whom she loved.

"Now therefore, I pray you, swear unto me by the Lord, since I have shewed you kindness, that ye will also shew kindness unto my father's house, and give me a true token: and that ye will save alive my father, and my mother, and my brethren, and my sisters, and all that they have, and deliver our lives from death!"

"Our life for yours," answered the men to their brave and generous preserver. "Behold," they afterwards said, "when we come into the land, thou shalt bind this line of scarlet thread in the window which thou didst let us down by: and thou shalt bring thy father, and thy mother, and thy brethren, and all thy father's household, home unto thee. And it shall be, that whosoever shall go out of the doors of thy house into the street, his blood shall be upon his head, and we will be guiltless; and whosoever shall be with thee in the house, his blood shall be on our head, if any hand be upon him."

They were gone, those men of Israel; Rahab had faithfully performed the duties of hospitality, of mercy, and now she remained awaiting in trembling hope the fulfilment of the promise which they had made. There hung the scarlet line from her window over the wall of the doomed city: on it was now suspended the safety of herself and her household. We picture to ourselves Rahab watching from that window the miraculous passage of the Jordan by Israel's hosts under Joshua; the priests descending into the bed of the river, bearing with them the Ark of the Covenant; and the waters standing on a heap to let the Lord's people go over dry-shod. She beholds the multitudes of Israel, — warriors and women, flocks and herds — streaming across the dry channel of the once rapid river, a countless, an irresistible force, because under the immediate guidance of Him who is omnipotent. We know what was the effect of the marvellous passage on the minds of the people of Canaan: *their heart melted, neither was there spirit in them any more.* Rahab might tremble like the rest; but when she looked on that scarlet cord she would yet thank God and take courage. Those terrible hosts of Israel came not as enemies to her.

Then followed the siege of Jericho, the city on whose wall stood the dwelling of Rahab. Day after day the woman of Canaan beheld that mysterious march of the Israelites round the city. Strange and terrible must have appeared the solemn procession which for seven days moved round its walls. First came the seven priests with their trumpets, preceding the Ark of God. The warriors of Israel followed in stern silence; there was no sound of voice from the hosts whose glittering arms were consecrated to the terrible work of executing the sentence passed by a righteous God upon His guilty creatures. Despair would have oppressed the soul of Rahab, who knew but too well that Jericho was given into the hands of its foes, but for that scarlet line, the pledge and token of mercy to her and all in her house.

The seventh day dawned, the last that the city of Jericho — as it then stood — ever should see. Seven times the march of the Israelites encircled the walls. Then with what terror must the household, gathered together in the dwelling on the wall, have heard the blast of the trumpet, followed by that thundering shout before which crashing fell bulwark and battlement — all Jericho's pride and strength! Fearful sounds succeeded; slaughter was raging in the streets; the swords of Israel were bathed in blood! Rahab and her family could not but have experienced emotions of pity and horror, as shuddering they listened to those sounds; but they needed to have no feelings of personal fear: that scarlet cord was to them a surer defence than strongest bulwark or loftiest tower; a surer defence than a phalanx of spears bristling around them. There was no danger to Rahab from falling wall or from enemy's sword; there was no stain on her threshold, no dying cry in her home. By faith, she perished not with them that believed not. She lived to be a mother in Israel, by adoption one of the people of God, if, as is supposed, it was this Rahab who became the wife of Salmon, and the mother of Boaz of Bethlehem, and thus an ancestress of the blessed Saviour Himself.[17]

17. [See Matthew 1:5.]

We naturally suppose that the scarlet cord would be preserved as an heirloom in the family at Bethlehem; that the gentle Ruth, herself a daughter of Abraham by adoption, looked with peculiar interest upon this relic of her husband's Gentile mother; and that young David often gazed with reverential awe on this memorial kept in his father's home of her who, in faith, preserved the Israelitish spies. We can scarcely conceive that such a family relic as this would lightly be cast away.

There is much that reminds us of Christ's Church, in the position of the pale, anxious woman of Jericho, watching from her casement the Israelites encircling the city doomed to destruction, she herself secure in a promise, saved by faith, reserved for blessedness and honour. A thousand years with the Lord is but as a day, and for nearly six such periods has the silent, solemn march of events, brought nearer the grand consummation before us. The Church knows that *the day of the Lord will come as a thief in the night; in which the heavens shall pass away with a great noise, and the elements shall melt with fervent heat, the earth also and the works that are therein shall be burned up.*[18] She is listening with trembling expectation for the sound of the *shout, and the voice of the archangel, and the trump of God,*[19] when the earth shall *reel to and fro,*[20] and the mountains shall shake, and the mighty cities shall fall![21] She has nothing to fear in that day: the blood of Christ is her salvation — the angel of destruction will see the token of living faith, and touch not the redeemed of the Lord.

Yes, faith in Christ is our scarlet cord, and there are two lessons which we may learn from the type. Rahab's cord was not left in her dwelling a useless coil; it was employed in God's service, and it was shown forth in sight of the world. What would the mere possession of a scarlet line have availed to Rahab, if she had not used it in doing God's work? Was not Rahab *justified by works, when she had received the messengers, and had sent them out another way?*[22] Nor was her scarlet cord hidden from men; it hung from her window over the wall. So should the Christian's profession of faith be open: he should not only believe in Christ, but serve Him — not only serve Him, but confess Him.

Source: A.L.O.E. [Charlotte Maria Tucker], *House Beautiful* (London: T. Nelson & Sons, 1868), 75–80.

---

18. [2 Peter 3:10.]
19. [1 Thessalonians 4:16.]
20. [Isaiah 24:20.]
21. [Ezekiel 38:20.]
22. [James 2:25.]

Rahab

ETTY WOOSNAM

True Conversion

Etty Woosnam (1849–ca. 1883) was born in India to James Bowen Woosnam and Agnes Bell Woosnam.[23] In 1860 she moved with her family to England to reside in Somerset, where she taught a Bible class for young ladies that became the basis for her two published volumes on women of the Bible. Woosnam returned to India in 1881 and married John R. Theobalds, Surgeon-General in Madras in 1882. She died a year later.

Woosnam wrote *Women of the Old Testament* (1881) and *Women of the New Testament* (1885) to edify, instruct, and one might even say preach to her female readers. She presented the characters of individual women through the lens of a particular characteristic or theme, drawing on a wide variety of contemporary sources to make her point. Woosnam was very interested in forming Christian character and often raised issues related to woman's nature, character, and role, and her writings reveal much about the lives of privileged English women.

Woosnam's "sermon" on Rahab focuses on the theme of conversion and illustrates the meaning of what Woosnam calls *the full gospel*. This entails both justification (being saved from the wrath of God) and sanctification (conquering sin in the here and now while preparing for the life to come). Woosnam praises Rahab's actions but states clearly that God is not dependent on them, as her belief in the sovereignty of God compels her to conclude that God does not need the services of his people but uses them to show that "the blackest of sinners" can be transformed into "workers in His vineyard." When Woosnam explores the morality of Rahab's lying, she concludes that it cannot be excused and claims that although it shows that Rahab had sided with the cause of God, she needed further instruction in the way of the Lord. Unlike Susanna Rowson, Woosnam does not explore the context or consider that lying might be the lesser of two evils. Lying is simply wrong regardless of circumstances.

Woosnam wonders why New Testament writers continue to label Rahab as a harlot when she is praised as a model of the Christian life. Woosnam

---

23. For a fuller discussion of Woosnam, see Donna Kerfoot, "Etty Woosnam: A Woman of Wisdom and Conviction," in *Recovering Nineteenth-Century Women Interpreters of the Bible*, ed. Christiana de Groot and Marion Ann Taylor (Atlanta: Society of Biblical Literature, 2007), 217–31.

suggests that while "men" continue to attribute old sins to reformed characters, God forgets our sins. This criticism of the use of "harlot" in the New Testament raises questions about Scripture's infallibility, though Woosnam would have defended a high view of Scripture. In addition to addressing this difficult issue, Woosnam expounds the story of Rahab as instruction for holy living as this is expressed both in the "home circle" as well as in public life.

Rahab: True Conversion

Two spies are sent out secretly to reconnoitre the enemy's land, and are received by Rahab. In the account of this extraordinary character we find for ourselves a *full gospel;* and in her case an example of true conversion, which may profitably be used as a gauge against which to measure our own souls and test whether we really be in the faith. First of all, our notice is attracted to Rahab's singular device for saving herself and her family, in the sack of the city, by a "scarlet line," that forcible type of the redeeming blood of Christ. Here is a most striking illustration of the safety of the sinner who takes shelter from the wrath to come in the atonement of Christ on Calvary — the central truth of Christianity — the lesson of God's forgiving grace and love in Christ which glitters on every page of the Bible and shines through all the sacrifices and offerings;[24] is taught by the Paschal Lamb;[25] Noah's Ark;[26] the cities of refuge;[27] the passage of the Red Sea;[28] and the washings in Jordan.[29] We gain, then, firstly the precious doctrine of justification by faith in the Cross of Christ. The sinner is only safe when he is in the household protected by the scarlet line. This is the foundation-stone of our Christianity; but a foundation-stone is not the whole edifice. And the doctrine of justification by faith is not the *full* gospel. It is indeed much to be delivered from going down to the pit and to be given a glorious hope of immortality with God in heaven....

But a message of forgiveness is not all that is contained in the glad tidings. Jesus is the Saviour who not only saves us from hell, but who will save His

24. [The offerings are primarily described in Leviticus 1–7.]
25. [That is, the Passover lamb; see Exodus 12:1–24.]
26. [See Genesis 6–8.]
27. [See Numbers 35:9–34.]
28. [See Exodus 14.]
29. [See the story of Naaman in 2 Kings 5:1–14.]

people even here on earth from those sins which constitute their misery and sorrow, who will give us His Holy Spirit to enlighten and lead us, to comfort and sanctify us, and make us meet for the place He is gone before to prepare for us. It was not only safety that was granted to Rahab. She did not merely escape with her life like Lot's family from a doomed city,[30] or like a shipwrecked mariner, destitute and breathless. She became a princess in Israel of the royal tribe of Judah — the ally and friend of God's people — the mother of Boaz, "a mighty man of wealth,"[31] and no less than Sarah, Rebekah, Rachel, and Ruth, the ancestress of King David and of our Divine Master Jesus Christ — mother, thus, of Him in whom all the families of the earth should be blessed.[32]

Two New Testament writers refer to Rahab to illustrate their point, each enforcing one of the two sides of God's eternal Truth. Neither side is it wise or safe or scriptural to overlook. The author of chapter xi.31 of the Hebrews cites Rahab as an instance of a notorious sinner's being saved by grace through faith. "She perished not with the unbelieving or disobedient when she had received the spies with peace." It makes our memory revert to the noble testimony she gave of her faith: "I know that the Lord hath given you the land and that your terror is fallen upon us." . . . and "the Lord your God, He is God in heaven above and in earth beneath." The Apostle James brings Rahab forward to demonstrate the difference between the dead faith which is not a saving faith, and the living faith, which brings forth the fruit of good works. She showed the genuineness of her faith by her conduct towards God's people and her own kindred. St. James says: "Likewise also was not Rahab the harlot justified by works when she had received the messengers and had sent them out another way? For as the body without the Spirit is dead, so faith without works is dead also."[33]

Conversion means a real change in the character, heart life, friendships, habits: forsaking the old leader to enroll oneself in the opposite army under the other Captain. . . .

What evidences did Rahab give of true conversion? — that her candle was divinely lighted?

(i.) She had implicit faith in the scarlet thread, the sign of the covenant agreed upon between her and God's messengers. . . . In the Epistle to the

---

30. [See Genesis 19:15–25.]
31. Ruth ii.1. [This footnote was marked by an asterisk in the original.]
32. [See Genesis 12:3 and 28:14.]
33. [James 2:25–26.]

Hebrews and in that of St. James, Rahab is spoken of as "the harlot." This is the way in which men allude to reformed characters; even long years after conversion, the memory and reproach of old sins cling to the child of God. It is well for us that though the world thus brands us indelibly, God has promised that our sins and iniquities He will remember no more.[34] Though He will never forget our wants, the depths of the sea will close over our sins.[35] "Let us fall now into the hand of the Lord, for His mercies are great; and let us not fall into the hand of man."[36]

(ii.) She gave practical help to God's people. . . .

(iii.) A third evidence of Rahab's sincerity was her request to the spies. She did not engage them to give her gold, or silver, or changes of raiment, or any reward whatsoever; she desired only her own safety and that of all her kindred. Her eagerness for their salvation is a great mark of the strength of her conviction. . . . True conversion is most severely tested by the demeanour in the home circle. It is *the real thing* indeed if it shows there, in more unselfish love, wiser thoughtfulness, and gentler patience. . . . "*Unto all* in the house." Not only must we shine in the eyes of a too indulgent father or mother, or uncle or grandfather, or to the favourite brother or specially genial sister; but to all the various characters in the house, servants included. . . . "Let your light *so* shine," says the dear Master to whom we belong, "that ye may glorify your Father which is in heaven."[37]

Source: Etty Woosnam, *The Women of the Bible: Old Testament*, 4th edition (London: S. W. Partridge & Co., 1881), 86–97.

Leigh Norval

Daring to Be Different

While Leigh Norval (fl. 1889) is virtually a forgotten author, we have one book to remember her by, which was published by the Methodist Episco-

---

34. [Hebrews 10:17.]
35. [See Micah 7:19.]
36. [2 Samuel 24:14.]
37. [Matthew 5:16.]

pal Church South — possibly her church affiliation. It appears from this book that Norval was involved in the Christian education of children as she adapted her language to young readers and omitted elements of the stories that she felt were not age appropriate.

Norval discusses many of the themes presented already. She is especially concerned to address the moral issue of God's destruction of the people of Jericho. She mentions a variety of means of divine destruction of "sinful heathen . . . so corrupt that even the little children are trained in wickedness." Unique to Norval is her description of Rahab as a three-dimensional character who was "bad, like the rest, and smart and resolute," "knew how to manage men," but was also kind, "for a warm heart beat in the bosom of this wide-awake, sensible, active woman." Norval writes that Rahab let the spies down in the basket with "her own strong hands" and "dared to be peculiar when it was right to be different from those around her." Norval does not dwell on the particular sins of Rahab, but paints a physically strong, pragmatic, and independent woman who takes risks to do what needs to be done.

Rahab, of Jericho

A strong walled city stood about seven miles from the river Jordan, and eighteen miles east from the site of Jerusalem. It was called Jericho. The sinful heathens of that city had a king and "mighty men of valor," but they were sore afraid. They had gone on in their own bad way a long time, and had grown so wicked that it was not good for them to live longer. Now and then when people get so corrupt that even the little children are trained in wickedness, God uses some means to destroy them. It is not always by a miracle, like the rain of fire on Sodom. Generally he destroys a nation by war. There are forms of sin, however, such as drunkenness, that produce diseases which kill people, so that God does not leave himself without a witness in this life that sin is "exceeding sinful." God had determined to destroy the people of Jericho. Moses had gone to heaven from Mount Pisgah, and the brave, good Joshua had been made the leader of the Hebrews. With more than six hundred thousand armed men he was about to cross the river Jordan. The inhabitants of Jericho had heard of God's dealings with the Egyptians and other heathens, and they were in a terrible fright. They knew they were as wicked as could be, and they suspected they were about to be punished.

WOMEN OF WAR, WOMEN OF WOE

It did not seem to occur to the people of Jericho to repent. One woman, however, was wise enough to desire God's mercy, and she got it. She was bad, like the rest, and smart and resolute. This woman, Rahab, had a house built in the high wall around Jericho. Two men came by night into the city, and were received into Rahab's house. They were Hebrews, or Israelites, sent out by Joshua as spies. The King of Jericho found out they had entered the city and sent to take them prisoners, but Rahab hid them on the flat roof of her house under stalks of flax. She was ready with a probable story when they were searched for, and told their pursuers they had gone out of the city gate when it was dark. She knew how to manage men, and got rid of the king's soldiers quickly by hurrying them off to try to catch the two Hebrews where they had not gone.

When Rahab had sent the men of Jericho on a fool's errand she went herself upon the roof of her house. There were solemn thoughts in her mind. She knew it was now a matter of life and death with her and her family to win favor with the Hebrews and with God. She told the two men, "I know that the Lord hath given you the land, and that your terror hath fallen upon us, and that all the inhabitants of the land faint because of you." Then she openly confessed, "The Lord your God, he is God in heaven above, and in earth beneath." For the kindness with which she had treated them she begged they would return kindness. Her request was not chiefly for herself, for a warm heart beat in the bosom of this wide-awake, sensible, active woman. She asked that her father and mother and brothers and sisters should be spared, and their property also. A promise was made her that all of her "father's household" should be spared when Jericho was destroyed. "As the body without the spirit is dead, so faith without works is dead also";[38] and Rahab had confessed her faith, and now she proved it by her works. With her own strong hands she let the two Hebrew spies down from her window to the bottom of the wall outside the city. She gave them excellent counsel, saying: "Get you to the mountain, lest the pursuers meet you; and hide yourself there three days, until the pursuers be returned; and afterward may ye go your way." They did as she told them, and went safely back to Joshua.

Joshua and his warriors gathered around Jericho. For six days they marched once a day around the city. Each time seven priests followed, blowing trumpets of rams' horns. The golden ark, or box, containing the Ten Commandments written with the finger of God, was carried behind. On the seventh day the city was compassed seven times, and the last time that great army of half a

---

38. [James 2:26.]

million went around Jericho the priests blew a loud blast with the trumpets, and a great shout went up. The walls fell flat before Joshua and the men who had obeyed God. At the appointed hour all difficulties give way before those who believe and obey God. Jericho was given up to the sword, and all in the city were killed but the one woman and her kin. Joshua had charged his army: "Rahab, the harlot, shall live, she and all that are with her in her house, because she hid the messengers that we sent." It had been agreed that she should hang from her window the red cord by which she had let the two Hebrews down the wall. All who were gathered of her kin under her roof were to be unhurt. "The young men that were spies went in, and brought out Rahab and her father, and her mother, and her brethren, and all that she had; and they brought out all the kindred, and left them without the camp of Israel."

Rahab had separated herself from her people because they were wicked, and she believed God would punish them. He accepted and blessed her, and he gave her a home among his chosen, and her name shines in the New Testament. She dared to be peculiar when it was right to be different from those around her; therefore "she perished not with them that believed not."[39]

Source: Leigh Norval, *Women of the Bible: Sketches of All the Prominent Female Characters in the Old and the New Testament* (Nashville, Tenn.: Publishing House of the M. E. Church, South, Sunday-School Department, 1889), 73–78.

Josephine Elizabeth Butler

The Saving Shelter of the Home

The parents of Josephine Butler (1828–1906), John Grey and Hannah Annett, were committed Anglicans who instilled in their daughter their strong convictions about abolition, alleviating poverty, and other social justice causes.[40]

39. [Hebrews 11:31.]
40. For more information on Butler see Timothy Larsen, "Evangelical Anglicans: Josephine Butler and the Word of God," in Timothy Larsen, *A People of One Book: The Bible and the Victorians* (Oxford: Oxford University Press, 2011), 219–46; Amanda Benckhuysen, "Butler, Josephine Elizabeth Grey (1828–1906)," in *Handbook of Women Biblical Interpreters: A Historical and Biographical Guide*, ed. Marion A. Taylor and Agnes Choi (Grand Rapids: Baker, 2012), 104–5; and Judith R. Walkowitz, "Butler, Josephine Elizabeth," in *The Oxford Dictionary*

Although Butler was raised an Anglican, she had a Methodist governess and regularly attended Wesleyan services. Her evangelical faith was her constant companion and source of empowerment in her life and work with the poor and the marginalized. In 1852 she married George Butler, who was ordained as an Anglican priest a year later. After the tragic death of their five-year-old daughter, Butler began a ministry to women in workhouses, seeing their pain as greater than her own. To these and other "outcasts," Butler devoted her life, campaigning for the repeal of the Contagious Diseases Acts, advocating for women's rights to education, property, and the vote, and creating awareness of the dark world of human trafficking of women in Europe, especially in time of war. Butler used the printed and spoken word to communicate with the public. She was a prolific author, producing numerous pamphlets, essays, and books on a variety of subjects, including women's education and work. A number of her most passionate and effective oral and written presentations showcase her sophisticated effort as a biblical exegete. Francis Newman said of her approach to biblical interpretation: "She reads Scripture like a child and interprets it like an angel."[41]

Butler's discussion of Rahab is found in an essay entitled "The God of Families," which is in a collection of essays titled *The Lady of Shunem*. Butler premises her essay on the promise in Jeremiah 31:1 that God would be the God of all the families of Israel and that Israel would be God's people. She makes two basic points: first, God is committed to the family as the basic unit that receives salvation, and second, God is committed to all families — Jews, Christians, Gentiles, and foreigners. Butler stresses Rahab's concern to protect her extended family. Her request is granted, and the narrative records that Rahab and her entire household were spared and eventually integrated into the Israelite people. Butler points out that the faith of one member of the family is sufficient to ensure the salvation of the whole family. She supports these claims with biblical examples and John Bunyan's *Pilgrim's Progress*.

Almost paradoxically, Butler criticizes Christians who would limit the love of God by comparing them to Jews, whose spirit she describes as exclusive and narrow. Her lack of insight into the faith of the Jewish community

---

of National Biography, ed. H. C. G. Matthew and Brian Harrison (Oxford: Oxford University Press, 2004), 9:180–86. See also Butler's essays in the chapter on the Levite's concubine.

41. Timothy Larsen corrected the mistake made by many who identified the Newman who described Butler's hermeneutical approach as Cardinal John Henry Newman. Larsen suggested instead that the quotation came from John Newman's freethinking brother, who was a strong supporter of the campaign against the Contagious Diseases Acts. See *A People of One Book: The Bible and the Victorians* (Oxford: Oxford University Press, 2011), 240.

contributes to her fear that Christians in her day might repeat the "fatal error" of the Jews and stands in sharp contrast to the inclusive message she seeks to promote in this essay. Butler's evangelical commitments emerge in several places in the essay, such as when she holds Rahab up as a model of faith and charity because of her kindness to the spies, arguing that she is an object lesson of God's benevolence because God had "elected" her, a Gentile.

The God of Families

"I will be the God of all the families of Israel, and they shall be my people."[42] So it is written. But was it of the families of Israel alone of whom God thus spoke? The most impressive answer possible to this question is given to us in the record of a strangely wonderful event occurring on the eve of the entrance of the people of Israel into the Promised Land, after their long wandering in the wilderness. Joshua was now their leader. They were approaching the shores of the Jordan. We may imagine that every heart beat high with hope, with expectation, with wonder, not unmixed, perhaps, with fear on account of the power of the hostile inhabitants of Judea, whom they were to supplant. The inhabitants of the land were idolators, ignorant of the true God. They were to be cast out, and this rich and beautiful country was to become the inheritance of the race chosen of God to be keepers and transmitters of his divine teachings and truth. But before the crossing of the Jordan, Joshua sent spies in advance to view the land, and especially to observe and report upon the great fortress and city of Jericho. The spies went forth, and the first dwelling they entered was that of the harlot Rahab; and it was this Rahab who was elected of God to proclaim, by the object-lesson of her charity, her active faith and its results, the truth that God, the God of Israel was, and is, also the God of all the families of the earth, of the families of every Gentile as well as Jew who should admit him into his heart and his home.

Rahab's Faith.[43] I need not recite the story, familiar to all, of Rahab's sheltering of this reconnoitring party sent by Joshua. That she recognized the

---

42. [Jeremiah 31:1.]

43. [These headings were not originally placed in the text but occurred next to the page numbers as subject guides; their current placement reflects an editorial decision based on paragraph content.]

divine government, and the presence and favour of God granted to the invading people, is shown by her words to the spies: — "I know that the Lord hath given you the land" . . . "for we heard how the Lord dried up the water of the Red Sea for you when you came out of Egypt"; and the close of her address to them is a confession of a faith which she alone, the harlot Rahab, appears to have possessed in that great city. Then, true woman as she was, though a sinful woman, she made her large-hearted request. She asked no personal gift in return for the kindness she had shown to the spies; I do not know if she was a mother: poor soul, she may have been so; but it is generally supposed that she, a woman of soiled life, had no closer relationships than those which she herself named in her comprehensive petition. She had at least the mother-heart, the yearning to gather around her, to shelter and to save all whom in any way she could call her own. Having recognized the spies as messengers of God, she prayed: — "Swear unto me by the Lord, since I have showed you kindness, that ye will also show kindness unto my father's house: and that ye will save alive my father, and my mother, and my brethren, and my sisters, and all that they have, and deliver our lives from death"; and the men sware unto her. Her prayer reached the heart of God, and his covenant mercy closed over all those of whom she had spoken. He inspired the messengers to reply to her, "Behold, when we come into the land, thou shalt bind this line of scarlet thread in the window, and thou shalt bring thy father and thy mother, and thy brethren, and *all thy father's household home unto thee.*" "Home unto thee"; what a beautiful word! A woman of an idolatrous tribe; unlike the Lady of Shunem — she had no dignified position, no lofty character, no virtuous record.[44] Yet her poor, ignoble house becomes, through her faith and humility, a city of refuge, an ark of salvation, a true *home* for all her kindred. "Home *unto thee.*" Without *her* presence there, without her faith, and her gathering-in love, it would have been no home, no refuge from the storm which was about to break over the doomed city.

Rahab's City of Refuge. Jericho fell, and a general massacre followed. But Joshua had said unto the two men that had spied out the country, "Go into the harlot's house and bring out thence the woman and *all that she hath,* as ye sware unto her." It seems as if the sacred historian had purposed by repetition to emphasize the complete, the absolutely and minutely faithful carrying out of the promise made to her by God through the messengers; as though he would count again and again all the relatives of Rahab, one by one, down to the most distant of her connections and belongings, in order

---

44. [2 Kings 4:1–37.]

to assure all who should read the record that not one was missing of all whom she had *brought home to herself.* For again it is recorded, "And the young men went in and brought out Rahab, and her father and her mother, and her brethren (sisters are included in the word brethren), and all that she had"; and again it is repeated, "And they brought out *all her kindred*" (in the Hebrew "families"). Probably among her brethren some had wives, with families of children, infants in arms, or aged parents. All, all were included in the asked, and promised, and fulfilled salvation.

Again there is a repetition, two verses further on: "And Joshua saved Rahab the harlot alive, and her father's household, and all that that she had; and she dwelleth in Israel unto this day." She had the honour of being ranked as an ancestress of the Messiah, for she became the wife of Salmon, who was the father of Boaz, husband of Ruth the Moabitess; and she obtained a place in the long honour-roll of the heroes of faith; (Hebrews, xi., 31) — "By faith the harlot Rahab perished not with them that believed not."

And so, in the opening act of the long history of the conquest of Palestine by the children of Israel, this beautiful idyll of a rescued Gentile family is bound up in the wonderful and tragic story of the destruction of Jericho; as if the great Father of all would teach his chosen and favoured people that, while they were the subjects of his special election, He, their God, was not alone the "God of all the families of Israel," but was also the God of families everywhere, in every land, and to the end of time; and that in the family bond, ordained by him the love and the faith of one may draw and gather in many, bringing them all within the saving shelter of the home marked by the symbolic scarlet line.

Source: Josephine Butler, *The Lady of Shunem* (London: H. Marshall, 1894), 93–99.

Elizabeth Cady Stanton

The Question of Motives

Elizabeth Cady Stanton (1815–1902), daughter of Judge Daniel Cady and Margaret Cady, was born in Johnstown, New York.[45] She was well educated and,

[45]. For a fuller discussion of Stanton, see Priscilla Pope-Levison, "Stanton, Elizabeth Cady

after her schooling, studied law in her father's office and became interested in women's legal status. She married abolitionist Henry Brewer Stanton in 1840, with whom she shared a passion for human rights. The challenges she experienced as a wife and mother of seven children while living in Seneca, New York, heightened her awareness of women's rights. With Lucretia Mott, Stanton convened the first women's rights convention in 1848 and helped to formulate the Declaration of Sentiments and Resolutions, modeled on the Declaration of Independence. The declaration included a resolution on female suffrage, an issue Stanton championed for five decades. She also lobbied for the Married Women's Property Act, for which she gave several speeches before the New York State Legislature. Over the course of her life, Stanton came to believe that the traditional view that the Bible taught women's subordination was impeding the progress of the battle for women's equality. She decided to take on the "enemy" and produce a book that critically evaluated the Scripture's teachings on women. She gathered together a female revising committee and a group of writers who produced the first volume of *The Woman's Bible* in 1895; a second volume followed in 1898. In the preface to the second volume, Stanton declared that the Bible had been "made a fetich [sic] ... long enough," arguing that it be read critically like any other book. She advocated "accepting the good and rejecting the evil it teaches."[46]

Stanton portrays Rahab as a complex character and entertains the possibility that her motives in saving the spies might have been mixed. She considers Rahab a typical woman in that she is marked with "keen insight and religious fervor," adding that Rahab's commitment to Israel could have been due to her genuine desire either to serve the cause of the Israelites or "to save her own life and that of her kinsmen." She may well have been a turncoat who aligned herself with the winner. As such, Rahab was more a shrewd woman than a sincere convert.

Stanton concludes her commentary on Rahab with a discussion of the nature of Scripture. She addresses the comments of a critic of the first volume of *The Woman's Bible* who said that "there is no more significance ... in commenting on the myths of the Bible than on Aesop's fables." Stanton however, argues that for many interpreters there is a difference and it is that difference she wants to change. She hopes to rid women of "superstitions" regarding the

---

(1815–1902)," in *Handbook of Women Biblical Interpreters: A Historical and Biographical Guide*, ed. Marion A. Taylor and Agnes Choi (Grand Rapids: Baker, 2012), 469–73.

46. Elizabeth Cady Stanton, "Preface to Part II," *The Woman's Bible* (New York: European Publishing Co., 1898), 8.

Rahab

divine inspiration of the Bible. Her contrast between the light of reason and the ignorance on which faith is based is typical of nineteenth-century rationalism.

In saving the spies from their pursuers, Rahab made them promise that when Jericho fell into the hands of Joshua, they would save her and her kinsmen. From the text, it seems that Rahab fully understood the spirit of her time, and with keen insight and religious fervor, marked characteristics of women, she readily entered into the plans of the great general of Israel.

Rahab was supposed to have been a great sinner, her life in many respects questionable; but seeing that victory was with the Israelites, she cast her lot with them. From the text and what we know of humanity in general, it is difficult to decide Rahab's real motive, whether to serve the Lord by helping Joshua to take the land of Canaan, or to save her own life and that of her kinsmen. It is interesting to see that in all national emergencies, leading men are quite willing to avail themselves of the craft and cunning of women, qualities uniformly condemned when used for their own advantage.

There is no more significance, as one of our critics says, in commenting on the myths of the Bible than on Aesop's fables. The difference, however, is this: that in the latter case we admit that they were written by a man; while in the former, they are claimed to have been inspired by God. Though at variance with all natural laws, it is claimed that our eternal salvation depends on believing in the plenary inspiration of the myths of the Scriptures; as the "higher criticisms," written by learned scholars and scientists, are not familiar to women, our comments in plain English may rid them of some of their superstitions.

Though the injustice to woman is the blackest page in sacred history, the distinguished Biblical writers take no note of it whatever. Even Hon. Andrew D. White, though he devotes several pages of his work to the statue of Lot's wife in salt, vouchsafes no criticism on the position of Lot's wife in the flesh, nor of Lot's outrageous treatment of his daughters.[47] The wonder is that women themselves should either believe that such unholy proceedings were

---

47. Andrew Dickson White (1832–1918), an educator, bibliophile, diplomat, historian, and cofounder of Cornell University, discussed the history of the interpretation of the story of Lot's wife in the second volume of *A History of the Warfare of Science with Theology in Christendom* (New York: D. Appleton & Co., 1896).

inspired by God, or make a fetich [*sic*] of the very book which is responsible for their civil and social degradation.

Source: Elizabeth Cady Stanton, "The Book of Joshua," in *The Woman's Bible, Part II: Joshua to Revelation,* ed. Elizabeth Cady Stanton (Boston: Northeastern University Press, 1898), 11–12.

STUDY QUESTIONS

1. The story of Rahab presents some ethical dilemmas, such as whether it is sometimes right to lie. How would you describe the ethical choices Rahab faces? Does the biblical text affirm her decisions? How do the commentators view her actions? Does a close reading of this biblical text affect your understanding of what is right and wrong?
2. There has long been some debate about whether Rahab was an innkeeper or a prostitute. What is at stake regarding how she earned a living? Was the evaluation the same or different in biblical times? The Victorian Era? Our own time?
3. The commentators "clean up" the story to various degrees. Why did they do this? How would you tell the story of Rahab? Would this change depending on who you were speaking to? How would you share the story with children? Young adults? Men? Women?
4. Many Christians read Rahab's story through the lens of the three New Testament texts that mention her (Matthew 1:5; Hebrews 11:31; and James 2:25). How do these lenses shape an interpreter's understanding of Rahab's story? Do these New Testament texts determine the only "correct" reading of the Rahab narrative?
5. How do theological, hermeneutical, and/or cultural assumptions shape nineteenth-century readings of the Rahab story. Provide examples. What assumptions do you bring to your reading of the Rahab story?
6. How do these commentators address the "massacre" of the men, women, and children in Jericho? Do those who attempt to explain this "genocide" convince you that God was just in requiring the extermination of the Canaanites?
7. How did the personal battles of the writers affect their interpretation of the conquest of Jericho?

2

Achsah, Caleb's Daughter

The twice-told story featuring Caleb's daughter Achsah is a compelling tale of inheritance, father-daughter relations, and shrewd property acquisition.[1] The account is part of the larger story of the Israelite conquest of the Promised Land. When Caleb is granted Hebron, as a reward for his faithfulness, he announces he will give his daughter's hand in marriage to the one who actually conquers Hebron, formerly Kirjath-sepher. Achsah urges the victor, Caleb's nephew Othniel, to ask her father for a field. Achsah also approaches her father more directly, asking for springs of water in addition to the land in the Negeb, which her father had given. Caleb grants Achsah the "upper springs and the lower springs."

Some commentators recognized parallels between this brief narrative and a number of social conventions being negotiated in their own time and place, including the rights of a father over his daughter and the rights of married women to own and manage property.[2] Both the text and the commentators grapple with three potential variations of how women relate to property: (1) women have the status of property and cannot own or control property; (2) women have the status of property but might be able to own or at least indirectly control property; and (3) women can (and should) own property and take the opportunity to control that property. The blurring of these three "states" provides the backdrop to the entire discussion, as the story of Achsah itself contains competing understandings of women's rights regard-

---

1. It occurs in Joshua 15:13–19 and Judges 1:11–15.
2. Over the course of the nineteenth century in America and Britain, both single and married women slowly gained increased economic rights relating to inheritance, control over income and property, and retention of individual legal identity after marriage. These changes did not happen quickly or without debate, confusion, and overlap of understandings and directives about women's legal and economic rights.

ing property. For example, when Caleb offers his daughter Achsah as a war prize to the hero, she is clearly treated as property to be exchanged between men. Less clear is the granting of her indirect request for land: the field from her father may be "her" dowry, but it appears that her husband is the sole recipient of the property. The matter of the springs, however, appears to be a direct transaction between father and daughter and at least suggests that Achsah would have some control over the water.

Most interpreters explored issues relating to how gender and property rights intersect in Scripture and different historical eras. For example, Grace Aguilar harmonizes the account of Caleb's family and the laws in the Pentateuch regulating inheritance practices. Aguilar views the presentation of Achsah as a prize of war to be "won" not as degrading to women, but rather puts women "on a pedestal," likening the practice to the treatment of women in the age of chivalry. Elizabeth Cady Stanton, however, focuses on Achsah's direct request to her father and calls on women in the United States to follow this example by asking clearly for what they need. While Marianne Farningham points out that Achsah was not consulted prior to becoming a prize of war, Farningham assumes from the silence in the text that Achsah was in agreement with this arrangement. Interestingly, both Aguilar and Farningham title their sections "Caleb's Daughter," implicitly drawing attention to the power of the father over his daughter, rather than to the initiative and agency of his daughter.

Sharply contrasting with interpreters who use the literal/historical sense of the story as a platform for discussing such contemporary issues as woman's rights and woman's nature are Lydia and Charlotte Tucker, who unpack its "hidden" spiritual meaning. The pseudonymous author Lydia advocates discerning "things spiritual beneath the surfaces of historical narratives" and finds in both the nature and manner of Achsah's request and in many other details in the story "lessons of deep import." Tucker similarly sees spiritual lessons about prayer and the character of God in Achsah's request of her generous father for springs of water in addition to the land he has already given: "[God, Our Sire] will gifts for us prepare, Beyond our hopes, beyond our prayer!"

Achsah, Caleb's Daughter

LYDIA

Achsah Spiritually Considered

Lydia (fl. 1830s–40s) is the penname used by the British author of a number of articles in *The Christian Lady's Magazine*, including an impressive series entitled "Female Biography of the Scriptures." Lydia's articles are interlaced with biblical quotations and allusions and show that she was well educated and had access to a fine theological library. She was also familiar with theories of child development and Christian education. She espouses a traditional view of woman's nature and role, suggesting that most women in Scripture "exhibit marks or blemishes which we might expect to meet with in the fallen descendants of [Eve] who was 'first in the transgression.'" It is likely that she knew Charlotte Elizabeth Tonna, who edited *The Christian Lady's Magazine* from 1834 to 1846.[3] Although traditional in her view of the status of women, Lydia uses inclusive language to refer to God, anticipating the concerns of feminists regarding exclusively masculine language for God. Lydia also echoes feminist concerns when she fills out the lives of the "daughters of the old dispensation."

Lydia begins her commentary on Achsah with a discourse on hermeneutics, beginning with Romans 15:4, which she uses as a reading lens for Old Testament stories. Achsah is one of the many "prototypes" or "living representations" in Scripture that "the great Parent of our common humanity" has used to provide "our lessons in divine wisdom." Lydia draws out the spiritual lessons of Achsah's story from "beneath the surface" of the Old Testament for Christian women, whose situation is "singularly analogous" to Achsah's: Caleb is analogous to the divine parent, Achsah is a figure of the Christian believer, her request for a blessing and springs of water and "her manner of asking" model the kind of prayer for spiritual blessings that Lydia encourages her readers to pray. "And how shall we approach the Father of Spirits? As Achsah approached her earthly parent, with the confidence of a child, but with the low prostration and meek reverence of an inferior, pleading his own rich gift as the ground of a further 'blessing.'"

---

3. For information on Charlotte Elizabeth Tonna, see Heather Weir, "Tonna, Charlotte Elizabeth (1790–1846)," in *Handbook of Women Biblical Interpreters: A Historical and Biographical Guide*, ed. Marion A. Taylor and Agnes Choi (Grand Rapids: Baker, 2012), 500–502. Tonna published under a number of pseudonyms; perhaps she herself was Lydia.

Achsah

"Whatsoever things were written aforetime were written for our learning, that we through patience and comfort of the scriptures might have hope."[4] This is the testimony of God, by the mouth of an inspired apostle, concerning the details of the Bible. It is an important declaration; for by it we learn that there is no fact recorded in that book, which is irrespective of ourselves; — no mention made of matters which had better not have been mentioned; — no disclosures, which had better not have been disclosed; — no event, so apparently trivial, as to be of no moment to us; — no subject so vast as to be unapproachable by us. . . .

As the earthly parent endeavours to smooth the roughness of the road to knowledge by spreading before the unpractised eye of his child the pictured alphabet, and pouring into his yet uncultivated ear the soft cadences of measured rhyme; so has the great Parent of our common humanity given us our lessons in divine wisdom, not in the dry didactics of ethical science; but by living representations of men of like passions with ourselves. . . .

There is no age nor station of life which is not furnished with a corresponding exemplar in this varied and extensive record. The king on the throne — the captive in the dungeon — the master and the servant — the buyer and the seller — the warrior in the camp and the "plain man dwelling in tents"[5] — the statesman and the artificer — the merchant and the mariner, may here all find their prototypes; . . .

St. Peter evidently draws the attention of his female converts towards the study of the character and conduct of the "holy women of old,"[6] as one means of acquiring that adorning which is in the sight of God, of great price. It is true that the sacred writings afford but few particulars concerning the lives of these daughters of Israel. Their memoirs, if we may so speak, occupy that subordinate place in the word of God, which that word assigns to them personally; and it is only in the relations of wife or mother, daughter or sister, that they are brought before our notice; except it be in those rare instances in which we find them invested by God with civil authority, or super-naturally

---

4. [Romans 15:4.]
5. [Genesis 25:27.]
6. [1 Peter 3:5.]

endowed with prophetic vision, as in the case of Deborah or Miriam, Huldah or Anna. For the most part too, they exhibit marks or those blemishes which we might expect to meet with in the fallen descendants of her who was "first in the transgression":[7] but whether it be in the continuous history of a female believer from the time of her being called "to turn from dumb idols to serve the living and true God,"[8] 'till the period when that dust which was once animate with life, and "fair to look upon"[9] is buried out of the sight of the husband whom she once obeyed, calling him lord: or whether it be in the brief narrative that introduces to our notice her who is the subject of the present sketch, — there is always something to arrest our interest, something to shew that "these things were written for our examples."[10]

To the daughters of the Christian covenant, the short but striking incident which brings Achsah under the brief mention of the sacred historian is, when spiritually considered, full of instruction and encouragement. Brought up under the care of a pious and devoted parent, in the most triumphant period of the Jewish theocracy when, we have reason to think, the knowledge and fear of the Lord prevailed more universally than at any former or subsequent period among the people of Israel; her situation is in this respect singularly analogous to that of those who at the present day have been nurtured amid gospel privileges, and have lived to behold the conquests of the true Joshua, extending "northward and southward," eastward and westward, and the possession of the true Canaan made secure. The daughter of Caleb must have obtained some eminence among "the virgins her fellows"[11] from the adventitious circumstance of her birth and parentage alone.

Among the tribes assembled at Gilgal, there were but two men of all the countless host of Israel who had survived the desert march, and the fiery trials of the wilderness: but two, who, "because they judged him faithful that promised,"[12] had entered into possession of the promised rest. With what reverence must the warriors of Israel have looked upon Caleb, when, at the age of fourscore and five, he stood before them, strong and vigorous, as when in Kadesh-Barnea he stilled the tumult of the unbelieving multitude by the bold declaration of his own unshaken faith in the promises of Jehovah; and now claimed the fulfilment of that which the law-giver had then spoken to

---

7. [1 Timothy 2:14.]
8. [1 Thessalonians 1:9.]
9. [Genesis 12:11; 1 Peter 3:6.]
10. [1 Corinthians 10:11.]
11. [Psalm 54:14.]
12. [Numbers 14:30; Hebrews 11:11.]

him, "Surely the land whereon thy feet have trodden shall be thine inheritance and thy children's forever."[13] His just demand was acceded to, and the blessing of his faithful fellow-soldier, the leader of the armies of Israel, accompanied the investiture of this promised inheritance.

The gigantic sons of Anak found their strength departed from them; and the family of Caleb was soon in possession of the fair fields and villages of Hebron. But other fortresses remained to be conquered; the Anakims were yet in the land, and as an alliance with an individual so distinguished among his people, could not but be an object of ambition, Caleb proposes to give his daughter Achsah (his only daughter she appears to have been) to him whose victorious hand should complete the conquest of his allotted portion.

From the filial reverence which Achsah displays in her deportment towards her father, and the parental pride and affection with which Caleb evidently regarded his daughter, we may judge that she "was worthy" for whom Othniel was willing to give battle to the giant sons of Anak. The expedition against Kirjath-sepher was successful, and Caleb not only bestowed his daughter upon Othniel, but gave him soon after, at his own request, the additional grant of a field, which it is probable the latter desired on account of its valuable pasturage; for the whole district inherited by the tribe of Judah was remarkable for its fertile fields and fruitful vineyards. Vainly however would the flocks and herds of Othniel have lain down in the green pastures of Debir, could he not have led them also to springs of living water, and without these, the dowry of Achsah was incomplete.

Achsah undertakes to procure this additional grant from her indulgent parent: "She lighted off her ass"; and Caleb said unto her, "What wouldest thou?" She answered, "Give me a blessing, for thou hast given me a south land; give me also springs of water." Both the nature of her request and her manner of urging it afford lessons of deep import to all who have access to a Father in heaven whom they can approach with filial confidence, albeit not unmixed with reverence and godly fear. He who was a father in Israel, knew how to give good gifts to his beloved child, and has not your Father which is in heaven endowed you with a rich and fertile inheritance? Has he not given you "a south land"?[14] Taken up out of the wilderness of this world, your lot has been cast among his people. "The lines have fallen to you in pleasant places,"[15] in the fold of Christ's church, where there are fair and large pastures

---

13. [Joshua 14:9.]
14. [Joshua 15:19.]
15. [Psalm 16:6.]

— in the vineyard of God, where there are pleasant fruits. Corn and wine were the literal blessings of that mountain[16] which was given to the faithful Caleb, for his children's inheritance. And have not you too been invested with "the blessings of the eternal mountains, the desirable things of the everlasting hills"?[17] . . .

Does not the true vine grow in the midst of the garden of God, and are you not invited to partake of its fulness? What can your heavenly Parent do more for you that he has not yet done? Has he but one blessing to bestow? Can you, by repeated solicitations, encroach upon his bounty? Can you ask more than he is able or willing to impart? Oh, no! he who said of old to his ancient people "open thy mouth wide and I will fill it,"[18] hath in these latter days enjoined us to "covet earnestly the best gifts,"[19] and to "count not ourselves to have attained."[20]

"Give me," said the daughter of Caleb, "a blessing, for thou hast given me a south land; give me also springs of water." "If thou knewest the gift of God, and who it is that saith to thee, Give me to drink, thou wouldest have asked of him, and he would have given thee living water,"[21] said Jesus to the Samaritan. . . . The pastures among which the people of God walk up and down may be fair, and large; and great may be the care with which the under-shepherds tend the fold of the Great Proprietor: but it will be of no avail that we dwell "in a south land," if we cannot also obtain possession of the springs of living water. To whom then shall we go to obtain "a blessing"? To him who said "if ye being evil know how to give good gifts unto your children, how much more shall your Father which is in heaven give his Holy Spirit to them that ask him":[22] to him who said, "I will pour water upon him that is thirsty, and *floods* upon the dry ground; I will pour my Spirit upon thy seed and MY BLESSING upon thine offspring."[23] And how shall we approach the Father of Spirits? As Achsah approached her earthly parent, with the confidence of a child, but with the low prostration and meek reverence of an inferior, pleading his own rich gift as the ground of a further "blessing." Thou hast given thine only-begotten Son, wilt thou not also freely give the Comforter,

---

16. Joshua xiv.12.
17. [Genesis 49:26.]
18. [Psalm 81:10.]
19. [1 Corinthians 12:31.]
20. [Philippians 3:13-14; 2 Corinthians 10:12.]
21. [John 4:10.]
22. [Matthew 7:11; Luke 11:13.]
23. [Isaiah 44:3.]

the Sanctifier, — the fruitful source of blessing, — the earnest of a future and far richer inheritance.

When the daughters of the old dispensation rested at eventide by the fountains of Judah, with the full water-urns, drawn from the springing wells, how must the more meditative and contemplative among them, who "desired to see the things which we see,"[24] and who loved to look beyond the mere vehicles of prophetic instruction, "searching what manner of thing the Spirit of Christ, which was in them, did signify"[25] how must they have recalled to mind at such intervals the inspired declaration, "With joy shall ye draw water from the wells of salvation."[26] The time of shadows is now over, the reign of grace and truth is begun: shall we then go to the broken cisterns of worldly pleasure to supply our daily need? Oh, no! "The Spirit and the Bride say come, and let him that heareth say Come, and let him that is athirst come, and whosoever will let him take of the *water of life freely.*"[27]

Source: Lydia, "Female Biography of the Scriptures: Achsah," *The Christian Lady's Magazine* 10 (July–December 1838): 156-63 (ed. Charlotte Elizabeth; London: R. B. Seeley & W. Burnside); paragraph breaks have been introduced into the original document for ease of reading.

Grace Aguilar

Achsah and the Age of Chivalry

Grace Aguilar (1816-47) was born in Hackney, Middlesex, a suburb of London, England, the eldest of Emanuel and Sarah Aguilar's three children.[28] Emanuel was the leader of a Spanish and Portuguese Jewish congregation in London. Aguilar's gifts as a writer showed themselves at an early age in the family home, where she received her education. In 1828, due to Emanuel

---

24. [Matthew 13:17; Luke 10:24.]
25. [1 Peter 1:11.]
26. [Isaiah 12:3.]
27. [Revelation 22:17.]
28. For information on Aguilar see Cynthia Scheinberg, "Aguilar, Grace (1816-47)," in *Handbook of Women Biblical Interpreters: A Historical and Biographical Guide,* ed. Marion A. Taylor and Agnes Choi (Grand Rapids: Baker, 2012), 31-37.

Aguilar's poor health, the family moved to Devon, and it was there that Aguilar associated with Christians and attended services at a Methodist church. After returning to London with her family, Aguilar continued her writing career while running a school for Jewish boys with her mother. When Aguilar died at the age of thirty-one in Germany, the Jewish communities in Britain and America deeply mourned the loss of this creative and brilliant female writer, theologian, and apologist. Much of her work was published after Aguilar's death by her mother, and many of these works were written in support of Judaism and religious tolerance at a time when British Jews were under great pressure to convert to Christianity.

In 1845, Aguilar published *The Women of Israel*, a book of essays on Old Testament heroines intended to refute the writings of women such as Sarah Ellis, who elevated Christianity as "the sole source of female excellence."[29] Aguilar wrote *The Women of Israel* to encourage young Jewish women to be proud of their heritage and to see the benefits of their own religion for women. Aguilar also intended her book to be "as instructive as interesting, as full of warning as example, and tending to lead our female youth to the sacred volume, not only as their guide to duty, their support in toil, their comfort in affliction, but as a true and perfect mirror of themselves."[30] While Aguilar's *The Women of Israel* was one of many books in the mid-nineteenth century addressing issues related to "woman's capabilities, influences and mission," it stood out — not only because she was a gifted writer but also because of the uniqueness of her experience as a devout Jewish woman familiar with Christian worship and tradition. *The Women of Israel* became a popular gift book for Jews and Christians alike.

Aguilar begins her commentary on Achsah by describing the glories of the medieval age of chivalry as a time when women enjoyed elevated status and were able to bring out the best in men who would risk all for the smile of a woman. Aguilar then argues that the biblical story of Caleb offering his daughter as a prize of war represents the first recorded example of chivalry, predating the Middle Ages by many centuries. With this apologetic strategy, Aguilar refutes the claim that Christianity elevates women's status and that Judaism, by contrast, degrades women. Noting that Israelite men would not

---

29. Sarah Stickney Ellis (1799–1872) was the prolific author of thirty-four books. Her most famous conduct book, *The Women of England: Their Social Duties and Domestic Habits* (1839), which voiced middle-class views of womanhood, was an important foil for Aguilar's views on women in the Old Testament. Grace Aguilar, *The Women of Israel* (London: Groombridge & Sons, 1845), 8.

30. Aguilar, *Women of Israel*, 20.

have been inspired to compete for a slave's hand in marriage, Aguilar argues that Achsah enjoyed a high status and, further, that this elevated position was typical for women of ancient Israel. Aguilar also notes the intertextual connections of this story to other biblical texts that addressed inheritance. While Caleb's decision to offer his daughter in marriage (and presumably a dowry of land along with her) appears to risk violation of the inheritance laws found in Numbers 27:1-11 and 36:1-9, Aguilar posits that God acts so that these laws are upheld as Caleb's nephew is victorious, and so the laws allowing a daughter to inherit, providing she marry within the tribe, are followed.

Aguilar claims that women should have the right to own property even after marriage, although in 1845 women in England were still denied these rights.[31] Aguilar's assertion that the Hebrew Scriptures promote the liberation of women is supported by her observation that Achsah enjoyed the right to own property and that, generally, women in the Hebrew Bible held a higher status than women in England. Aguilar also finds the courtesy Achsah shows to her father to be an important feature of the story. Like Lydia, she sees Achsah's dismount — prior to requesting her present — as a sign of appropriate filial respect and interprets Caleb's immediate reply as indication that he views his daughter as a capable adult. This is but one example of how Aguilar points to scriptural models of how contemporary men and women ought to deal with each other — both showing mutual respect and confidence.

Aguilar sums up the narrative by describing masculinity and femininity in very stereotypical ways: women are pure and holy and are charged with the responsibility to inspire men to deeds of valor. She maintains that chivalrous values should be upheld because they are consistent with the teaching of Scripture. Aguilar does not, however, suggest how these values correspond with the right of a woman to own and negotiate property independent of her husband.

The age of chivalry is generally supposed to be a powerful proof of the respect and consideration with which women were regarded among the

---

31. Through the course of the nineteenth century, women's rights to own and manage property, even when married, slowly expanded.

Achsah, Caleb's Daughter

Gentile nations during the middle ages. Their position was marked; their love, their hand, the greatest reward, the most powerful incentive for the young warriors to distinguish themselves. Marvellous deeds were done, and dangers dared, all for the smiles of woman; nay, evil passions were often subdued: generosity, magnanimity, kindness, and many other virtues, were called into play by woman's influence, without which those ages would have been dark indeed. Her individual position might have been too elevated; but still, that elevation was far more often used for good than evil. Chivalry *did* bring forth good with regard to woman's influence on man, and no one assuredly will deny, but that to have been held up as the reward of valor, the incentive of virtue, must have made her a subject of consideration, respect, and love, very different to slavery and degradation.

Now, the very first instance of chivalry which history records, is found in the Bible, and in the history of that very people to whose women similar privileges are denied. [Aguilar quotes/summarizes the narrative here.]

Caleb seems to have been, like Joshua, a prince and warrior of high repute, dauntless, and faithful before God and before man. His daughter (though not an only child, for we read in 1 Chron. iv.15, that he had also three sons) shared the consideration proffered to her father. Caleb must have seen the high respect and admiration in which she was held, or he never would have dreamed of offering her as the reward of valor. That which is of no value, lightly won, and lightly held, and, when obtained, to sink merely into a household slave, was not at all likely to excite young men to the arduous task of smiting and taking a fortified city, defended as it was by the sons of Anak, whose immense stature and extraordinary prowess had formerly caused them to be considered as "giants," in whose sight the children of Israel were but as "grasshoppers." Nor can we regard this as merely a solitary instance: it is a proof of the *general condition* of Hebrew women at that period; and also that Othniel was not Achsah's only admirer.

"He that smiteth and taketh it, to him will I give Achsah my daughter to wife," is a general appeal, supposing her hand to be a sufficient incentive to all the young men of the tribe; and that His Law, regarding the inheritance of daughters, should not be transgressed, the Eternal blessed the valiant efforts of Othniel, Caleb's own nephew, with success; and the coveted maiden became his wife.

That it was solely Achsah herself who was sought and won, with no idea of her wealth, is clearly proved by the simple words "she moved him [her husband] to ask of her father, a field or piece of land"; the wish for possession came from her, not from Othniel, who was in all probability fully satisfied with the recompense he had gained; and when Caleb had granted this request, as we know by the words in which she afterward addresses him, she approached him herself, and lighting off her ass, a token of the respect natural to Israel, Caleb asked her, "What wilt thou?" and she answered him, "Give me a blessing": meaning, possibly, a further token of his love for her; "for thou hast given me a south land [alluding to that already given at Othniel's request], give me also springs of water: and Caleb gave her the upper and the nether springs."

Without springs, land, in so hot a country as Judea, was of little value; and therefore is it that Achsah craves this boon in addition to that already granted. The affectionate confidence subsisting between the father and daughter is beautifully illustrated in this simple little incident. Though Achsah held her father in such respect as not to prefer her request while *sitting* on her ass before him, yet she feared not to make her wishes known, fully conscious that, were they in his power, he would grant them unhesitatingly; and his instant reply proves how much reason she had for her confidence.

We learn too from this, that woman must undoubtedly have had the power of possessing landed property in her own right, and in a degree exclusive of her husband;[32] else Caleb would have made over the portion intended for her to Othniel on his marriage, instead of waiting for Achsah to ask, and granting it to her alone.

The beautiful law of our God was then in full force among every rank and condition of man; and surely we can find no trace in the history of Achsah to confirm the false position of our being degraded. Does it not rather elevate us to a perfect equality with our brother man, and prove undeniably that the Israelites were the very first nation in the world to hold forth the love and hand of woman as the pure and holy incentive to deeds of manliness and valor?

Source: Grace Aguilar, *The Women of Israel* (London: Groombridge & Sons, 1845), 199–202.

---

32. And exclusive also of her brothers; for if landed inheritance were to be man's only, she could have had no claim to any portion. The above was written originally under the impression that Achsah was Caleb's only child: a further study of the genealogies in Chronicles proves that she was not. [This footnote was marked by an asterisk in the original.]

Achsah, Caleb's Daughter

Charlotte Maria Tucker

The Hebrew Daughter's Prayer

Charlotte Maria Tucker (1821–93) was an evangelical Anglican author and educator of considerable means who published between two and seven books a year between 1852 and 1875 under the pseudonym A.L.O.E. (A Lady of England).[33] Tucker wrote most of her books for children, but also published for adults. Her poem on Achsah is one of ten poems on "Women of Holy Writ" included in the collection of poetry published in 1854.[34] Like Lydia, Tucker read the story analogically. Achsah's request of a blessing is interpreted as a prayer that her father would add the gift of water to the gift of land he had already bestowed. God's children are similarly encouraged to ask for more blessings: "Their Sire . . . will gifts for us prepare, Beyond our hopes, beyond our prayer!"

Achsah

"Father! Give to me a blessing!"
Such the Hebrew daughter's prayer;
"Through thy love this land possessing,
Oh! let thy paternal care
Add the gift of springs that flow
And fertilize the plains below!"

Caleb blessed his suppliant daughter
(Bride of him whose valiant sword
Won her in the day of slaughter);
More than asked will he accord,
Both the low and upper tide
Shall lave the land of Othniel's bride.

---

33. For a fuller discussion of Tucker, see the Rahab chapter and Heather Weir, "Tucker, Charlotte, Maria (A.L.O.E.) (1821–93)," in *Handbook of Women Biblical Interpreters: A Historical and Biographical Guide*, ed. Marion A. Taylor and Agnes Choi (Grand Rapids: Baker, 2012), 511–14.

34. Tucker wrote poems on eight Old Testament women (Eve, Hagar, Rebekah, Jochebed, Miriam, Rahab, Achsah, and Jael) and two New Testament figures (the Penitent and Mary).

Thus before their Sire in heaven
Let His blood-bought children bend;
"Much hast Thou already given,
Father! Let Thy grace descend,
Bid the barren desert live,
Give what Thou alone canst give!"

God will yield the wished-for blessing,
Nor the *upper springs* alone;
Once the Father's love possessing,
Earth and Heaven are our own!
He will gifts for us prepare,
Beyond our hopes, beyond our prayer!

Source: A.L.O.E. [Charlotte Maria Tucker], "Achsah," in *Glimpses of the Unseen: Poems* (Edinburgh: Gall & Inglis, 1854), 98–99.

Elizabeth Cady Stanton

Assertiveness Training

Elizabeth Cady Stanton (1815–1902) was a prominent American social activist, abolitionist, and advocate for women's legal, social, and spiritual equality.[35] Her comments on Achsah are taken from the second volume of *The Woman's Bible* (1898), the collaborative work she hoped would change the traditional understanding of the Bible's position on women, which she felt was hindering women's progress toward full equality with men.

Stanton's brief commentary is a striking counterpoint to Grace Aguilar's. Like Aguilar, Stanton reads the narrative in conjunction with the story of the inheritance given to the daughters of Zelophehad (Numbers 27:1–11; 36:1–9). Unlike Aguilar, Stanton calls attention to the double standard of the law in Numbers, which mandated that daughters could inherit only if there were no sons. Stanton, along with the other women excerpted in this

---

35. For more information on Stanton, see "The Question of Motives" in the Rahab chapter.

chapter, holds Achsah up as a model to follow, but the values and qualities she elevates are different than those identified by Lydia, Aguilar, and Charlotte Tucker. Stanton looks to Achsah as a model woman who asks directly for what she needs and calls on the women in the United States in 1898 to act accordingly. We see Stanton's core ideas and values in her list of demands, which is followed by her claim that these demands correspond seamlessly with the fundamental ideas of the Protestant religion. Whether Stanton was aware of how she privileged Protestant Christianity and of the consequences of doing so (i.e., the denigration of Judaism and Roman Catholicism) is not clear in this passage, but her approach certainly contrasts with Aguilar's project to disprove Christianity's singular role in elevating women's status in the world.

In giving Achsah her inheritance it is evident that the judges had not forgotten the judgment of the Lord in the case of Zelophehad's daughters.[36] He said to Moses, "When a father dies leaving no sons, the inheritance shall go to the daughters. Let this henceforth be an ordinance in Israel." Very good as far as it goes; but in case there were sons, justice demanded that daughters should have an equal share in the inheritance.

As the Lord has put it into the hearts of the women of this Republic to demand equal rights in everything and everywhere, and as He is said to be immutable and unchangeable, it is fair to infer that Moses did not fully comprehend the message, and in proclaiming it to the great assembly he gave his own interpretation, just as our judges do in this year of the Lord 1898.

Achsah's example is worthy the imitation of the women of this Republic. She did not humbly accept what was given her, but bravely asked for more. We should give to our rulers, our sires and sons no rest until all our rights — social, civil and political — are fully accorded. How are men to know what we want unless we tell them? They have no idea that our wants, material and spiritual, are the same as theirs; that we love justice, liberty and equality as well as they do; that we believe in the principles of self-government, in individual rights, individual conscience and judgment, the fundamental ideas of the Protestant religion and republican government.

36. [See Numbers 27:1–11; 36:1–9.]

Source: Elizabeth Cady Stanton, "The Book of Joshua," in *The Woman's Bible, Part II: Joshua to Revelation,* ed. Elizabeth Cady Stanton (Boston: Northeastern University Press, 1898), 13–14.

Marianne Farningham

Giving Good Gifts

Coming from humble beginnings and having only sporadic formal education, Marianne Farningham (1843–1909) was to become a household name in evangelical circles in England by the time of her death.[37] The daughter of Joseph Hearn, a tradesman and postmaster, and Rebecca Bowers, whose father was a papermaker and Baptist preacher, Farningham (one of the pseudonyms adopted by Mary Anne Hearn) supported herself and eventually members of her extended family through her writing. During her lifetime, her views on theology and women developed and changed; from her beginnings as a Baptist with Calvinist and Sabbatarian leanings, she adopted a more inclusive and less judgmental understanding of the Christian faith, while at the same time becoming more open and sympathetic to the matter of women's rights. Farningham was a prolific author of poems, hymns, stories, biographies, Sunday School lessons, a book on women in the Bible entitled *Women and Their Work,* and her memoirs, *A Working Woman's Life.* She was also a champion of women's rights (especially economic) and a popular lecturer and held public office as a member of the Northampton School Board. She believed that women should work for the common good in the public arena after fulfilling their primary obligations in the domestic sphere.[38] Although her book on women in Scripture was not published in the nineteenth century, it reviews and develops ideas previously expressed in her earlier public lecture, "The Women of the Bible," and so we include an excerpt from it here.

Farningham reads the story of Caleb's daughter through a lens of sympathy for the biblical story and its values. While she notes that Caleb has the

---

[37]. See Linda Wilson, *Marianne Farningham: A Plain Woman Worker* (Colorado Springs: Paternoster, 2007).

[38]. Not surprisingly, Farningham's memoir was entitled *A Working Woman's Life* (1907).

right to give his daughter away, she softens the harshness of this practice by assuming that daughters seemed to go along with the practice. She further asserts that Othniel was a good as well as brave man in order to have won the prize of Achsah's hand in marriage. Again the text is brought into conformity with nineteenth-century marriage customs. Just as good Israelite women married good Israelite men, good Christian women should marry good Christian men. Farningham claims that the culture of ancient Israel was more progressive than its neighbors because instead of the dowry being given to the bride's father, it was given to the bride.

The request for springs of water leads to a reflection on the necessity of water for life and an example from South Africa to prove her point. Although not drawing explicit attention to it, Farningham's world reflects England's role as a colonial power in the nineteenth century. The lesson ends with a moral on gift giving: gifts should reflect the affection of the giver and also be of service to the recipient.

Caleb's Daughter

"And she said unto him, Give me a blessing."

Judges i.15

It was only now and then that great women were given to Israel. They are not evident in the Book of Joshua, and between him and Saul, the first King of Israel, a period of two hundred years passed of which we know very little, except about the wars of Israel. Under Joshua's leadership the Hebrews went over the Jordan into the land of Canaan, which was their "Promised Land." The successor of Moses had an enormous task before him, but Moses had blessed him, and the children of Israel listened to him, and Joshua the son of Nun was "full of the spirit of wisdom."[39] "When the people had wept and mourned thirty days for their great leader, his minister Joshua began to urge them to cross the river and take possession. His word to them was always "Be strong and of good courage,"[40] and after many vicissitudes, and much fighting with the Canaanites, Joshua distributed Canaan among the Jews.

---

39. [Deuteronomy 34:9.]
40. [Deuteronomy 31:6.]

He lived a strenuous life; but when he was eighty-five years old he had not forgotten the days when Moses sent twelve men to spy out the land which they were to possess, nor the fact that only Caleb and himself brought back a good report. It was Caleb who stilled the panic-stricken people and said the brave words, "Let us go up at once and possess it, for we are well able to overcome it,"[41] and to him God promised "the land that he had trodden upon, and to his children, because he had wholly followed the Lord."[42] The inheritance which Joshua gave Caleb, with his blessing, was Hebron, though he had a battle to fight before he could secure his own.

Now, Caleb had a daughter, and when he was sorely pressed by difficulties he offered her as a prize to the man who gave him the best help: "He that smiteth Kirjath-sepher, and taketh it, to him will I give Achsah my daughter to wife." Fathers evidently had the power and the right to choose husbands for their daughters, who, knowing this, do not seem to have objected. He was a brave, good man who won this prize. "And Othniel the son of Kenaz, Caleb's younger brother, took it." The city must have been worth taking; its name, Kirjath-sepher, signifies its importance. The city of books, the city of scribes, the city of letters, the city of archives, the city of the oracle — all these interpretations have been given to this name. And the man who had taken it, Othniel, whose name signifies "lion of God," received from Caleb his daughter Achsah for his wife.

"And it came to pass that she moved him (her husband) to ask of her father a field." It was common to the Hebrews to give their daughters a dowry. Achsah knew what she wanted, and urged Othniel to ask of her father a field, a word which stands for a very valuable gift. The request was complied with; and this indicates not only the high social rank of Caleb, but also the dignified position held by the Israelite wife. This dowry was not given, as was usual with Orientals, to the father of her husband, but to the bride herself. And she wanted this her marriage portion to be as perfect and valuable as possible; and therefore, meeting her father, she "lighted down from off her ass."

"What wilt thou?" said Caleb to her.

"Give me a blessing," was her reply. "Thou hast set me in the land of the south; give me also springs of water."

The words have a winsome sound as of summer music. The south country is warm and sunny, rich with flowers and fruits, and greatly to be desired — if only there be plenty of water. In Palestine everything depends on that. A

---

41. [Numbers 13:30.]
42. [Deuteronomy 1:34.]

south field would be comparatively valueless if it were in a dry and thirsty land where no water was. Water, cool, health-giving, life-giving, is longed for always in the East. In our own colonies there is often much suffering from the lack of it. There was great sickness and weakness a short time ago in a South African town. The doctors were very busy giving medicine, but they said to their patients, "What you want is the rain." The very smell of it is good. Job was right when he said, "There is hope of a tree, though the root wax old in the earth and the stock die in the ground; yet through the scent of water it will bud and put forth boughs."[43] Caleb's present depended on the watercourses of the land. And the daughter beloved was satisfied, for Caleb gave her the upper springs and the nether springs.

Is there not a lesson for some of us here? Do we never give gifts without thinking of that which alone can render them of true value? The field without the water was not worse than any gift without love. Generous gifts are twofold, service and affection.

Source: Marianne Farningham, *Women and Their Work* (London: J. Clark, 1906), 39–42.

STUDY QUESTIONS

1. The commentators assert that the story of Caleb's daughter had important insights and lessons for gender relations, women's rights, and faithful living as experienced in their own day. Do their findings ring true? Can we find insights and lessons in this story for our own place and time? How can we evaluate whether a particular interpretation is appropriate?
2. Both Grace Aguilar and Marianne Farningham claim that Achsah's silence indicated her willingness to go along with her father's plan to offer her as a prize of war. Is silence always assent? Would another interpretation be reasonable? How, why, and when should we "fill in the gaps" in Scripture, if at all?
3. The commentators suggest a number of texts that relate to this Bible passage, including 1 Chronicles 4:15; Numbers 27:1–11; 36:1–9. Are there other Bible texts, such as Proverbs 31:10–31, which you use to illumine Achsah's story?

43. [Job 14:7–9.]

4. Each commentator offers a claim about how things should be in the future and attempts to support that claim through analysis of this Bible story. What are these claims? How successful were the commentators in supporting them?
5. Several commentators draw lessons from Achsah's "ask"; some develop a spiritual lesson on prayer whereas Elizabeth Cady Stanton interprets the "ask" as modeling for women a direct and assertive way of seeking out necessities. Assess these applications of the story. Is it more faithful to be direct in asking for something? Is it sometimes more faithful to be patient?

3

Deborah

The Deborah story begins by describing the twenty years of cruel oppression Israel experienced under King Jabin of Canaan due to the Israelites again doing what "was evil in the sight of the Lord, after Ehud died."[1] The pattern of history set up in Judges 2:11–22 replays here; God's response to idolatry is to allow neighboring peoples to attack and subdue Israel. In this context, Deborah is introduced as a prophetess, the wife of Lapidoth, who judges Israel while sitting under a palm tree in the hill country. It is she who summons Barak and commands him to engage the enemy, telling him where to position his men and that he must engage Sisera, the enemy's general. Barak agrees on the condition that Deborah accompany him into battle, and while Deborah agrees, she foretells that Barak will not end up with the glory, as Sisera will be delivered into the hands of a woman. The battle between Israel and the forces of King Jabin led by Sisera ends in panic for his army and their chariots. Barak and the Israelites pursue them, and Sisera is killed at the hand of Jael. The victory for Israel is complete. In response, Deborah and Barak sing the song found in Judges 5, where Deborah praises God for the victory and calls herself "a mother in Israel." The song recounts the day of battle and concludes with a vignette from the point of view of Sisera's mother, who comforts herself by assuming that her son is late because he is dividing the spoil, a girl or two for every man, and choosing with special care the loot that he will bring home as a gift for her. The reader knows, meanwhile, that Sisera is dead, killed at the hand of a

---

1. Judges 4:1–16 and 5:1–31. The intervening passage, Judges 4:17–24, focuses on Jael, and although the narrative is integral to the final victory of the Israelites, this book will treat the account of Jael separately. A few of the Jael commentators also include a brief discussion of Deborah.

woman. The song ends with final praise to God, contrasting God's treatment of God's enemies and friends. The chapter concludes with the note that the land had rest for forty years.[2]

For nineteenth-century women interpreters who were beginning to question the narrow roles traditionally assigned to women, the story of Deborah raised a number of issues. Presented as a judge, prophet, military leader, poet, and singer, Deborah was also a wife who called herself "a mother in Israel." Because she embraced such diverse positions in public and private life, Deborah became a lightning rod for discussions on the Woman Question.[3] Commentators were not uniform in their opinions about what aspects of the narrative were most significant or in their understanding of what changes, if any, should ensue regarding women's roles in society. A survey of their work demonstrates the richness, depth, and diversity of their interpretations and applications of the Deborah story. The issue of war was occasionally engaged, often indirectly. The more important issue for them was Deborah's transgression of expected gender roles, which invited reflection on appropriate spheres of women and men. Because the narrative shows Deborah coleading a military action with Barak, some commentators also explored how the two domains ought to relate to one another. For example, Grace Aguilar and Elizabeth Baxter understand Deborah's engagement in the public sphere to be an exception, inferring that her household duties suffered due to her public involvement. A corollary to the discussion of what place men and women should occupy in society was the question of whether men and women were fundamentally different. Commentators who presumed that "womanly" qualities such as compassion, humility, and intuition defined women were troubled by Deborah's demonstration of the "masculine" traits that enabled her to excel in public leadership. Others, however, questioned this traditional dichotomy. Julia McNair Wright, for example, contested the description of what masculinity and femininity entailed, while Clara Balfour argued that a woman could enter public life and still keep her womanly qualities. Clara Neyman criticized the public/private distinction, arguing that women and men should

---

2. Recently, Joy Schroeder published *Deborah's Daughters: Gender, Politics and Biblical Interpretation* (New York: Oxford University Press, 2014), a history of the interpretation of the Deborah narrative beginning with early Judaism and Christianity and continuing to the present. The book is an excellent study of the reception history of this challenging narrative.

3. The "Woman Question" refers to discussions and arguments about the shifting understanding of women's nature and women's roles in society and the family taking place in the nineteenth century. See the introduction for a fuller presentation.

be involved in both spheres, as their goals and abilities were essentially the same. For Neyman, Deborah and Barak modeled an ideal male/female relationship characterized by equality and harmony.

Deborah's role as a judge and public officer also raised the issue of female education. For example, Aguilar drew on Deborah's role as judge, and the assumption that she was therefore well educated, to promote religious education for Jewish girls. Balfour and Wright likewise praised Deborah's intelligence as a judge and poet while advocating equal education for women.

Some interpreters included here read the Bible in light of their current context, which also included conversations with traditional and contemporary scholarship across the academic disciplines. Harriet Beecher Stowe, for example, worked with an evolutionary model of human development as it related to the story of salvation and cited German biblical scholar Johann Gottfried Herder in her discussion of the poetry of the Song of Deborah.[4] Wright employed a developmental model of human history to claim that we should move beyond war as a means to resolve conflict.

Grace Aguilar

Superwoman

Grace Aguilar (1816-47) was a gifted Anglo-Jewish author of short stories, novels, poetry, and religious writings.[5] In 1845 Aguilar published *The Women of Israel* to encourage Jewish women to be proud of their heritage and to see the benefits of their own religion for women.

Deborah was one of many biblical women Aguilar used as a platform to address issues related to women's abilities, influences, and mission. Aguilar's presentation of Deborah — as a prime example of women's high status in ancient Israel — forms part of her argument against some Christian commentators' claim that Jewish women should convert because Christianity affords women a higher standing. Aguilar notes Deborah's multiple

---

4. J. G. Herder (1744-1803), a German philosopher, theologian, poet, and literary critic, first published his influential two-volume work on Hebrew poetry in 1782-83.

5. For further biographical details, see "Achsah and the Age of Chivalry" in the Achsah chapter.

roles, concluding that ancient women must have had "high and intellectual training, as well as natural aptitude for guiding and enforcing the statues of their God."

Aguilar also sees the narrative teaching that women and men are the same in matters of the heart, concluding that God can choose a woman as well as a man to be judge, prophet, and military leader. Aguilar combines this notion of men's and women's essential equality in the eyes of God, however, with the idea that women and men have naturally different abilities. She writes that God, in choosing Deborah, is "heeding neither the weakness nor apparent inability of one sex, compared with the greater natural powers of the other."

Aguilar applies the lessons learned from the life of Deborah to the lives of married and single women. Here too she holds to the traditional division of the public and private sphere, claiming that women should exercise their judging ability only at home and should participate in the public arena indirectly by influencing their husbands. Single women are likewise advised to seek out ways of serving God that cohere with the traditional nurturing roles assigned to women. In the end, Aguilar declares to nineteenth-century women: "Deborahs in truth we cannot be."

Deborah

[Aguilar sets the stage for her discussion of Judges 4–5 with a review of the conquest of the Promised Land and Israel's subsequent disobedience. She addresses the ethical issue of holy war and defends God's command to possess the land by the sword.] But even in these periods of anarchy and rebellion, all were not idolatrous. There must still have been many "seven thousands who had not bowed the knee to Baal,"[6] else would not the Lord have thus repeatedly compassionated and relieved them. Among these faithful few, the law was of course followed, and the people judged according to the statutes given through Moses. Had there been the very least foundation for the supposition of the degrading and heathenizing the Hebrew female, we should not find the offices of prophet, judge, military instructor, poet, and sacred singer, all *combined* and all *perfected* in the person of a woman; a fact clearly and almost startlingly illustrative of what

---

6. [1 Kings 19:18.]

must have been their high and intellectual training, as well as natural aptitude for guiding and enforcing the statutes of their God, to which at that time woman could attain.

"And Deborah, a prophetess, the wife of Lapidoth, she judged Israel at that time. And she dwelt under the palm-tree of Deborah, between Ramah and Bethel, in Mount Ephraim: and the children of Israel came unto her for judgment." This simple description evinces that the greatness of Deborah consisted not at all in outward state, in semblance of high rank, or in any particular respect or homage outwardly paid her; but simply in her vast superiority of mental and spiritual acquirements which were acknowledged by her countrymen, and consequently revered. The office of judge in Israel was not hereditary. It only devolved on those gifted to perform it; and, by the example before us, might be held by either sex: rather an *unsatisfactory* proof of the degradation of Jewish women. We are expressly told that Deborah was a prophetess, and "the wife of Lapidoth." Now, by the arrangement of this sentence, confirmed by the context, it is very evident that Deborah was a prophetess in her own person, wholly and entirely distinct from her husband, who was a mere cipher in public concerns. The Eternal had inspired her, a WOMAN and a WIFE in Israel, with His spirit expressly to do His will, and make manifest to her countrymen how little is He the respecter of persons; judging only by hearts perfect in His service, and spirits willing for the work: heeding neither the weakness nor apparent inability of one sex, compared with the greater natural powers of the other.

Yet so naturally are her public position and personal gifts described, that we cannot possibly believe her elevation to be an extraordinary occurrence, or that her position as a wife forbade her rising above mere conjugal and household duties. We never hear of a slave, or leper, or heathen, being intrusted with the prophetic spirit of the Eternal, simply because the social condition of such persons would and must prevent their obtaining either the respect, obedience, or even attention of the people. For the same reason, had woman really been on a par with these, as she is by some declared to be, she would never have been intrusted with gifts spiritual and mental, which Deborah so richly possessed. She never could have been a prophetess, for her words would only have been regarded as idle raving. She could never have been a judge, from the want of opportunities to train and perfect her intellect, and to obtain the necessary experience. Now it is clear that instead of this, her natural position must have been so high, that there needed not even adventitious state and splendor to make it acknowledged; and her intellect and judgment so cultivated, as not only to bring the people flocking to her for judgment, but to occasion Barak's refusal to set out on a warlike expedition unless she accompanied them.

We find the first recorded instance of her using her prophetic power in Judges iv.6: [Aguilar quotes verses 6–9]. . . .

We should be at a loss to understand the feeling in Barak, which impelled his reply, might we not infer it from Deborah's rejoinder. It would appear that, like many of his countrymen, while he obeyed, he was still wanting in the perfect faith which would have given him a glorious triumph in his own person. The presence of Deborah could in no way give him greater increase of safety and glory, than had he gone without her. She was but the instrument of the Lord, making His will known to her fellows. The words were not hers, but God's; and Barak should have acted on them without either reservation or doubt. Instead of which we find him making a *condition* to his obedience; and refusing to obey, if that condition were not complied with. What could the presence of a woman avail him? Her being a prophetess gave him no more assurance of conquest than the word of the Lord had already done; and *because he trusted more in the woman than in her God,* the journey would not be to his honor; a *woman's* hand should accomplish that complete downfall of Sisera, which would otherwise have accrued to his individual glory. It is evident that this is the real rendering of this rather obscure sentence, else we should not have it so expressly stated that the "journey would not be for his honor." . . .

We next find Deborah exercising that glorious talent of extempore poetry only found among the Hebrews; and by her, a woman and a wife in Israel, possessed to an almost equal degree with the Psalmist and prophets, who followed at a later period. Her song is considered one of the most beautiful specimens of Hebrew poetry, whether read in the original, or in the English version. We find her taking no glory whatever to herself, but calling upon the princes, and governors, and people of Israel, to join with her in "blessing the Lord for the avenging of Israel." In the fourth and fifth verses, she alludes, by a most beautiful figure, to the power of the Eternal. That before Him "the earth trembled, and the heavens dropped, and the clouds dropped water. And the mountains trembled, even Sinai, before the Lord God of Israel," thus manifesting that His power, not man's, had brought delivery to Israel. Then in the sixth and eighth verses she describes the condition of the people before she arose a mother in Israel; that they were compelled to travel in by-paths, because of the high roads all being occupied by their foes; and from villages all the inhabitants had ceased, from their being continually exposed undefended to the enemy. Nor was

Deborah

there a shield or spear seen in the forty thousand of Israel. The simplicity and lowliness of the prophetess's natural position, is beautifully illustrated by the term she applies to herself — neither princess, nor governor, nor judge, nor prophetess, though both the last offices she fulfilled — "until that I, Deborah, arose, until I arose a MOTHER in Israel." She asked no greater honor or privilege for herself individually, than the being recognized as the mother of the people whom the Lord alone had endowed her with power to judge. "My heart is toward the governors of Israel," she continues, "that offered themselves willingly among the people. Bless ye the Lord," meaning those who, rising from the idolatry and sloth which had encompassed the people, offered themselves willingly for the service of the Lord. She bids them speak — all classes of people — from those princes who rode on white asses, and those who sat in judgment, and those who walked by the way, to even the drawers of water who had before been harassed by the noise of the archers coming forcibly to disturb their domestic employments; and all were to rehearse the righteous acts of the Lord, for to Him alone they owed their preservation. "The Lord made ME have dominion over the mighty," she says, in verse thirteen, thus retaining her own dignity and power in Israel, yet tracing it to the Eternal, not to herself. The poetry describing the downfall of their foes, calling forth the imagery of nature to give it force and life; the death of Sisera, and the waiting and watching of his mother at her lattice — "Why is his chariot so long in coming? why tarry the wheels of his chariots?" and the answer, alike from her ladies and her own heart, "Have they not sped? have they not divided the prey; to every man a damsel or two; to Sisera a prey of divers colors, a prey of divers colors of needlework, meet for the necks of them that take the spoil?" as if to fail with his mighty armament were impossible; and thus sung by the lips of the conquerors, infused with a species of satire, giving indescribable poignancy to the strain; and then the glorious conclusion, "So let all thine enemies perish, O Lord: but let them that love thee be as the sun when he goeth forth in his might"; form altogether one of the sublimest strains of spiritual fervor in the Bible; and mark forcibly, by her conduct, both as prophetess and judge, that in Deborah, even as in Gideon, David, and the prophets of later years, God disdained not to breathe His spirit, but made a WOMAN His instrument to judge, to prophesy, to teach, and to redeem.

"And the land had rest forty years," we are told at the conclusion of Deborah's song; words which, as no other judge is mentioned, would lead us to infer that Deborah continued "a mother in Israel" all that time, retaining the people in fidelity, and consequently in temporal and spiritual peace. Even if she did not live herself to govern all those years, it is evident that her influence and instructions were remembered and acted upon, for it was not till *after* these forty years that "Israel again did evil in the sight of the Lord," and so again required a redeemer, which was granted in the person of Gideon.

The silence preserved regarding the subsequent life and death of Deborah, is a simple confirmation of the meekness and humility with which we found her judging Israel under her own palm-tree, before being called to a more stirring scene. The land was at peace, the power of prophecy and foresight in military matters was no longer needed, and Deborah resumed her personally humble station, evidently without any ambitious wish, or attempt to elevate her rank or prospects. It was enough that she was useful to her countrymen; that she was a lowly instrument in the Eternal's hand to work them good. What, now, did she need to satisfy the *woman nature*, which she still so evidently retained? Her judgments, her works, are covered with the veil of silence, but we learn their effects by the simple phrase, that "the land had rest forty years" — the land, the whole land, not merely that which was under her direct superintendence. Virtue, holiness, and wisdom, though the gifts of but one lowly individual, are not confined to one place, when used, as were Deborah's, to the glory of God, and the good of her people. Silently, and perhaps unperceived, they spread over space and time; and oh! how glorious must be the destiny of that woman, who, without one moment quitting her natural sphere, can yet by precept, example, and labor produce such blessed effects as to give the land peace, and bring a whole people unto God!

In a *practical* view, perhaps, the character of Deborah cannot now be brought home to the conduct of her descendants, for woman can no longer occupy a position of such trust and wisdom in Israel; but, *theoretically*, we may take the history of Deborah to our hearts, both *nationally* and individually. With such an example in the Word of our God, it is unanswerably evident that neither the Written nor the Oral Law could have contained one syllable to the disparagement of woman.

Men were in no condition to have permitted the influence of woman, had they not been accustomed, by the constant and emphatic enjoinments of the law, to look on her with respect, consideration, and tenderness. Mentally and spiritually, Deborah was gifted in an extraordinary degree, leading us to infer that the women of Israel must have had the power to cultivate both mind and spirit, and to delight in their resources, for we have the whole Bible to prove that the Eternal never selected for the instruments of His will, any but those whose hearts were inclined toward Him, even before He called them — witness the history of Abraham, Joseph, Moses, David, and others. All and every talent comes from God, but will not work and influence by His sole gift alone. They are given to be improved, persevered in, perfected, by those to whom they are intrusted, and then used in the service of their Giver. It is evident, then, that Deborah had the *inclination* and the *power* to cultivate, perfect, and use the gifts of her God; and this would have been quite impossible, had her social condition been such as the enemies of *scriptural* and *spiritual* Judaism declare. With the history of Deborah in their hands, the young daughters of Israel need little other defence or argument, to convince their adversaries that they require no other creed, nor even a denial of the Oral Law, to teach them their proper position, alike to themselves and their fellows, and in their relative duties toward God and man.

Deborah being a wife, confirms this yet more strongly. There must not only have been perfect freedom of *position*, but of *action*; even more than is found in the history of any modern nation, for we do not find a single instance of a wife being elected to any public office requiring intellect and spirituality, secular and religious knowledge, so completely distinct from her husband. Yet the history of Deborah in no way infers that she was neglectful of her conjugal and domestic duties. There is an unpretending simplicity about her very greatness. The very fact of those she judged coming to her under her own palm-tree, supposes her quiet and retired mode of living. She never leaves her home, except at the earnest entreaty of Barak, which urges her to sacrifice domestic retirement for public good. To a really great mind, domestic and public duties are so perfectly compatible, that the first need never be sacrificed for the last. And that Lapidoth in no manner interfered with the public offices of his wife, called as she was to them by God Himself through His gifts, infers a noble confidence and respectful consideration toward her, evidently springing at once from the national equality and freedom tendered to Jewish women; and from a mind great enough to appreciate and value such talents even in a woman; a greatness not very often found in modern times.

To follow in the steps of our great ancestors is not possible, now that the prophetic spirit is removed from Israel, and the few public offices left us fall naturally to the guardianship of man; yet many and many a Jewish woman is intrusted with one or more talents direct from God; and if she can stretch forth a helping hand to the less enlightened of her people, let her not hold back, from the false and unscriptural belief that woman cannot aid the cause of God, or in any way attain to religious knowledge. His Word is open to her, as to man. In Moses's command to read and explain the Law to all people, woman was included by name. And now the whole Bible, Law, Historical books, Psalms, and Prophets, are open to her daily commune, and shall it be said that she has neither the right nor the understanding to make use of such blessed privilege? Shame, shame on those who would thus cramp the power of the Lord, in denying to any one of His creatures the power of addressing and comprehending Him, through the inexhaustible treasure of His gracious Word!

Every married woman is judge and guardian of her own household. She may have to encounter the prejudices of a husband, not yet thinking with her on all points; but if she have really a great mind, she will know how to *influence,* without in any way *interfering.* She will know how to serve the Lord in her household without neglecting her duty and affection toward her husband; and by domestic conduct influence society at large, secretly and unsuspectedly indeed, but more powerfully than she herself can in the least degree suppose.

To unmarried women, even as to wives, some talent is intrusted, which may be used to the glory of its Giver. . . . Have we not all some precious talent lent us by our God, and for the use of which He will demand an account? Is there not the whole human family from which to select some few objects of interest, on whom to expend some of our leisure time, and draw our thoughts from all-engrossing self? Were there but one object on whom we have lavished kindness, and taught to look up to God and heaven, and to walk this earth virtuously and meekly — but one or two whom, had we the pecuniary means, we have clothed and fed — a sick or dying bed that we have soothed — a sorrowing one consoled — an erring one turned from the guilty path — the repentant, or the weak, strengthened and encouraged — we shall not have lived in vain; or, when we come to die, look shudderingly back on a useless life and wasted gifts; on existence lost in the vain struggle to arrest the flight of time, and still seek hope and pleasure in thoughts and scenes, whose sweetness has been too long extracted for aught to remain but bitterness and gall. Deborahs in truth we cannot be; but each and all have talents given, and a sphere assigned them, and, like her, all have it in their power, in the good performed toward man, to use the one, and consecrate the other to the service of their God.

Source: Grace Aguilar, *The Women of Israel* (London: Groombridge & Sons, 1845), 202–11.

Deborah

Clara Balfour

Redefining Femininity

Clara Lucas (1808–78) was the daughter of John and Sarah Lucas of Gosport, England, and was married at fifteen to James Balfour.[7] The marriage was difficult due to her husband's drinking problems. Clara Balfour educated herself by reading extensively, and her ability to write and to speak publicly enabled her to help support her husband and their six children. Although raised Anglican, Balfour joined the Baptist church and the temperance movement at thirty-two, and her husband also signed the temperance pledge when he gave up drinking. Balfour lectured on temperance in ladies' drawing room meetings and later addressed larger audiences in a variety of cities in Britain on temperance and eventually on literature, history, education, the rights of women, and Scripture. Balfour became a popular and prolific writer of novels, journal articles, and stories over a forty-year period. Four of her books focused specifically on women: *Women of Scripture* (1847), *Working Women of the Last Half Century: The Lessons of Their Lives* (1854), *The Bible Patterns of a Good Woman* (1867), and *Women Worth Emulating* (1877).

Balfour's comments on the Deborah story in *Women of Scripture* address a number of issues related to the Woman Question. Balfour identified with Deborah; they were both thoughtful, spiritual, and intellectual leaders working in the public sphere at a time when it was dominated by men. Balfour is adamant that Deborah did not sacrifice her femininity when she entered public life, claiming it is a "vulgar error" to suppose that when a woman enters public office she thereby sacrifices womanly qualities. Indeed, she ascribes Deborah's success in inspiring the troops to her feminine qualities. It would seem to the reader, however, that while Balfour is resolute in her claim that Deborah's leadership expressed womanly characteristics, Balfour is actually redefining what counts as feminine.

Similarly, Balfour defends Deborah's remarkable intellectual ability as feminine in nature and calls attention to Deborah's poetic genius, highlighting the particularly feminine parts of her song. Balfour's contemporary, Irish novelist Lady Sydney Morgan (1783–1859), went further in her praise of the beauty of the poetry of the Song of Deborah in her response to those who argued that women could not write as beautiful poetry as men:

---

7. Kirstin G. Doern, "Balfour, Clara Lucas," in *The Oxford Dictionary of National Biography*, ed. H. C. G. Matthew and Brian Harrison (Oxford: Oxford University Press, 2004), 3:514–15.

> This canticle of Deborah was sung 2285 years before the birth of Christ. A fine immortality! A grand celebrity! There are among the learned some who believe that Homer took it as his model, and found in it the germ of his own immortal poem. In an article in the *British Quarterly Review,* in which the intellectual nature of Woman is treated with contempt, their supporters (few in number) are called upon to produce anything that can compare to the poetry produced by men. The first ode on record was the joint effusion of a brother and sister, Moses and Miriam; and Deborah's canticle, which succeeded it, besides its higher poetic inspiration, has the distinction of preceding Homer's epic by thirteen centuries.[8]

Like Morgan, Balfour uses Deborah's song to applaud women's poetic genius. Similarly, she elevates "the dear and holy name of mother," arguing that Deborah's natural motherly abilities enabled her to do her job as judge and leader more effectively: "A mother in her sympathies . . . a mother in her anxieties, a mother in her energies, a mother in her rapture at their deliverance."

In addition to exploring the Woman Question, Balfour addresses themes that are more traditionally considered devotional in the story of Deborah. She invites readers to identify with the depravity of the Israelites, to repent, and to commit themselves anew to follow the God who gave Israel the victory. Deborah is a model for Christians desiring to live a faithful life. That Deborah composed the victory song on the same day the battle was won suggests that Christians bring to God their thanksgivings immediately, rather than taking the credit for themselves.

Deborah

> . . . In this crisis of the national affairs, when Israel seemed deserted by their justly offended God, and when intestine division and despondent supineness had crept in amongst them, it pleased the Almighty to raise up a woman as a judge and deliverer of Israel: "And Deborah a prophetess, the wife of Lapidoth, she judged Israel at that time."[9]

---

8. Lady Sydney Morgan, "Women of the Hebrews under the Judges: Deborah," in *Woman and Her Master* (Philadelphia: Carey & Hart, 1840), 1.109n.

9. Judges iv.4.

Deborah

There is something in the style of this announcement that seems to convey the idea of Deborah, notwithstanding her office, being a peculiarly feminine character. "The wife of Lapidoth," though elevated to the highest station a human being could fill,[10] yet the relative obligation pertaining individually to Deborah is announced, and though the husband was evidently not associated with her in the high office she filled, yet she chooses to be known as a wife. The common opinion that when a woman is called in the arrangements of Providence to fulfil any great public office, if she fill it well it is by the sacrifice of womanly qualities, is a mere vulgar error. Doubtless there have been many women eminent on the page of history, whose characters have been remarkable for masculine attributes, and whose distinction has been mainly attributable to their want of all feminine gentleness, benevolence, and modesty. But instances of personal ambition, morbid craving for power, and an unscrupulous mode of obtaining it, are very different cases from power bestowed by the Almighty, — such a leading of events in the arrangements of Providence, as makes it the duty of the individual to fulfil the responsibility bestowed. It matters not then how onerous the duty, or how public the office; God can magnify Himself in the weakness of His instruments.

The record of the state of Deborah is equally interesting. "She dwelt under the palm tree of Deborah, between Ramah and Bethel in Mount Ephraim: and the children of Israel came up to her for judgment." Here is no human pomp, none of the parade and circumstance that excite the admiration and awe of vulgar minds. It is manifest that Deborah's was an authority based alone on intellectual superiority. Beneath that verdant canopy whose broad impervious leaves spread tent-like over and around her, sat the female lawgiver dispensing justice and awarding judgment. How simple the actual environment, how august the mental splendour.[11] Undepressed by the condition of Israel, the strong soul of Deborah — strong in reliance upon God — rose to meet the exigencies of her people. She sent a message to Barak in the name of the Lord, commanding him to go towards Mount Tabor with ten thousand men, and assuring him that Sisera and his host, who were the

---

10. "The greatest trust between man and man is the trust of giving counsel" — *Lord Bacon*. [Original footnote marked with asterisk.]

11. Similarly, Emily Dibdin suggested Deborah as a role model for simplicity. The lesson she gave to Anglican women focused on Deborah sitting under a solitary palm tree. "No pomp here, no great palace, no costly carpets, no soft divans, no choice perfumes. In the open air, protected from the hot sun only by the branches of the tree, sits Deborah the wife of Lapidoth." Emily Dibdin, *Lessons on Women of the Bible* (London: Church of England Sunday School Institute, 1893), 8.

captain and warriors employed by Jabin, king of Canaan, should be delivered into his hand. The faith of Barak lacked both the firmness and energy that distinguished Deborah's. What were ten thousand apprehensive, dispirited men compared with the confident and well trained multitude commanded by Sisera? Some extraordinary stimulus was needed by Barak, and therefore he replied, "If thou wilt go with me, then I will go: but if thou wilt not go with me, then I will not go." We can readily imagine that the strife and agony of a battle field would be indeed a painful change to one who had dwelt under the quiet meditative shelter of her palm tree, and uttered the calm words of wisdom. But personal dislike, feminine benevolence, natural reserve, were all secondary to the grand duty of delivering her people from the oppressor. She regretted that Barak had not sufficient implicit faith to undertake the enterprise alone, and while consenting to go with the host, yet in the language of mingled reproof and prophecy she tells Barak that Israel shall be delivered, but the deliverance shall not be for his honour; for Sisera shall fall by the hand of woman.

It may be considered another proof of the essentially feminine character of Deborah, that Barak should have laid so much stress on her appearance among the children of Israel at that time. The human mind is far more affected by contrasts than by similarities. Had Deborah been a fierce, stern, masculine woman, she would have aroused no enthusiasm, her character would have approximated too closely to their own — she would have been a sort of second-rate man, instead of being, as she was,

"A perfect woman, nobly plann'd
To warn, to comfort, to command."[12]

It was the presence of a thoughtful, spiritual, intellectual woman as a leader of the armed host, that awakened energy and strengthened hope....

The signal triumph of the Israelites was followed by that glorious song, which so clearly elucidates the circumstances of the Jewish nation at that time, and which is such a splendid monument of the genius and piety of Deborah. Certainly the name of Barak is associated in that song, "Then sang Deborah and Barak in that day," but the meditative reader will find abundant rational evidence in the song itself to prove its being a feminine production.

In the first place, we have to consider the time of its composition — "In that day," on the very day of the battle. The grateful heart of Deborah admit-

---

12. Lines from William Wordsworth, "Perfect Woman."

ted no delay. Her soul, accustomed to spiritual communion with her Maker, poured out its thanksgiving at once. How instructive is this lesson. In the time of sorrow, most thoughtful people hasten to commune with God: pain and trouble often drive even the careless to devotion; but is it not a truth — a humiliating truth, that in the hour of success and triumph, while we fully and freely congratulate ourselves and each other, often "God is not in all our thoughts"?[13] Not so Deborah. And yet she might plausibly have pleaded fatigue as a motive for delay. She felt the deliverance had been as swift as it was signal; and equally prompt should be the devotional acknowledgment: she would not give rest to her frame, or slumber to her eyelids, before she had called her people to a pious and joyful thanksgiving. The feelings of the true woman's heart were too strong to admit of cold or tardy utterance.

The splendid exordium of Deborah's song combines a grateful solemn address to Deity, with an invitation to the great and mighty of the earth to join the devout homage.[14] She then, in the next three verses, describes the desolation of Israel from the persecutions of the enemy, "The highways were unoccupied, and the travellers walked through the by-ways." No description could convey a more vivid picture of abject wretchedness. It was unsafe to pass along the usual roads; and those whose business compelled them to journey to a distance, went in secrecy and mortal fear through the obscure by-ways, as the only method of escaping their cruel oppressors. This state of things continued so long that "the inhabitants of the villages ceased in Israel." Persecution and sorrow had depopulated a great portion of the flourishing land, "until," as the prophetess triumphantly exclaims, "that I, Deborah, arose — that I arose a mother in Israel." There is something peculiarly feminine and tender in this sentence. The names of prophetess, judge, leader, might all or each have been appropriately used by Deborah: but she chooses the dear and holy name of mother. How much is conveyed in that appellation! a mother in her sympathies with the sufferings of her people, a mother in her anxieties, a mother in her energies, a mother in her rapture at their deliverance. In the 11th verse, we have incidentally a further description of the miseries that the Israelites had endured, during the twenty years that Jabin had mightily oppressed them. "They that are delivered from the noise of archers in the places of drawing water!" Water, the indispensable luxury of the east, was not to be obtained but at the peril of life and limb. The enemy waylaid and attacked the children of Israel by the wells; and, in a beautiful

---

13. Probably from John Wesley's Sermon 43, "On Wandering Thoughts."
14. Judges v.2–5.

spirit of truly feminine devotion, Deborah proposes that in those very places where they had suffered attack they should unite in worship. "There shall they rehearse the righteous acts of the Lord."

At this period of the song, as if afraid that her thanksgiving too feebly expressed her gratitude, she bursts forth with sublime enthusiasm, "Awake, awake, Deborah: awake, awake, utter a song. Arise, Barak, and lead thy captivity captive, thou son of Abinoam." The concluding clause of the appeal to Barak is peculiarly feminine. She seeks to arouse him to increased enthusiasm by the mention of his father, a domestic filial allusion of exceeding delicacy and tenderness. Then follows an enumeration of the tribes who had rendered patriotic service in the struggle, with graphic mention of the supine and lukewarm, dispersed throughout. The disapprobation expressed is equally of a feminine character. It derives peculiar point and force from the sex of the speaker. The tribe of Reuben was divided and supine during the contest, and, with a fine vein of irony, Deborah exclaims, "Why abodest thou among the sheepfolds, to hear the bleatings of the flocks?" This remark was the most pungent in its sarcasm that the lip of woman could utter. An imputation of cowardice is probably the most intolerable charge that can be received by man from woman. Yet this severe covert censure is redeemed from any manifestation of unhallowed anger, by the sorrowful apostrophe, repeated twice, with slight variations, "For the divisions of Reuben there were great searchings of heart."

Then follows the magnificent passage so expressive of faith in God's merciful providence, "they fought from heaven, the stars in their courses fought against Sisera," winding up this part of the song with the awful stanza — "Curse ye Meroz (said the angel of the Lord); curse ye bitterly the inhabitants thereof, because they came not to the help of the Lord — the help of the Lord against the mighty." The attentive reader in this denunciation will not fail to perceive the same womanly character. The curse is not uttered by Deborah in her individual character, but by celestial command as a special message — "said the angel of the Lord." . . .

The whole account of this distinguished woman concludes with the words, "And the land had rest for forty years." No fuller testimony is needed in reference to the wisdom of Deborah's government. Prosperity, peace, enjoyment, are all included in the word "rest."

Strict as is the unvarying impartiality of Scripture in relating the errors of its most distinguished characters, nothing appears to detract from the excellence of Deborah. Her genius, wisdom, energy, and piety are conspicuous throughout the whole narration; and her administration, if judged by the results that followed — a peace of forty years continuance — is as worthy to rank with that of the most able of the leaders of God's ancient people, as her sublime song is to compare with their loftiest compositions. Altogether, the history of Deborah is perhaps the most memorable instance on record of the Almighty elevating a woman to public dignity and supreme authority.

Source: Clara Lucas Balfour, *The Women of Scripture* (London: Houlston & Stoneman, 1847), 88–104.

Barbara Kellison

Helpmeet and Head

Most of what is known about the life of the American preacher Barbara Kellison (1823–79) is found in her forty-four-page pamphlet *The Rights of Women in the Church,* published in Dayton, Ohio, in 1862. In this work, Kellison identifies herself as living in Winterset and a member of the Des Moines Christian conference in Iowa. While her call to preach was criticized widely, it was supported by her husband, Elder Kellison. Her pamphlet suggests that Kellison was well read, acquainted not only with Scripture but also biblical commentaries and a number of Quaker works. Kellison intended her work to "be productive of good and advance the cause of truth, and especially aid and encourage my Christian sisters in their pilgrimage journey."[15] Arguing that women were less able to use their gifts for preaching than were slaves, she engages Scripture and contemporary discussions about the spiritual and emotional nature of women to defend women's right to preach.

The chapter in which Kellison reflects on Deborah is titled "The Prophetess" and includes brief studies on Miriam, Deborah, Huldah, Hannah, Ruth, Anna, and the daughters of Philip. Kellison describes Deborah both as a "helpmeet" (Genesis 2:18), a term often understood to indicate woman's subordinate status, and as the "head" (1 Corinthians 11:3), a term typically understood to designate the authority a husband has over his wife and, by extension, the authority men have over women. However, she detaches the

---

15. Barbara Kellison, *Rights of Women in the Church* (Dayton, Ohio: Herald & Banner Office, 1862), iii–iv.

terms from their usual gender assignments and instead has them simply describe a role: Deborah is the "helpmeet" to Barak when she gives him the support he needs to engage the army of King Jabin, and she is the "head" when she commands the army. Kellison concludes that, because Deborah's authority came from God, Deborah was not usurping Barak's place but was divinely intended to take on the role of leader.

The Prophetess

The prophetess is a woman who foretells future events; which is the highest and most divine order of heaven. . . .

Turn next to Judges 4:4, 6.

Deborah — the prophetess, the mother in Israel, judged her people; for the children of Israel came up to her for judgment. She occupied a very high station in life, as she was judge over all the land of Israel. Of course she was higher in office than the men. In this our day, if a woman was placed as judge, or even to counsel in church business, some people would think she was doing wrong, since man has the power to govern. But this woman called Barak, and said unto him, "hath not the Lord God of Israel commanded, saying, go and take with thee ten thousand men," that is to meet the enemy. This woman prophesied things that have come to pass, and no one can doubt it, with the Bible in their hands, for she was a true prophetess of God, and also judge at the same time.

Sisera was captain of Jabin's army, the enemy of Israel. Deborah's name signifies a bee, and she answers her name by her industry. It is said that she was intimately acquainted with God, and was instructed by God. She judged, not as a princess by any civil authority, but as a prophetess, and as a mouth for God to them. When the children of Israel came up for judgment by God's direction, she ordered Barak to raise an army and engage Jabin's forces that were under Sisera's command. Josephus says, when Barak saw Sisera's army drawing up to surround the mountain, on the top of which he and his forces lay encamped, his heart quite failed him, and he determined to retire to a greater place of safety.[16] But Deborah said to him, this day the victory should be obtained; for the Lord would go before him. She was surely an helpmeet

---

16. *Antiquities of the Jews* 5.3.

to him, for no doubt he and his enemy would have been slain if she had not spoken as she did. This day, she, as the head, gave the command, though ordinarily man is the head; but this time, woman was placed head over the army, and that by the order of God, and the enemy was overthrown, just as she prophesied. When she commanded Barak to gather the army of men by the order of God, he said he would not go unless she would go with him; although she told him it would not be for his honor, for the Lord would sell Sisera into the hands of a woman. She arose and went with him. She was blessed with the spirit of prophecy, was judge, and also placed in high authority at the head of the army. By searching the word of God we find that women have rights as well as men, and that by the authority of God. She is filling her station in life as an helpmeet for man.

Source: Barbara Kellison, *Rights of Women in the Church* (Dayton, Ohio: Herald & Banner Office, 1862), 8–9.

Julia McNair Wright

Knowledge Is Power

Julia McNair Wright (1840–1903), born in Oswego, New York, was the daughter of John McNair, a well-known civil engineer who made sure she was given a fine education at private schools and academies. At nineteen she married William Wright, a graduate of Union College who went on to study theology at Princeton and Union and later mathematics and metaphysics in Europe. His career included ordained ministry in several different Presbyterian churches, army chaplaincy, and teaching mathematics and metaphysics at Wilson College, Pennsylvania, and Westminster College, Missouri. Wright shared her husband's interest in education, theology, and travel, was involved in the temperance movement, and pursued a career in writing. She published on a variety of subjects, including history, nature, ethnography, theology (some of which was sharply anti-Catholic), and the Bible. Her 620-page book *Saints and Sinners of the Bible,* first published in 1872 and reissued three years later under the title *Lights and Shadows of Sacred Story,* shows Wright's progressive approach to the study of Scripture, which drew on "general reading and classical studies, and the severer researches of modern criticism," which she likened to "comely priestesses" who "minister at its shrine."[17] Wright also encourages readers to use their imaginations to enter into the world of the text: "We must go out of our homes and dwell with them in the storied east where the world was young . . . [then] we must make them part of our own lives."[18]

Wright's interests in such contentious issues as the Woman Question and women's education also influence her interpretations of Scripture. Her position on the Woman Question is nuanced. She makes the claim that Deborah was womanly and that she mostly stayed in her domestic sphere because she judged Israel from under the palm tree, waiting for people to come to her rather than traveling around the countryside as male judges might. She fleshes out Deborah's character by describing her as a woman of prayer, a "true woman" who did not seek renown. Wright holds that there are essential differences between men and women, even claiming that Deborah's high status did not unsex her and that she remained, as her title indicates, "a mother in Israel." She explains: "There are times when a woman can do a man's work more nobly and fitly than he can do it himself. When that time has come let her do the work as God has called her." If a woman is doing her duty, she is to be applauded, but Wright is critical of women "who have been loudly vaunting their fitness and demanding opportunity."

When Wright turns to the subject of education, she sounds most egalitarian, asserting that women and men have the same intellectual capabilities and should receive the same education. She further refutes the stereotypical description of women as intuitive and instinctual and claims, "Women's weakness is *not* her strength; for her as for man knowledge is power. Intuition is no more the peer of education than the dog's instinct is the equal of his master's knowledge." Wright calls for universal education of girls and boys. But she also claims that women, by nature, will choose the home as their sphere of activity, but will seek additional ways to use their "surplus" power outside of the home. They have a call from God, which men should not impede. Wright sums up her position, going back to the creation story of Genesis 2 to ground her anthropology: "The scriptural assertion of the unity of their flesh is the assertion of their equality; to claim equality is not to deny a difference. In religion only these two find their true oneness, their highest destiny."

---

17. Julia McNair Wright, *Saints and Sinners of the Bible* (Philadelphia: Ziegler & McCurdy, 1872), 9.

18. Ibid., 8.

Deborah

Wright briefly addresses war and reflects pacifist commitments. She argues that womanhood and war are incompatible, but states that war is also incompatible for "all good men."

Under that solitary land mark, the palm tree in Ephraim, later called Baal Tamar — the sanctuary of the palm, dwelt Deborah, the wife of Lapidoth. . . .

At this time God put his spirit upon Deborah, a woman of Ephraim, the wife of Lapidoth, and Israel recognizing her prophetic gift, went to her for judgment. From her lips they received instruction, advice, exhortation, reproof. To her they unfolded their griefs and difficulties, and from her they learned the error of their ways, the wrath and the forgiving mercy of their God.

The high position of Deborah, as a judge of her people, did not militate against her true womanliness, or her domestic life. She judged Israel, but she exercised her office as the wife of Lapidoth, dwelling in the sanctity of his home. She did not go up and down the land to proclaim her abilities; to call the people to her standard; to inquire into their wants, or their wrong doing; to exhibit her gifts and power. On the contrary, she *dwelt* under her palm tree, and when she was wanted, the people went to her.

In courage, faith, patriotism, self-sacrifice, and humility, she was the very person suited to Israel's dire extremity; this fitness in herself secured her the dominion, and that dominion she exercised just as circumstances demanded. . . .

A woman of unusual faith, Deborah must also have been a woman of prayer, and under her palm tree, day and night, she had cried to her God for the salvation of her people. She mourned before the Lord, as afterwards she sung jubilantly to him. It was this woman's faith and prayerfulness which made her a prudent ruler; this, her godliness, was her crown and her shield.

At length the answer to her prayers came. She was informed from heaven that God would lead out Sisera and his host to the river Kishon. This should be the river of death to the army of Jabin, and its mighty waters should sweep away the oppressors of the Hebrews.

The chariots and foot soldiers should perish; the proud head of Sisera should bow down under the clods of the valley beneath Tabor. Here was military glory waiting for some one, but Deborah did not seek it.

It was written in her destiny that she should lead that line of warrior women who shine on the historic page; but a true woman, she did not covet such renown, and would willingly have waited for another victor, to sing his achievements beneath her palm.

She sent for Barak, the son of Abinoam, a dweller in Kadesh-Naphtali....

Barak promptly obeyed the summons of the prophetess, and appeared before her. Deborah addressed him in words of fervent faith and patriotism, which would have stirred the most sluggish soul:

"Hath not the Lord God of Israel commanded, saying, Go and draw toward Mount Tabor, and take with thee ten thousand men of the children of Naphtali, and of the children of Zebulun? And I will draw unto thee, to the river Kishon, Sisera, the captain of Jabin's army, with his chariots and his multitude; and I will deliver him into thine hand."

Listening, Barak had more faith in the rapt prophetess than in his God! Deborah's grand courage drank its strength from the fountains of the Infinite, but Barak dwelt more in the seen.

The enthusiasm of Deborah fired him; she grasped the promise of the coming triumph, and her holy confidence rang in every tone.

> "Her warbling voice, a lyre of widest range,
>   Struck by all passion, did fall down and glance
> From tone to tone, and glided through all change
>   Of liveliest utterance.
>
> "When she made pause, I knew not for delight:
>   Because with sudden motion from the ground
> She raised her piercing orbs, and filled with light
>   The interval of sound!"[19]

This woman could command victory, thought Barak, even in the face of six hundred armed iron chariots.

And straightway he spoke his thought: "If thou wilt go with me, I will go: but if thou wilt not go with me, I will not go!"

We can imagine the look that swept over the noble face of that mother in Israel. Indignation, surprise at the faith in flesh and lack of confidence in God, half scorn, and abundant self-sacrifice. She had not sought to lead the army; she had avoided it, but the fate of Israel rested on her heroism. It was needful for her to lead the advance of the ten thousand Hebrews; this being so, she could do it.

---

19. Lines from the poem "A Dream of Fair Women" by Alfred, Lord Tennyson.

Deborah

There was reproof in her answer. "I will surely go with thee: notwithstanding the journey which thou takest shall not be for thine honor; for the Lord shall sell Sisera into the hand of a woman."

Even this prophecy and reproach did not alter Barak's resolution. He probably reasoned that as her prophetic gift was so well known, her presence in the army would be a pledge of victory. Zebulun and Naphtali were much more likely to come at his summons, if their beloved Judge were with him.

As he in no wise abated his demand, "Deborah arose, and went with Barak to Kedesh."

"And Barak called Zebulun, and Naphtali to Kedesh; and he went up with ten thousand men at his feet; and Deborah went up with him."

There were men enough in Israel to judge the people and exhort Barak; there were warriors, priests, legists, and the princes of Judah; but God called this woman to stand in the breach, to destroy Jabin, free the tribes, and judge them. She had such inspiration and fitting for her office as Gideon and other judges. We see her grandly suited to her position; she is never in advance of demand; never behind it; she keeps majestic pace with necessity.

When the hosts of the Canaanites and Hebrews were arrayed against each other, Deborah gave the signal of battle, saying to Barak: "Up! for this is the day in which the Lord hath delivered Sisera into thine hand; is not the Lord gone out before thee?"

... The day of slaughter closed with song. Deborah and Barak meeting when the oppressor was vanquished, and their people were made free, burst forth into the praise of God. Instead of self-congratulation there was worship, "Praise ye the Lord!" "I will sing praise to the God of Israel." This began the paean, and when the glowing numbers ceased, they ceased in praise. "So let all thine enemies perish, O Lord; but let them that love him be as the sun, when he goeth forth in his might."

After this deliverance "the land had rest forty years." The passing of each Hebrew generation seemed to mark a new lapse into idolatry.

Behold this Deborah! her piety, her discretion, her wisdom, her patriotism, are an inheritance for a world.

She grew up at her birthplace; there she married; there when called to lofty station she still abode; and Israel went up to her for judgment. Her high position and mighty deeds did not unsex her; she was not a king, but *a mother in Israel*. The trouble-tossed, worn, grieving, penitent people, needed a *mother*, and that mother was Deborah. She sang them songs of salvation and of patriotism comforting them. Hers was no feeble lullaby; she sang gloriously as David, Isaiah and Habakkuk. That swelling triumphal ode seals her a prophet.

The history of Deborah, of her prophesying, judging and warring, shows us that in the thought of God there is no unfitness in woman's undertaking those toils, and filling those positions, if need be, which more ordinarily belong to men. There are times when a woman can do a man's work more nobly and fitly than he can do it himself. When that time has come let her do the work as God has called her. And we shall see that the women thus needed and thus employed are not the women who have been loudly vaunting their fitness and demanding opportunity; but those who with souls intent on duty, rather than renown, have given their hearts to each toil as it found them; and having been faithful in least were found to be equally faithful in much.

Since before women under Divine government lie these possibilities, we work in the line of the Divine intent, when women are educated, as men are educated, in the ratio of their capacity. The capacity of women for learning is, on the whole, the same as that of men. More than half of each sex is unequal to a liberal education. Given unlimited opportunities, each growing mind will by natural selection receive that for which it is best suited, and which will in the end be found to be a proper furnishing for the exigencies of its future.

Not every Paduan maiden could have become professor of six languages in the university, as did Elena Cornaro;[20] and, as was proven by the fact, not every Paduan lad; for she found none to compete with her.

Fenelon taught that feminine purity was as incompatible with learning as with vice.[21] God being the great fountain of knowledge, we do not presume that he has ever fashioned a creature so holy as to be defiled by wisdom.

Dr. Channing is horror struck at woman's meddling with theology.[22] The excellent divine would not have had Miriam prophesy; Deborah deliver the oracles of God; or Priscilla be one of the professors of theology, of whom Apollos the eloquent learned. The good doctor is not the only man who has been wiser than God.

---

20. Elena Cornaro Piscopia (1646–84) earned a doctor of philosophy degree from the University of Padua; the degree was granted in 1678. Her studies were not confined to languages, but included mathematics, philosophy, and theology. The six languages she studied in addition to her native Italian were Latin, Greek, Hebrew, Spanish, French, and Arabic.

21. François Fenelon (1651–1715), Archbishop of Cambrai, was a French Roman Catholic priest and theologian.

22. William Ellery Channing (1780–1842) was a Unitarian theologian. Fenelon and Channing are linked in the same way that Wright linked them on page 141 of an unsigned article called "Ought Women to Learn the Alphabet?" published in *The Atlantic Monthly* 3 (February 1859): 137–50. It seems very likely that Wright used this article for her examples, particularly as her positive example, Elena Cornaro, is also mentioned in this article (144).

Deborah

There has been much prating about woman's *intuition* and *instinct,* and her weakness being her strength. Woman's weakness is *not* her strength; for her as for man knowledge is power. Intuition is no more the peer of education than the dog's instinct is the equal of his master's knowledge. Instinct and intuition are well enough when they are all that can be had — and no longer.

Given a sound religious, moral, and mental training, and we think other problems will work themselves out — when it is time. It took many years to teach men that there is a better implement than the sword; and that woman could manage anything beyond her spinning wheel; and the lesson in either case is yet far from well learned.

The fear of the Lord is the beginning of all wisdom. The Creator bestows this on women as he does on men. He demands of each the best exercise of the talents, whether few or many, which he has bestowed. In proportion as the soul and brain are educated, women will appreciate the dignity and extent of what is evidently their first sphere, the sphere of home. When they go beyond this, it will be because their home work demands *less* than their capacity; because outside work calls for the surplus power; because they are equal to the new demand made upon them.

In considering this "woman question" most people ignore the fact that marriage is the God-implanted instinct of the race. The majority of men and women will marry. Unconquerable nature will then set the claims of husband, children, home life *first* in the heart of every educated and godly woman. Therefore, there need be no more masculine trepidation lest women usurp the pulpit and the gubernatorial chair, the general's star, and the sea captain's floating kingdom, because wifehood and motherhood will interpose their mysterious ban. There may be no legal disability, but there will be in general the natural disability and disinclination. When there is an exception, it will be so fitting and so necessary that, as in the case of Deborah, Miriam and Huldah the prophetess, no one will wish to condemn. For any body of men to legislate against the entrance of woman into any honest sphere, we hold to be action running before the face and will of God, which will be forced to run back again.

Woman shines fitly in her home, as shines a jewel in a ring; but, as says John Quincy Adams: "Women are not only justified, but exhibit the most exalted virtue, when they do depart from the domestic circle, and enter on the concerns of their country, of humanity, and of their God."[23] For the first

---

23. John Quincy Adams, "Speech . . . Upon the Right of People, Men and Women, to Pe-

specification, we see a bright array of those who have been warriors, rulers, martyr-patriots. We admit the vast incompatibility between womanhood and war; that, however, is an argument against war and not against the sex. We see an incompatibility between God's ministers and war; between all good men and war. Leaving home, women have blessed the earth, as nurses and teachers — as missionaries, and the sustainers and pioneers of missions.

"Times change, and we change with them."[24] The nineteenth century has demanded more of and for women than any precedent. The next century may do more, but loud outcry, and wild demands for that, for which the fulness of time has not come, will not hasten the years, slipping like sands from the hand of the Creator.

The status of woman under the Divine Government is a mental and spiritual equality with man. Add to this piety, and only in those exceptional cases where there is a clear need and call will woman trench on the *office work* of man.

The honorable women of the centuries, whose names are written in light, have not been those who clamored for great honors in public places, but who, doing whatsoever their hands found to do, grew into fame without intending it. If there is a loftier good, a higher sphere for woman, she will reach it by showing herself equal to all the emergencies of the present.

If the day comes when the affairs of State government, diplomacy, and politics need her guidance, she will find herself standing quietly at her post, lifted there *because she was needed.*

In such need, while manhood ignores the sentimentalism of a Dunois,[25] it will possess the unselfish recognition and reverence of Barak, for one whom God has animated and molded for the occasion.

"If Barak had believed like Deborah, he would have been as near to God as she was," says Lange.[26] Faith was the measure of valor. Not legions, but prophets, guard the kingdom of our God. God has called his prophets from

---

tition; on the Freedom of Speech and Debate in the House of Representatives" (Washington, D.C.: Gales & Seaton, 1838), 68.

24. A Latin proverb, *Tempora mutantur, nos et mutamur in illis.*

25. Jean d'Orléans, comte de Dunois (1402–68), fought with Jeanne d'Arc at the siege of Orleans and following. The reference here draws parallels between Dunois and Barak and by implication Deborah and Joan of Arc.

26. Johann Peter Lange, *A Commentary on the Holy Scriptures: Critical, Doctrinal, and Homiletical, with Special Reference to Ministers and Students,* trans. Philip Schaff (New York: Charles Scribner's Sons, 1871), 4.88.

Deborah

either sex as it pleased him; but in the main the duties of the prophetic office have been suited rather to the physique of the man than the woman.

When all men and women have faith, when all are Christians, then all fear of mutual aggression and oppression will be done away. The scriptural assertion of the unity of their flesh is the assertion of their equality; to claim equality is not to deny a difference. In religion only these two find their true oneness, their highest destiny:

"As Heaven's high twins, whereof in Tyrian blue
    The one revolveth, through his course immense
Might love his brother of the damask hue,
    For like, and difference.

For different pathways evermore decreed
    To intersect, but not to interfere;
For common goal, two aspects, and one speed,
    One centre and one year."[27]

Source: Julia McNair Wright, *Saints and Sinners of the Bible* (Philadelphia: Ziegler & McCurdy, 1872), 189–99.

Harriet Beecher Stowe

An Inspired Poet

Harriet Beecher Stowe (1811–96) was the seventh of thirteen children of seminary president Lyman Beecher and his second wife, Roxanna, who died shortly after giving birth to Harriet Beecher.[28] Harriet Beecher received a fine

---

27. Lines from a poem "The Love of Sympathetic Souls," by Jean Ingelow.
28. For a fuller discussion of Stowe as a biblical interpreter, see Marion Ann Taylor, "Harriet Beecher Stowe and the Mingling of Two Worlds: The Kitchen and the Study," in *Recovering Nineteenth-Century Women Interpreters of the Bible,* ed. Christiana de Groot and Marion Ann Taylor, Society of Biblical Literature Symposium Series 38 (Atlanta: Society of Biblical Literature, 2007), 99–115. See also Marion Ann Taylor, "Stowe, Harriet Beecher (1811–96)," in *Handbook of Women Biblical Interpreters: A Historical and Biographical Guide,* ed. Marion A. Taylor and Agnes Choi (Grand Rapids: Baker, 2012), 482–87.

theological and academic education at home and later at Hartford Female Seminary, a school established by her older sister, Catharine. After Harriet's marriage to distinguished biblical scholar Calvin Ellis Stowe in 1836, she wrote for local religious periodicals and newspapers to supplement her husband's inadequate salary. Her most successful novel, *Uncle Tom's Cabin*, initially published serially (1851–52), brought fame, financial gain, and international recognition. Stowe continued to publish novels and articles for religious periodicals and newspapers. In her later prose writings on the Bible, *Woman in Sacred History* (1873) and *Footsteps of the Master* (1877), Stowe effectively drew on the resources of the male academy recommended by Calvin, her "Rabbi," and her experiences as wife and mother of seven children.

Stowe's elegant gift book, *Woman in Sacred History*, featured her own essays and lithographs of great paintings of the women in Scripture as well as poems and reflections authored by both men and women. Her essay on the Deborah narrative is the most sympathetic to Judaism of the selections written by the Christian commentators in this chapter. Stowe begins by describing in very positive and modern terms the ideal of Mosaic law, which she claims sought to create "an ultra-democratic community, so arranged that perforce there must be liberty, fraternity and equality." Stowe claims that the law set out an especially honorable position for women in their various roles as wives and mothers.[29]

Although Stowe elevates Judaism and especially the law of Moses, she still reads the narrative from an explicitly Christian point of view. She operates with a notion of progressive revelation; just as revealed religion in the Old Testament was superior to that of the surrounding nations, so Christianity is superior to Judaism. Stowe also traces the progression from Deborah, the first of an inspired line of female prophets, to the virgin Mary, "the last and greatest of a long and noble line of women." Because Judaism elevated women to such a high degree, Stowe concludes that we should not think of Deborah as an exception. Her abilities and her role were consistent with the view of women promulgated by the law. Her use of J. G. Herder's work on the Song of Deborah also allows her to speak of Deborah's poetic work "as one of the noblest expressions of devout patriotism in literature." Unlike

---

29. In the introduction to *Woman in Sacred History*, Stowe spells out in much more detail how the laws dealing with wives, concubines, divorce, polygamy, and mothers all elevate and care for women, setting up the ideal that they are equal with men; *Woman in Sacred History* (New York: J. B. Ford & Co., 1873), 17–28. Stowe does not cite Grace Aguilar's popular book, *The Women of Israel*, in her discussion, but many of her arguments are also found in Aguilar's extensive writings on women in the laws of the Pentateuch.

many of the authors excerpted in this chapter, Stowe does not connect the high view of women in ancient Israel with the Woman Question of her time.

Deborah the Prophetess

The Book of Judges is the record of a period which may be called the Dark Ages of the Jewish Church, even as the mediæval days were called the Dark Ages of Christianity. In both cases, a new system of purity and righteousness, wholly in advance of anything the world had ever before known, had been inaugurated by the visible power of God, — the system of Moses, and the system of Christ. But these pure systems seem, in each case, to have been allowed to struggle their own way through the mass of human ignorance and sin. The ideal policy of Moses was that of an ultra-democratic community, so arranged that perforce there must be liberty, fraternity, and equality. There was no chance for overgrown riches or abject poverty. Landed property was equally divided in the outset, and a homestead allowed to each family. Real estate could not be alienated from a family for more than a generation; after that period, it returned again to its original possessor. The supreme law of the land was love. Love, first, to the God and Father, the invisible head of all; and secondly, towards the neighbor, whether a Jewish brother or a foreigner and stranger. The poor, the weak, the enslaved, the old, the deaf, the blind, were protected by solemn and specific enactments. The person of woman was hedged about by restraints and ordinances which raised her above the degradation of sensuality to the honored position of wife and mother. Motherhood was exalted into special honor, and named as equal with fatherhood in the eye of God. "Ye shall fear every man *his mother* [emphasis original] and his father, and keep my Sabbaths: I am the Lord." (Lev. xix.3.) . . .

The history of the Jewish nation, in the Book of Judges, presents a succession of these periods of oppression, and of deliverance by a series of divinely inspired leaders, sent in answer to repentant prayers. It is entirely in keeping with the whole character of the Mosaic institutions, and the customs of the Jewish people, that one of these inspired deliverers should be a woman. We are not surprised at the familiar manner in which it is announced, as a thing quite in the natural order, that the chief magistrate of the Jewish nation, for the time being, was a woman divinely ordained and gifted. Thus the story is introduced: — . . .

In all this we have a picture of the reverence and confidence with which, in those days, the inspired woman was regarded. The palm-tree which shaded her house becomes a historical monument, and is spoken of as a well-known object. The warlike leader of the nation comes to her submissively, listens to her message as to a divine oracle, and obeys. He dares not go up to battle without her, but if she will go he will follow her. The prophetess is a wife, but her husband is known to posterity only through her. Deborah was the wife of Lapidoth, and therefore Lapidoth is held in remembrance even down to our nineteenth century.

This class of prophetic and inspired women appear to have been the poets of their time. They were, doubtless, possessed of that fine ethereal organization, fit to rise into the higher regions of ecstasy, wherein the most exalted impressions and enthusiasms spring, as birds under tropic sunshine. The Jewish woman was intensely patriotic. She was a living, breathing impersonation of the spirit of her nation; and the hymn of victory chanted by Deborah, after the issue of the conflict, is one of the most spirited specimens of antique poetry. . . .

There is a beautiful commentary on the song of Deborah in Herder's "Spirit of Hebrew Poetry."[30] He gives a charming translation,[31] to which we refer anyone who wishes to study the oldest poem by a female author on record. The verse ascribed to Miriam seems to have been only the chorus of the song of Moses, and, for aught that appears, may have been composed by him; but this song of Deborah is of herself alone. It is one of the noblest expressions of devout patriotism in literature.

[At this point Stowe includes a version of this poem, modified according to Herder.]

And as this song dies away, so passes all mention of Deborah. No other fragment of poetry or song from her has come down from her age to us. This one song, like a rare fragment of some deep-sea flower, broken off by a storm of waters, has floated up to tell of her. We shall see, as we follow down the line of history, that women of this lofty poetic inspiration were the natural product of the Jewish laws and institutions. They grew out of them, as certain flowers grow out of certain soils. To this class belonged Hannah, the mother of Samuel, and Huldah, the prophetess, and, in the fullness of time, Mary, the mother of Jesus, whose *Magnificat* was the earliest flower of

---

30. See J. G. Herder, *The Spirit of Hebrew Poetry*, trans. James Marsh (Burlington: Edward Smith, 1833 [originally 1782–83]), 2.182–91.
31. Ibid., 187–91.

Deborah

the Christian era. Mary was prophetess and poet, the last and greatest of a long and noble line of women, in whom the finer feminine nature had been kindled into a divine medium of inspiration, and burst forth in poetry and song as in a natural language.

Source: Harriet Beecher Stowe, *Woman in Sacred History* (New York: J. B. Ford & Co., 1873), 99–106.

Elizabeth Baxter

An Imperfect, But Useful Woman

Elizabeth Baxter (1837–1926) was born into a Quaker home, where she was educated by a governess before being sent to boarding school at the age of eleven.[32] She had a significant conversion experience as a teenager that changed the trajectory of her life. She became involved in the Anglican deaconess movement and at thirty-one married the Reverend Michael Paget Baxter (1834–1910), an eccentric endtimes lecturer and author of the popular book *Louis Napoleon: The Destined Monarch of the World* (1863). For fifteen years the Baxters toured Britain; Michael lectured on the second coming, and Elizabeth preached. During this time they joined in the British crusades of the celebrated American evangelist Dwight L. Moody and his associate, Ira D. Sankey, with Elizabeth teaching Scripture to as many as fifteen hundred women each week. The couple also initiated a number of publishing projects that facilitated Baxter's writing career, but strained her health. Baxter published some forty books on Scripture and the Christian life, weekly Sunday School lessons in her husband's successful paper, *The Christian Herald,* numerous booklets, tracts, and brief appeals. Most of her writings grew out of her various teaching ministries, including *The School of the Patriarchs* (1903) and her commentaries on the books of Proverbs (1891), Job (1894), Revelation (1896), and Ezekiel (1902). *The Women in the Word* (1897), as its title suggests, contains studies on the lives of women in the Bible.

---

32. Nathaniel Wiseman, *Elizabeth Baxter: Saint, Evangelist, Preacher, Teacher, and Expositor* (London: The Christian Herald, 1928).

The story of Deborah challenged many of Baxter's traditional views about the place and nature of women in God's economy. Because Deborah's role as prophet, judge, and military leader cannot be reconciled with her understanding of the difference in men's and women's capacities and roles, Baxter argues that Deborah was an exception to the rule that men's nature equips them for leadership. Similarly, she argues that when modern women "dare things which men are not courageous enough to undertake, it is not intended to institute a new order of things, but rather to provoke men to jealousy, that they may take the first place, which God has given them."[33]

Baxter criticizes Deborah's self-presentation in her song, because, unlike many of the other commentators, she interprets Deborah's naming of herself as "a mother in Israel" as prideful rather than as a sign of humility. Baxter then sees Deborah's singing, "I, even I, will sing unto the Lord," and later, "The highways were unoccupied ... until I arose," as further evidence that Deborah thought too highly of herself.

Critical as Baxter is of Deborah's lack of humility, she does assume with other interpreters that Deborah was faithful in fulfilling her duties in the domestic sphere. Speaking from her personal experiences as a wife and mother who worked in the public sphere as an evangelist, preacher, teacher and expositor, Baxter stresses that involvement in public life does not nullify responsibilities at home, claiming that God will make it possible for a woman to do it all. "The being a worker together with God can never excuse her from being a helpmeet to her husband; but the two things can go blessedly together where the public call is really from God." Still, Baxter is much more negative about Deborah than other female interpreters, concluding, "Deborah was an imperfect, but a useful woman."

---

33. Similarly, American Methodist educator Leigh Norval (fl. 1889) argues that Deborah was an exception: "Occasionally [God] makes a woman who is wiser to lead and to rule than any man of her day. The girls who wish the Lord had made them boys would like to be one of these famous women. Remarkable people, however, are not the happiest; and the girl who is fitted to render a home pleasant, and does it, is the fortunate girl. Yet there are different people for different purposes, and those who use the talents given by God for the glory of God are blessed, whether they make bread or rule a kingdom. Deborah, the prophetess, was fitted to instruct, to govern, and to free a nation. She was the only good woman the Lord ever appointed to govern Israel, and was, like Joan of Arc, an exceptional character.... She roused and led her people to victory, but tried to put a man forward. He fell back on her as the weaker leans on the stronger. Her remarkable position was not from choice, but because she was fitted for it and put in it by circumstances." From Leigh Norval, *Women of the Bible: Sketches of All the Prominent Female Characters in the Old and the New Testament* (Nashville, Tenn.: Publishing House of the M. E. Church, South, Sunday-School Department, 1889), 83–87.

Deborah

Deborah

"I will surely go with thee: notwithstanding the journey which thou takest shall not be for thine honour; for the Lord will sell Sisera into the hand of a woman."

Judges iv.9.

It is not the usual order of God to put woman in the place of authority: "Adam was first formed, then Eve." (1 Tim. ii.13.) Deborah was an exception. The children of Israel had sinned grievously against the Lord, and apparently there was no man that could serve His purpose as judge over Israel. Just as, later on, He was driven to employ the child Samuel when the high priest Eli was not equal to the occasion,[34] so now, a woman must do the part of a man.

It is always sin which puts things out of God's order, and all kinds of complications follow. [Baxter quotes in full Leviticus 26:11-17 and references Psalm 107:6, 13, 19, 28.]

After twenty years of oppression by the king of Canaan, "the children of Israel cried unto the Lord," "And Deborah, a prophetess, the wife of Lapidoth, she judged Israel at that time: . . . and the children of Israel came up to her for judgment." (Jud. iv.1–4.) As their cry rose up to heaven, God, in answer, stirred the heart of this remarkable woman, and she knew how to understand the mind of the Lord, and the way of His deliverance, for she was in the secret of her God, and she knew that all things were possible to Him.

[Baxter quotes Judges 4:6-7 and then comments:] Had Barak possessed the same faith in his God which characterised Deborah, and had he possessed true manliness, he might, perhaps, have gone out alone and unaided; but Barak feared to undertake the command of an army against Sisera, except he had some one by his side to encourage him. Barak was not himself sufficiently acquainted with his God to receive direct communications from Him, but he was wise enough and humble enough to learn from a woman when he knew she was sent of God. He said to the prophetess:

"If thou wilt go with me, then I will go but if thou wilt not go with me, then I will not go."

There is a mightier power than many know in the fellowship of kindred

---

34. [1 Samuel 1–3.]

spirits. In the work of the Lord, he that preaches to a difficult congregation does not know the difference it makes when some half-dozen who are in full sympathy are sitting near him, with closed eyes, and hearts engaged in prayer. Nevertheless, a true man of God is not dependent upon any man; and when Barak refused to go except Deborah should go with him, there was an evident want of manliness in his character, which gives one easily to understand why a woman should have been used in such an exceptional way to be over him in Israel....

Sometimes there are things to be done and dared in the Church of God which men fear to attempt. An Elizabeth Fry was a leader in prison work; a Sarah Foster, of Newcastle, in the rescue of the fallen. It was women who began the great temperance movement in America. It was a woman, the late Mrs. Daniells, of Aldershot, who first thought of Soldiers' Homes and systematic work amongst the soldiers as a class.

It was a woman, Miss Marsh, who first began work among the navvies. The policemen's work, the work among railway men, sailors, etc., has generally in England had its origin with one or more godly women. A woman may give the inspiration to a work as Deborah did to Barak.

But there was One who went before him and before his host. It was no power of Deborah's, nor yet of Barak's, nor any military genius in his officers, which won that victory....

When it so happens that, in politics, in the affairs of nations, in Church matters, and in Christian work, women are found to dare things which men are not courageous enough to undertake, it is not intended to institute a new order of things, but rather to provoke men to jealousy, that they may take the first place, which God had given them. But God gave the glory neither to Jael, nor to Deborah, nor to Barak. "*God* subdued on that day Jabin the king of Canaan before the children of Israel. And the hand of the children of Israel prospered, and prevailed against Jabin, the king of Canaan, until they had destroyed Jabin, king of Canaan."

Deborah's Song

"I arose, a mother in Israel."

Judges v.7.

The unusual call of Deborah the prophetess ended with the conquest of Jabin. She still remained a judge and a prophetess, but her military campaign was at an end; she was no longer a Joan of Arc in Israel, but she gave herself to her ordinary work, and composed a song of victory, which was doubtless set to music, and sung by the priestly tribe.

But there is one thing that strikes one in the song of Deborah. There was so much of herself in it. The position had been too much for her; she could not forget the part she had played in it. "Then sang Deborah, and Barak the son of Abinoam, saying: Praise ye the Lord for the avenging of Israel, when the people willingly offered themselves." These first words witness how strong was the impression made on the people by this remarkable woman. Doubtless, the ten thousand men gathered by her and Barak were volunteers, and their military service was neither a forced matter nor an affair of money, but there was all the enthusiasm of the voluntary principle in it. "They willingly offered themselves."

"Hear, O ye kings," sings Deborah, "I, even I, will sing unto the Lord: I will sing praise to the Lord God of Israel." Barak was singing as well as Deborah; but Deborah was most present to her own mind: yet this woman lived in communion with the Unseen. She saw the Lord go out of Seir, marching out of the field of Edom, the earth trembling, the heavens dropping, the clouds dropping water, the mountains melting, even Sinai itself, before the Lord God of Israel. And then she discoursed on the desolation of the land through the destruction of Jabin. "The highways were unoccupied" — the Canaanites made them dangerous — "and the travellers walked through byways." The country villages became so unsafe that they were hardly to be found in Israel "until that I," said Deborah, "arose,

That I Arose

a mother in Israel." Here we see the danger of her position. O how much more blessed would it be if she had said, "Until the Lord arose." Deborah was no small person in her own eyes.

She speaks of the idolatry of the people. "They chose new gods; then was war in the gates"; and yet their armour was so poor that she asks, "Was there a shield or spear seen among forty thousand in Israel?" And again she sounds the strain of the willingness of the people: "My heart is toward the governors of Israel, that offered themselves willingly among the people." "*My* heart" — Deborah continues somebody, great in her own eyes! She is not simply an instrument of the Lord, although she intersperses her song with His praises.

"Awake, awake, Deborah"; she sings, "awake, awake, utter a song: arise,

Barak, and lead thy captivity captive, thou son of Abinoam." Deborah first, and Barak second! This was reversing the order of God; but this old prophetess did not perceive it; she had not learnt by the example of the meek and lowly One to take the last place, and to be among the people of God as one that serveth. It was to His little flock that Jesus taught: "He that will be chief among you, let him be as the younger."[35] It is true she said: "The Lord made me have dominion over the mighty"; but it would have been more womanly to have taken the place by constraint, and not to have boasted of it. . . .

After extolling highly the deed of Jael, and turning into irony the expectation of Sisera's mother that he should come back victorious and laden with the spoil, Deborah closes her song:

"So let all Thine enemies perish, O Lord; but let them that love Him be as the sun when he goeth forth in his might."

Deborah was an imperfect, but a useful woman. Let every redeemed and truly converted woman who reads these pages learn that, bought by the blood of Christ and saved by His life, our responsibilities are infinitely greater than hers, and God's grace in Christ for us is equal to them all.

This is all we hear of the history of Deborah. Of her private life we know nothing — what kind of wife, what kind of mother, what kind of mistress she made; and yet how many there are who would like to know how, such a woman dealt with the details of home life. No prophetic gift, no calling of the Spirit of God into active and public service can excuse a woman for unfaithfulness in family and domestic matters. The being a worker together with God can never excuse her from being a helpmeet to her husband; but the two things can go blessedly together where the public call is really from God. In His economy, one call does not necessarily supersede another, and "he that is faithful in that which is least," can be "faithful also in much." (Luke xvi.10.)

Source: Mrs. M. [Elizabeth] Baxter, *The Women in the Word*, 2nd edition (London: Christian Herald, 1897), 72–82.

---

35. [Matthew 20:27.]

Deborah

Clara B. Neyman

Genius Knows No Sex

Clara Neyman (fl. 1890s) likely came from Brooklyn, New York.[36] Fluent in German, she was a suffragette who became a member of the revising committee of Elizabeth Cady Stanton's *Woman's Bible*. Stanton spoke of Neyman's contributions to the history of suffrage, noting that she addressed the first meeting of the German suffragette organization formed in New York in 1872 and afterward became a popular speaker with many suffrage and free-religious associations.[37] Her theological views are evident in her writings; she is clearly critical of Christianity and was influenced by New Thought.[38]

Neyman marks the other end of the spectrum from Elizabeth Baxter, as Neyman understands men and women to be essentially the same, each being called by God to the same tasks. In a vision of a utopian future she sees them working together to combat the common enemies of humanity: ignorance, superstition, and cruelty. Both Deborah and Barak emerge as role models, and their cooperation is a further model of how men and women should relate to each other as equals.

Neyman is critical of how Christianity has used the Bible to delineate the roles of women and men. In her understanding, women's originally high status has deteriorated over time. Like many in her time, Neyman held to the idea that the original societal structure was matriarchal and that women have been losing power since ancient times. Like Grace Aguilar, she regards Deborah an example of women's high status in ancient Judaism, and she blames Christianity for lowering women's position, understanding Paul's teaching that women should be silent as a prime example of Christianity's oppression of women. She looks forward to a new Bible written by women and men together that would promote a vision of life on earth, "when love and justice reign supreme."

36. See also Neyman's comments on Manoah's wife and Delilah.

37. See *History of Woman's Suffrage*, ed. Elizabeth Cady Stanton, Susan B. Anthony, and Mathilda Gage (Rochester: Charles Mann, 1887), 405.

38. New Thought, also known as "Higher Thought," was a spiritual movement that began in the 1880s involving the understanding that divine thought, or prayer, could be efficacious in healing sickness.

WOMEN OF WAR, WOMEN OF WOE

The woman who most attracts our attention in the Book of Judges is Deborah, priestess, prophetess, poetess and judge. What woman is there in modern or in ancient history who equals in loftiness of position, in public esteem and honorable distinction this gifted and heroic Jewish creation? The writer who compiled the story of her gifts and deeds must have had women before him who inspired him with such a wonderful personality. How could Christianity teach and preach that women should be silent in the church when already among the Jews equal honor was shown to women? The truth is that Christianity has in many instances circumscribed woman's sphere of action, and has been guilty of great injustice toward the whole sex.

Deborah was, perhaps, only one of many women who held such high and honorable positions. Unlike any modern ruler, Deborah dispensed justice directly, proclaimed war, led her men to victory, and glorified the deeds of her army in immortal song. This is the most glorious tribute to woman's genius and power. If Deborah, way back in ancient Judaism, was considered wise enough to advise her people in time of need and distress, why is it that at the end of the nineteenth century, woman has to contend for equal rights and fight to regain every inch of ground she has lost since then? It is now an assured fact that not only among the Hebrews, but also among the Greeks and the Germans, women formerly maintained greater freedom and power.

The struggle of today among the advanced of our sex is to regain and to reaffirm what has been lost since the establishment of Christianity. Every religion, says a modern thinker, has curtailed the rights of woman, has subjected her to man's ruling; in emphasizing the life beyond, the earthly existence became a secondary consideration. We are learning the great harm which comes from this one-sided view of life; and by arousing woman to the dignity of her position we shall again have women like Deborah, honored openly and publicly for political wisdom, to whom men will come in time of need.

Genius knows no sex; and woman must again usurp her Divine prerogative as a leader in thought, song and action. The religion of the future will honor and revere motherhood, wifehood and maidenhood. Asceticism, an erroneous philosophy, church doctrines based not upon reason or the facts of life, issued out of crude imaginings; phantasms obstructed the truth, held in check the wheel of progress. Let our church women turn their gaze to such characters as Deborah, and claim the same recognition in their different congregations.

The antagonism which the Christian church has built up between the male and the female must entirely vanish. Together they will slay the enemies — ignorance, superstition and cruelty. United in every enterprise, they will win; like Deborah and Barak, they will clear the highways and restore

Deborah

peace and prosperity to their people. Like Deborah, woman will forever be the inspired leader, if she will have the courage to assert and maintain her power. Her aspirations must keep pace with the demands of our civilization. "New times teach new duties."

God never discriminates; it is man who has made the laws and compelled woman to obey him. The Old Testament and the New are books written by men; the coming Bible will be the result of the efforts of both, and contain the wisdom of both sexes, their combined spiritual experience. Together they will unfold the mysteries of life, and heaven will be here on earth when love and justice reign supreme.

Source: Clara B. Neyman, "The Book of Judges, Chapter II," in *The Woman's Bible, Part II: Joshua to Revelation,* ed. Elizabeth Cady Stanton (Boston: Northeastern University Press, 1898), 21–23.

STUDY QUESTIONS

1. Commentators did not agree about what aspects of the story were most significant or about women's roles in society. What nineteenth-century assumptions about the roles of men and women did this story challenge? How did they engage the Deborah story?
2. Comment on nineteenth-century women's responses to Deborah's identification as "wife of Lapidoth" and "mother in Israel." What do their comments reveal about their views of marriage and motherhood? Are these details significant in the narrative?
3. Provide examples from these excerpts of how presuppositions (i.e., about the nature of Scripture, the nature and roles of women) shape or influence interpretation.
4. Julia McNair Wright encourages readers to use their imaginations to enter into the world of the text: "We must go out of our homes and dwell with them in the storied east where the world was young . . . [then] we must make them part of our own lives." How do authors in this chapter use their imaginations in the interpretive process? Do you think it's possible to enter a place that is far away and was long ago?

4

Jael

Nineteenth-century interpreters were deeply troubled by the story of the inhospitable, treacherous murderer, Jael, whom Deborah names as "most blessed of women."[1] Jael's story is told first in narrative form in Judges 4:17–22 and again in poetry in the Song of Deborah in Judges 5:24–27. The account begins with the defeat of King Jabin's army under the leadership of Deborah and Barak. King Jabin's general, Sisera, escapes on foot and comes to the place where Heber the Kenite had erected his tent. Heber's wife, Jael, greets Sisera and invites him into the tent. She covers him with a rug and when he asks her for water she brings milk instead and covers him again. He falls asleep after ordering Jael to stand by the entrance of the tent and to lie to anyone who asks for him. Jael then takes a tent peg and drives it into his temple, through his head, and into the ground. When Barak comes in pursuit of Sisera, Jael welcomes him and brings him into the tent to show him his enemy, dead. The poetic rehearsal of the story in Judges 5 differs in small details from the narrative account in Judges 4 and includes Deborah's encomium of Jael: "Most blessed of women." It ends with the words of Sisera's mother and her wisest ladies, which introduce the theme of the victimization of women in times of war.

It is not surprising that the story of Jael's murder of Sisera provoked considerable controversy and commentary. Her unladylike actions run counter to nineteenth-century expectations that women are peacemakers, nurturers, trustworthy, hospitable, and passive in the realm of politics and war. Many commentators react in horror to Jael's duplicity and murderous act.

---

1. Judith received similar praise when she returned to the Israelite camp with the head of Israel's enemy, Holofernes (Judith 13:17). Compare also Elizabeth's declaration that Mary, the mother of Jesus, was "blessed among women" (Luke 1:42).

Elizabeth Cady Stanton, for example, regards Jael's action as "more like the work of a fiend than of a woman." In light of Deborah's praise of Jael, many interpreters felt a need to justify Jael's behaviour. Most highlighted the differences between primitive and enlightened cultures and between peaceful and warlike conditions to make sense of this story, which valorized Jael's actions. Constance de Rothschild and Annie de Rothschild aver that treason "was accepted and even praised by an oppressed and struggling people in that early dawn of civilization." Others invoke the notion of situational ethics. Etty Woosnam argues that Deborah and Jael had "to act the part of champions and warriors, *which ill becomes them*" because "men had been so neglectful of their duty." Eliza Steele and Harriet Beecher Stowe develop the theme of violence against women introduced by Sisera's mother's princesses to justify Jael's actions. Stowe argues that Jael killed the tiger who ravished women and children. Emily Owen and Anne Mercier defend Jael's womanly nature, imagining that Jael suppressed her "natural" feelings in order to murder Sisera.

The story's interpretive challenges invited reflections on the nature of Scripture. On the one hand, Stanton and Elmina Slenker used this story as evidence for the uninspired origin of Scripture. Mercier, who held a revised view of inspiration, judged Deborah's adulation of Jael as poetic rather than inspired. On the other hand, Elizabeth Jane Whately set out to defend Scripture in light of challenging texts like Judges 4–5.

Interpreters who read the text as God's revelation were motivated to find its religious or moral significance. Some followed the long tradition of reading Judges 4–5 allegorically and typologically. Woosnam calls every woman to "be a spiritual Jael and nail down to the ground her Sisera [that is] . . . coldness and hardness of heart and our grievous besetting sins." M.G. similarly calls women and girls to fight Satan and his army "as bravely as men." Eliza Smith's grandfather figure mentions a more negative typological reading of Jael as "a type of worldly pleasure, which promises only to betray; and Sisera . . . a type of those who trust for happiness in the things of this world."

Most interpreters, however, did not find spiritual and moral meaning hidden in the details of the story. Rather, they studied the story within its historical and canonical setting, drawing on traditional and contemporary resources, including the customs of the time, to help them discern its meaning. They considered Jael's effectiveness, God's role in the events, Sisera's status as the enemy, and Sisera's culpability in asking Jael to lie for him in order to arrive at sophisticated evaluations. Even the protocol of Eastern hospitality receives attention by Owen.[2] Whately draws attention to translation issues in her effort to soften the horror of Jael's actions, introducing an alternative translation of the Hebrew text that suggests that Jael struck Sisera when he was standing rather than sleeping.[3] Some commentators pondered Jael's ethnic identity. She is described in Judges as the wife of Heber the Kenite, but was she also a Kenite? M.G. claims that she was not an Israelite and, for that reason, Sisera could assume that he would find a welcome in her tent. The Rothchilds describe Jael as "a true Hebrew woman at heart." Most interpreters do not address the issue, treating Jael as an Israelite and judging her by her own actions. Smith makes the case that the Kenites also worshipped the God of Israel and knew the Ten Commandments, so that, whether or not Jael was an Israelite, her actions can be evaluated by Israelite standards.

Nineteenth-century women commented on the Jael story for a variety of audiences using a variety of literary genres. The selections excerpted in this chapter include catechetical commentaries for children and youth, Bible studies for young women, a sermon/address for women, an apologetic work, character studies for a mixed adult audience, historical fiction, and a traditional and a not-so-traditional commentary.

Sarah Ewing Hall

Jael's Masculine Resolution and Cruelty

Sarah Ewing Hall (1761–1830) of Philadelphia was well acquainted with the city's literary figures and published on a number of subjects, including

---

2. Similarly, Mary Carus-Wilson makes the case that Sisera was at fault for seeking refuge in Jael's tent and that if he had been discovered there, presumably by Jael's husband, there would have been a "bloody feud for twenty generations." Carus-Wilson's support for this claim is, "Mrs. Mountford (nee von Finkelstein), who, though of European parentage, was born in Palestine, learned Arabic as her first language, and has been entertained in Bedouin tents"; Mary L. G. Carus-Wilson, *Unseal the Book: Practical Words for Plain Readers of Holy Scripture* (London: Religious Tract Society, 1899), 99.

3. J. W. H. van Wijk-Bos argues similarly and offers an alternate translation to Judges 4:21: "Then took Jael, / wife of Heber, / the tent peg and picked up / the hammer in her hand. / She came to him quietly, / she drove the peg in his head, / so it hit the ground; / he, *stunned, passed out and died*"; *Reformed and Feminist: A Challenge to the Church* (Louisville: Westminster/John Knox Press, 1991), 72.

Jael

women's education and Scripture.[4] Her only major work, *Conversations on the Bible* (1818), paraphrases and comments on the Old Testament using the form of a conversation between a mother and her children.

Hall's brief discussion of Jael's questionable conduct is introduced by the daughter Fanny, who declares, "Her masculine resolution is in my mind no apology for her cruelty." This comment brings together the high regard for what were traditionally thought to be masculine attributes, with disgust at Jael's treachery and violence. Mother's response contains a careful statement of the command to love our enemies. She adds that this law applies insofar as it coincides with our own safety — an interesting addendum that allows Christians to support just-war theory. Still, Mother justifies Jael's actions, reasoning that she was moved by God to help win the battle against Israel's enemies. Mother also reminds Fanny that Sisera was not a victim but was the cause of much suffering among the Israelites.[5] She concludes that Jael's actions, which secured liberty for Israel, were to be celebrated. Fanny compares Jael to Deborah, and a discussion of woman's nature and right to equal education follows.

MOTHER. . . . About this period we find two women celebrated as the instruments of great benefit to their country.

After the death of Shamgar, the sins of Israel had brought them under the dominion of Jabin a powerful king of Canaan. Penitence as usual obtained mercy, and to Deborah the wife of Lapidoth, at once a *Judge* and a prophetess, a plan of deliverance was graciously imparted. . . .

Barak immediately fell upon the Canaanites and swept them off with a terrible slaughter! Their chariots of iron, were a feeble defence against the persevering courage of Barak: the whole army was destroyed, and the despairing Sisera himself compelled to abandon the field, and endeavour to save his own life! Leaving his chariot, he fled towards a district inhabited

---

4. For more details on Hall, see "A Sanitized Rahab."
5. By contrast, American poet Hannah Flagg Gould (1789-1865) portrayed Sisera as a victim in her poem "Sisera." She pondered the blood "thick around" Sisera's brow and "on the matted hair" as a result of the piercing by "the fatal nail" that "pillowed [him] on the ground!" causing his "long and deep" sleep. She asks: "Was the fair captive's needlework to deck, / With many colors, this poor severed neck?" Gould, "Sisera," from *Poems* (Boston: Hilliard, Gray & Co., 1839), 2.83-85.

by the descendants of Hobab, the brother-in-law of Moses, who had left their own country and dwelt amongst the Naphtalites. In this extremity he was met by Jael the wife of Heber, near the door of her house, and invited to accept its protection. As the Kenites, the denomination of this colony, were at peace with the king of Hazor, Sisera fearlessly entered, entreating his hostess to conceal the place of his retreat, and to give him a cup of water to drink. The better to allay any apprehension that might arise from the avowed friendship of her people to the Israelites, the wife of Heber presented a bowl of refreshing milk to the wearied warrior. Confiding now in her officious kindness, and overpowered by disappointment and vain exertion, he fell into a slumber, to awaken no more! For Jael seized the opportunity and put him to death by her own adventurous hand!

FANNY. I presume, mother, you do not vindicate the treachery of Jael to a vanquished man who had confided in her honour. Her masculine resolution is in my mind no apology for her cruelty.

MOTHER. You are not ignorant, my dear, that wars were formerly conducted by every nation with unrelenting severity. It is a peculiar glory of our amiable religion that it has abolished unnecessary violence, and strictly enjoins tenderness to our enemies so far as it can possibly consist with our own safety. Very many of those brilliant actions that have inscribed the names of heroes on the tablets of fame would be detestable in our view of moral obligation. These remarks, however, although they may serve to palliate the conduct of many celebrated men in both sacred and profane history, may not perhaps be applicable to the case of Jael any more than they would be to some acts of the Israelites in their contests with the natives of Canaan, which are repugnant to our opinions. He who commanded the end, directed also the means: and here we must rest the vindication of Jael, who is believed by correct commentators to have been moved by a divine impulse to put Sisera to death. This victory over the king of Hazor, was a great blessing to the suffering Israelites. Sisera his captain, was the hated instrument of his tyranny; the zeal of Heber's wife in the cause of religion and liberty, was therefore celebrated in rapturous gratitude by Deborah and Barak in the sacred Song[6] which they composed for this remarkable deliverance.

[Hall includes her own versification of Judges 5.]

FANNY. Difficult as it is to reconcile our present notions with the conduct of Jael — or indeed to the participation of women in warlike exploits at all, I must plume myself on Deborah. The appointment of a woman to the dignity

6. Judges, Chap. 5.

of a ruler and a prophet, by unerring wisdom, is in favour of my opinion, that the mental powers of the sexes are naturally equal.

MOTHER. That is a question, my dear, which we can never determine until their natural powers are alike cultivated by education. So long as one and twenty years are unremittingly given to the improvement of the one, and not more than half that time to the other, and that besides, in a desultory manner, it will be altogether unfair to estimate the minds of men and women by their subsequent conduct.

That the Creator, has separated their respective spheres of action by a line almost impassible, there ought to be no question, and perhaps the entire devotion of females to study for so many years, might be somewhat incompatible with their peculiar destination, still we may be allowed to contend, that a large portion of knowledge, the early and careful improvement of every talent, is necessary to qualify women for the useful discharge of those duties — as well as to sustain them, under the sufferings to which they are peculiarly liable. Neglected as they are, and unfurnished with adequate armour, they often meet the ills of life with surprising fortitude, and have even governed empires with ability. I cannot however gratify you with the elevation of another female besides Deborah in this period of sacred history. A female sovereign arose some centuries after in Israel, but we derive no honour from her character.

Source: Sarah Hall, *Conversations on the Bible,* 4th edition (Philadelphia: Harrison Hall, 1827 [originally 1818]), 156–60.

MARY CORNWALLIS

Using the Only Means in Her Power

Mary Cornwallis (1758–1836) was married to Reverend William Cornwallis, the Anglican priest of the parish of Elham and Wittersham in Kent, England, for more than fifty years.[7] Cornwallis's four-volume commentary on the

---

[7]. For a fuller discussion of Cornwallis, see Marion Ann Taylor, "Cornwallis, Mary (1758–1836)," in *Handbook of Women Biblical Interpreters: A Historical and Biographical Guide,* ed. Marion A. Taylor and Agnes Choi (Grand Rapids: Baker, 2012), 142–45; Marion Ann Taylor, "Words of a Mother: Mary Cornwallis, Nineteenth-Century Biblical Interpreter," in *Recovering Nineteenth-Century Women Interpreters of the Bible,* ed. Christiana de Groot and Marion

Bible, entitled *Observations, Critical, Explanatory, and Practical, on the Canonical Scriptures,* was first published in 1817 with a second edition appearing in 1820. Cornwallis's commentary began as study notes for her own use, were used to teach Scripture to her daughters, and eventually were reworked for her grandson. When her grandson tragically died, Cornwallis published her work, using the proceeds to endow a free primary school in his memory.

Cornwallis's interpretation of Jael's conduct is found within her comments on Judges 4–5. Like Hall, Cornwallis reasons that, because Jael's actions were directed by divine impulse, she was excused from judgment. Cornwallis regards Jael as neither base nor cruel; she praises her for ridding the world of an idolater and oppressor. Cornwallis's interpretation is shaped by her awareness of the story's historical and cultural context. She infers from data about contemporary Arab living quarters, which had separate apartments for women, that Jael would have lived in the women's quarters and that this explains why Sisera felt safe enough to fall asleep. Cornwallis's comment that the customs of the Arabs have remained constant since the time of Jael is typical of Western interpreters, who contrasted their own dynamic, progressive culture with the backward, static culture of the East.

Jael acted no doubt by Divine impulse, as an instrument of vengeance upon an idolatrous commander, and does not afford any more than Ehud an example for imitation in common life; where treachery and falsehood of every description are abominable in the sight of God, and liable to severe punishment. Deborah showed her prophetic knowledge, by anticipating this event in ver. 9. Jabin was a name common to the kings who reigned in the territory of Hazor; as Pharaoh and Abimelech were to the kings of Egypt and Philistia; it appears that he had oppressed the Israelites during twenty years. It is probable that the Kenites, the descendants of the pious Jethro, priest of Midian, separated themselves from the Israelites when they fell into idolatrous practices; and that God permitted Sisera to be taken off by Jael, as a reward for their fidelity, and adherence to the true worship. It must be remembered that, when the honour of God was concerned, the Jews were taught to overlook every other sentiment; even the ties of nature were to

---

Ann Taylor, Society of Biblical Literature Symposium Series 38 (Atlanta: Society of Biblical Literature, 2007), 39–44.

Jael

yield, and give place to this first consideration. Jael, therefore, zealous in the cause of religion, and acting under a Divine impulse, was neither base nor cruel in using the only means in her power to deliver the nation from such an oppressor, and the world from a vile idolater. As the manners of the Arabs are scarcely changed in any respect, it is probable that then, as now, the women's apartments were by established custom secure from the entrance of men, or strangers. This accounts for the confidence of Sisera being so great, as to admit of his consigning himself to sleep.

Source: Mary Cornwallis, *Observations, Critical, Explanatory, and Practical, on the Canonical Scriptures,* 2nd edition (London: Baldwin, Cradock & Joy, 1820 [originally 1817]), 2.343–44.

Eliza R. Stansbury Steele

A Mother's Love

Little is known about the life of the American author who published as Mrs. Eliza R. Stansbury Steele (fl. 1840–50s). Her writings suggest she was wealthy and well educated. The first of her three books, *A Summer Journey in the West*,[8] is valued by scholars as a well-written account of a woman's four-thousand-mile summer tour through New York State, the Great Lakes, the Illinois River, down the Mississippi to the mouth of the Ohio River, up the Ohio across Pennsylvania and Maryland. Steele's other publications demonstrate her knowledge of Scripture and theology; *Heroines of Sacred History* (1841) features female figures in Scripture, and *Sovereigns of the Bible* (1851) focuses on the kings of Israel. The dedication of *Sovereigns of the Bible* to her "revered pastor," the great American pulpit preacher Dr. Ichabod Spencer, suggests that she was a member of Second Presbyterian Church of Brooklyn, New York, and likely involved in some kind of teaching ministry in the church.[9]

In *Heroines of Sacred History,* Steele tried to redeem seven biblical women — namely Miriam, Deborah, Ruth, Esther, Jehosheba, Jephthah's daughter, and the apocryphal character Judith — from the disdain she felt they some-

---

8. Eliza R. Steele, *A Summer Journey in the West* (New York: J. S. Taylor & Co., 1841).
9. Eliza R. Steele, *Sovereigns of the Bible* (New York: Dodd & Mead, 1851).

times elicited. Her goal was to "render [them] more attractive," by portraying them with "the costumes, scenery, and manners" of the times in which they lived.[10] Steele's retelling of the story of Jael is embedded in her chapter "The Heroism of Deborah." Steele embellishes the story freely, adding a colorful scene about the kidnapping of Jael's fictional daughter, Zillah, which provides Jael with motivation for murder. In her conclusion Steele justifies Jael's conduct further, suggesting, "We must take into consideration the rude age in which she lived; the commands which the Israelites had received to slay the Canaanites if they would preserve themselves; and the danger in which the country stood should Sisera escape."

Steele's additions show that she is a careful reader of Scripture and especially sensitive to issues concerning women. She draws from Old Testament laws, narratives, and even the prophetic books to fill in gaps to enhance the story of Jael. She develops the theme of women as innocent victims of war raised in Judges 5:30 and introduces the idea that Sisera like Jephthah (Judges 11:30–31) made a vow that would involve the sacrifice of the innocent. Steele's Jael leaves her idolatry to renew her faith in the God of Israel.

Night with her lustrous stars, her silence and repose, had passed away, and soft eyed dawn heralded by gentle zephyrs, and breathing out perfume, arose from Asia's mists like the poet's Venus from the sea, all smiles and gladness. Each flower threw out its fairy petals, and wafted forth its fragrant incense to the day. Almond and citron blossoms, brilliant pomegranate, and oleander tossed the dew from their delicate heads, and shook their fragile branches in the morning breeze. The birds were on every bough singing their rejoicings to the coming day; for as yet the sun had not appeared, but clouds of rose and purple told of his near approach, and threw a softened radiance over plain and hill and valley. A clear and gentle river — Kishon, "that ancient river, the river Kishon," wound through the verdant plain. By its side arose a sloping hill, whose summit was crowned by a grove of oaks and elms, among whose shadows a lordly temple was just made visible as the sun's first rays fell on the hilltop, while all below still lay in shade. The rising light revealed its snowy porticoes and lofty arches, and graceful columns of rare proportion;

---

10. Eliza R. Stansbury Steele, *Heroines of Sacred History*, 4th ed. (New York: John S. Taylor & M. W. Dodd, 1851), vi.

then passing down the hill shone on a procession of solemn worshippers who were winding along the river's bank, and ascending to the temple above. Conspicuous among the throng were the sacred oxen, who gaily decorated with ribbons, and wreathed with roses, were led by young boys clad in white robes and crowned with garlands, behind them came a train of women dancing, and singing to instruments of music; while preceding and around the victims were several hundred priests whose black robes threw the only shadow over a landscape now brightly illumined by the broadly risen sun. The procession ascended the hill; the temple doors were thrown open; the priests entered and advanced to the altar. There upon two pedestals, stood the gods they came to worship. The one, a man cast in brass, having an ox's head — the other of marble, and human shape, clothed in a coat of golden mail, wearing a crown and wielding a sword; the former was Moloch, and the latter Baal. To these gods of marble and gold the priests and people had come to ask for protection from a powerful enemy, who in predatory bands made inroads upon them, and carried away flocks, and people, and goods.

Reader, canst thou say in what land arose this temple, these images of marble, and these idol worshippers? Canst thou believe it was in Israel? In the promised land? Alas — it was the dear-bought land of Canaan, and these deluded idolaters were the sons of Judah, once God's own peculiar people! No remembrance of their former errors and their previous punishment could wean this stiff-necked race from their love of idol worship. Forgotten was all the forbearing love of their gracious God — forgotten was his power which led them out of Egypt, and placed them in this lovely land — forgotten were all the denunciations of Jehovah against idolatry — again they sinned, and now again, in consequence of this sin, were plunged in misery and woe. The Canaanites, whom the Israelites had subdued and confined to their cities subject to tribute, had now been stirred up against them. For many years they harassed them by coming suddenly upon them in small bands, carrying away every thing or person which fell in their power.

In consequence of these incursions, the highways were deserted, the fields were uncultivated, and the children of Israel were sorely oppressed. To arrest this evil, the mass of the people sought not for protection from their all-powerful God, but blindly hewed them out gods of stone, and built groves in their high places, and called on their images to save; "yet can they not answer or save them out of their trouble!"[11]

The last of the priests had but just entered the temple, when, bursting

---

11. [Isaiah 46:7.]

through their ranks and uttering shrieks of terror, a woman, one of the dancers, threw herself before the statues; it was Jael, the wife of Heber the Kenite — the roses which had wreathed her lank locks, had fallen on her shoulder, and the white fillets were waving in disorder over her sallow shrivelled cheeks in bright contrast to their tawney hue. "O, Baal, save us!" she cried in distraction. "Now save us, for the enemy is upon us!" A chorus of shrieks arose from the women without, who came pressing confusedly into the temple. "The Canaanites are upon us!" they cried — "O Moloch shield us!"

Eager to save themselves from the invaders, the priests hastily closed the iron-studded doors of the temple, heedless of the many shrieking women whom they thus cruelly shut out. Their hopes of admission vain, the worshippers fled to the groves or down the hill, followed by the affrighted oxen, and their youthful leaders.

Jael arose from the ground and endeavoured to pass out of the door. "O my child!" she cried — "my Zillah is without — O let me go forth and shield her, or die with her!"

The priests however were bent upon saving themselves from harm, and the wailings and passionate entreaties of the miserable mother were unheeded by hearts as hard as the marble gods they worshipped.

At last the shouts of the enemy and cries of their victims were hushed and the noise of trampling steeds receded. The temple doors were slowly opened, and their safety being ascertained, the priests of Baal came forth. There was nothing to be seen near them, but afar off they descried a band of horsemen riding rapidly away, each bearing a captive upon his horse; while behind them the sacred oxen were goaded by a powerful escort. As the last of the horsemen turned into the wood which hid them from sight, it was perceived he bore away upon his horse a young girl, who, with arms uplifted, was loudly calling for aid. In her struggles a scarlet girdle fell to the ground; Jael swiftly ran down the hill, and hurriedly examined it.

"They have taken my daughter!" she cried, with a burst of woe — "O Zillah, that I could have died to save thee!"

Prostrate upon the ground, the miserable woman threw dust upon her head, invoking curses upon the Canaanites, and vowing deep vengeance for this cruel wrong.

* * *

During these troubles the Judge of Israel died, and Deborah became a "mother in Israel." Deborah, the widow of Lapidoth, was a woman of a

Jael

strong and masculine mind; more capable of ruling the affairs of the nation than many of her countrymen. Of this they were well aware; and came to her for counsel in any emergency. The piety of Deborah was great, and her God had bestowed upon her the gift of prophecy; thus using her as a means of keeping the faith in Israel, and drawing her country-people from the dreadful crime of idolatry, into which they had fallen. The grief of Deborah at their delinquency was great; as she foresaw the certain punishment their guilt would bring upon them. The present distress with which the country was afflicted, had been threatened them by their prophetess; but she was unheeded except by a few, who still worshipped at the tabernacle which was stationed at Shiloh.

* * *

... One morning Deborah restored to her favorite palm tree, and placed herself upon her usual seat, which was a long divan of costly structure, having cushions covered with embroidered silk. Her dress was a dark colored stuff of Damascus, having a deep border of gold embroidery, confined with a girdle wrought with scarlet and jewels; a bandean was around her head, from which projected a short horn of gold, supporting a veil of thin muslin of India, which fell to her feet. She was surrounded by many of her people who had come to her for judgment. A voice of wailing was heard outside the gate, when, followed by a large concourse of people, Jael, the wife of Heber the Kenite entered the court. She wore a sackcloth dress woven of black goats-hair, confined by a rope girdle, while her dark locks were thickly strewn with ashes.

"O help me, noble lady!" she cried; "help me, great Deborah! For I am stricken unto death!" — with a deep groan she sank on the ground before the feet of the Prophetess.

"What moves thee thus Jael?" asked Deborah, raising her. "Why art thou thus mourning in sack-cloth?"

"My daughter, my sweet child Zillah, hath been carried away by the enemy!" she exclaimed weeping. Others joining their cries to hers, bewailed the loss of relative, or cattle, and entreated Deborah for help against the invaders. Deborah listened while the outrage at the temple, just related, was described, as well as many similar inroads of the Canaanites.

"Where didst thou say thou wast, Jael, when thy child was ravished from thee?"

"At the temple of Baal, where we were going to sacrifice. O Deborah, hear the prayer of the people! Awake! Collect an army, and punish the invaders of our land!"

"Is it to me, a worshipper of Jehovah, that the children of Baal come for succor? Away! Go to your gods for aid. I will not raise a hand to save you!"

"Nay Deborah, hear us!" they cried. "Give us soldiers to defend our villages, or we shall all be taken captive — we and our little ones!"

"And ye would be well punished for your senseless idolatry!" said the indignant Deborah. "Do you not know — have ye not heard, that God has sworn he will punish you if you forsake him? Have ye forgotten the words of holy Joshua who said, — 'If ye forsake the Lord and serve strange gods then will he turn and do you hurt, and consume you!'[12]

"Had ye approached the Tabernacle of your father's God at Shiloh, instead of resorting to the high places of Baal, ye might have heard the words of Joshua read, and these your sufferings fully foretold; yea foretold to be inflicted by this same nation. 'Know for a certainty,' saith Joshua, 'the Lord your God, will no more drive out any of these nations before you; but they shall be *snares* and *traps* unto you and *scourges* in your sides, and *thorns* in your eyes, until you perish off this good land, which the Lord your God hath given you!'[13] Ungrateful people that ye are! ye have forsaken a kind and powerful God, who hath ever cherished and exalted you, to worship metal and stone! ...'"

While Deborah addressed her people, the mists of error departed from before their eyes; and when, as one inspired, she thundered in their ears the denunciations of Jehovah against idolatry, and the words of his servant Moses, the fear of God and remorse for their sin smote upon their hearts.

"We are guilty before the Lord!" they cried in terror. "We will indeed serve the Lord our God, and his voice alone will we obey!"

"Away then!" cried Deborah. "Prove your sincerity! Cut down your groves, — throw down your images, — that the anger of the Lord be no more hurled against you. If ye truly obey him, I will pray to him to raise up an army, and destroy your enemies from off the land."

[In what follows, Steele describes the destruction of the idolatrous images, Deborah's discussion with Barak about battle plans, and the battle itself.] ...

Sisera fled in his chariot, but finding the waters rising fast, he abandoned it, and ran up a neighboring eminence. For many hours he wandered about, and when the day dawned, found himself at some distance from the scene

---

12. [Joshua 24:20.]
13. [Joshua 23:13.]

Jael

of action. He was in the plain of Zaanim. Before him he beheld an encampment of tents, which, from their peculiar construction, he knew belonged to the Kenites, and he felt assured of safety. At the door of one stood a woman towards whom he ran for protection. Pursued by an avenging God, Sisera has been sent to the tent of his foe. It was the encampment of Heber the Kenite, whose family had joined the Israelites, and she to whom the marauder flew for safety was his bitter enemy Jael. She recognised him at once as the ravisher of her daughter, and the oppressor of Israel, and rejoiced to see him approaching.

"Turn in my lord! Turn in to me," she said. He gladly entered, and threw himself exhausted upon a pile of mats which she spread for him.

"Give me, I pray thee, a little water to drink," he said, "for I am very thirsty."

Jael opened a skin bottle and poured him out some milk, and gave him with it bread with butter in a dish of carved gold which her husband had taken in war. After he had eaten, she at his request threw over him a pile of clothes to conceal him from view.

"Stand in the door of the tent, good woman," said Sisera, "and if any man doth come and enquire of thee 'Is any man here?' thou shalt say, 'No.' If I am saved this day it will go well with thee, for Jabin shall reward thee, and give thee a place in his palace. Then thou mayest rule the Israelite women, for there are many in our houses whom we have carried away captive!"

Jael, repressing the various emotions with which her bosom was bursting, when she saw her enemy in her power, now, in a voice of affected indifference, asked, "Saw ye anything my lord, of Zillah, a young girl, who was taken from the temple of Baal when the sacred oxen were carried away?"

"Aye, indeed — she is in my house, and is as goodly to look upon as the goddess Ashtaroth. When I left home, I made a vow to Moloch to sacrifice her, and several others at his altar, if he brought me safe to Hazor again."

Jael rushed from the tent. "Now God I thank thee!" she cried, "that my enemy and Israel's oppressor is in my power. Zillah, thou art saved! for Sisera shall not return. In thy place he shall be sacrificed to the gods! Moloch! I devote him to thee! Baal! Give strength to my arm! O Jehovah, pardon me! why call upon false gods? thou alone art the only true God, and now that thou hast given me my enemy in my hand, I will worship thee alone."

Jael returned to the tent and lifted up the curtain of the doorway. Her enemy was plunged in a deep slumber. Fearful some of his followers might wander there and rescue him from her hand, and knowing her daughter's life was the price of his safety, she resolved to put him to death, and thus render Israel free from one who had cruelly used them. She tore out one of the large nails with which the tent ropes are fastened to the ground, and with a hammer smote the robber on the head. In triumph Jael rushed from the tent — Barak was riding rapidly past.

"Ho! Barak!" she cried, "come, and I will shew thee the man thou seekest." Barak followed her into the tent, and behold, dead before him, Sisera, the redoubtable oppressor of Israel. "Praises be to God!" he cried, "who hath this day subdued Jabin, King of Canaan, before the children of Israel! Truly did Deborah declare he should die by the hand of a woman. I thought the prophecy alluded to her, but to Jael is this honor due. Come with me, that I may show Deborah and the Princes this thy noble act."

The next morning saw Deborah at the height of her glory and popularity. She was again seated under her palm tree, surrounded by the princes and nobles of Israel, who gave to her the honor of freeing Israel from their oppressors. Deborah's heart bounded, but checking all pride, she said — "Not to me, — not to Deborah be the glory, my lords; let us ascribe it all to our merciful Jehovah, of whom I am the humble instrument. But where is our good general Barak? Is he still in pursuit of Sisera?"

"Behold where he comes, followed by a train of people," said the Prince of Issachar. Deborah looked up, and beheld Barak approaching, leading Jael; both were crowned with garlands, followed by men bearing a corpse upon a bier, and women dancing, and singing triumphant songs.

"Behold the deliverer of Israel!" cried Barak. "Sing praises to Jael, for she hath slain Sisera, the enemy of Israel. Blessed above women be Jael the wife of Heber!"

Jael was hailed as Israel's avenger, by all the people, when the death of Sisera by her hand became known. For one moment a pang smote the heart of Deborah when she thus saw the glory given to another, but she was a woman of too lofty a spirit, and devoted piety, to envy another. "I am punished," she said, "for my proud thoughts of yester-night." Throwing off all feeling save joy for the death of Sisera, she approached and greeted Jael, as a saviour in Israel. Then taking her timbrel, burst out in the following triumphant song: [There follows a poetic version of Deborah's Song from Judges 5].

The Moral

One of the most striking features in the character of Deborah, is her fearless avowal of the truth. While all the country was given up to idolatry, she upheld the religion of Jehovah. In the presence of the worshippers of Baal she was not ashamed to avow her own faith publicly, however unfashionable it had become; but declared herself decidedly upon the Lord's side. Nor did she swerve from the duty of shewing them the error of their way but severely rebuked them for their wickedness. Let us endeavor to imitate her example, and when in the company of unbelievers testify to the truth as it is in Jesus, unabashed by sneers and unawed by persecution.

In judging the conduct of Jael, we must take into consideration the rude age in which she lived; the commands which the Israelites had received to slay the Canaanites if they would preserve themselves; and the danger in which the country stood should Sisera escape.

Source: Eliza R. Stansbury Steele, *Heroines of Sacred History*, 4th edition (New York: John S. Taylor & M. W. Dodd, 1851 [originally 1841]), 33–58.

Eliza Smith

The Worst Woman Ever

Eliza Smith (fl. 1850–52) was one of a number of nineteenth-century British women who published pseudonymously as "A Clergyman's Daughter."[14] Though Smith's full identity is hidden, her writings suggest that she was a Scottish Presbyterian involved in the Christian education of children and youth in her father's church. She published two novels in 1850: *Chapters on the Shorter Catechism: A Tale* and *The Mingled Yarn; or, Prosperity without Peace and Adversity without Pain*. *The Battles of the Bible* (1852) showcases her sophisticated knowledge of the Bible. Like Sarah Hall, Smith adapts the traditional catechetical genre for her exposition of Bible stories and uses a series of conversations between Grandfather and his three grandchildren as a way of addressing both the content and the interpretive challenges of biblical stories. The subject of battles was ostensibly chosen by Grandfather in an attempt to get George more interested in the Bible, but his sister Marianne was reluctant to hear about the battles because she did "not like to hear of

---

14. Other women who published under this name include Ellen Clacy, Mary E. Simpson, Selina Gaye, Frances L. Bingham, and Emma F. Lloyd.

people killing one another" and had to be encouraged to listen and to see what she could learn.

The Grandfather figure explains many of the interpretive difficulties found in Jael's story. He adds information about the relationship between the Kenites and the Israelites, for example, to explain why Sisera thought he would be safe in Jael's tent. Similarly, Grandfather rationalizes the praise heaped on Jael by noting that people tend to applaud actions that are successful, whether or not they are good. When Marianne condemns Jael's actions, Grandfather cautions her to consider the context, explaining that killing the enemy in time of war is different than killing in a time of peace — an example of situational ethics. In addition, Grandfather suggests that Jael's intentions toward Sisera changed when he commanded her to lie: his duplicity led to hers. Grandfather then draws the moral lesson that "the sins of others can never excuse our own." In addition, he mentions (but does not seem to endorse fully) a traditional figural reading that views Jael as a type of worldly pleasure "which promises only to betray" and Sisera as a type of those who "trust for happiness in the things of this world."

MARIANNE. But you have not said anything, grandfather, about the woman who was to conquer Sisera.

GRANDFATHER. I shall tell you of her now. A people called the Kenites, who were descended from Jethro, the father-in-law of Moses, and priest of Midian, lived in the land of Canaan. They worshipped the true God and kept the law of Moses, so they lived on amicable terms with the children of Israel. However, in this war with the king of Hazor the Kenites were neutral. Knowing this, Sisera thought he might be secure with them. He fled to their tents; for when I told you that all the host of the Canaanites fell by the sword, I meant all except Sisera himself. He escaped to the tent of Heber, the chief of the Kenites. They were a pastoral people living in tents, whose riches consisted of flocks and herds. Jael, the wife of Heber, went out to meet the defeated general. She welcomed him with seeming kindness, and offered him shelter in her tent. He gladly accepted her offer, and asked for a little water to quench his thirst. The best drink she possessed was milk, which she gave to him, the richest she had, and in her finest dish. Then Sisera, thinking that his only chance for safety was in concealment, told Jael that if those passing by were to ask if any one were within, she must deny the fact. The wife of Heber

Jael

made no reply to this; but no sooner did she see that the enemy of Israel was sound asleep, than she took a long nail, one of those used for fastening the tents, and with a hammer she drove the nail through the temples of Sisera, and fastened his head to the ground.

MARIANNE. Oh! that would kill him, grandfather. How cruel; that surely was not right.

GRANDFATHER. I cannot defend the conduct of Jael to invite a man into her house, — to proffer him hospitality; and then, when he trusted in her, to put him to death, was false and treacherous. Though Deborah, in speaking of this action, says, — "Blessed above women shall be Jael, the wife of Heber, the Kenite"; still we need not understand that as intimating that the action itself was right, but rather that those who had suffered from the oppression of Sisera would load with approbation the woman who had taken his life. It is not always those actions that are best in themselves that are most praised by the world; it bestows its loudest approval on those which are most fortunate in their results.

MARIANNE. I think Jael was very wicked, the worst woman I ever heard of.

GRANDFATHER. We must not judge too severely of her, Marianne; when we think the conduct of any one deserving of blame, we ought always to take into view those circumstances which may make the blame appear less. There is little doubt that Jael was an Israelite at heart, looking on them as the peculiar people of the God whom she worshipped. She thought what was done for them was right; what was done against them was wrong. She wished that Sisera might be conquered; but when she saw that proud general of the Canaanites a miserable fugitive, it may have been pity alone that impelled her to offer him protection, for if she did not take him in, his death was certain. She took him in and treated him kindly; but when he asked her to tell a falsehood, she may have thought it no longer necessary to keep faith with him. In this she was wrong, for the sins of others can never excuse our own. If we learn this lesson from Jael it will be good for us to have heard of her. It has been observed by some that the wife of Heber is a type of worldly pleasure, which promises only to betray; and Sisera may be considered as a type of those who trust for happiness in the things of this world.

Source: A Clergyman's Daughter [Eliza Smith], *The Battles of the Bible* (Edinburgh: Paton & Ritchie, 1852), 111–15.

Emily Owen

Jael: A Heroine?

Emily Owen (1822-85) was born in Gloucester, England, to Mary and William Montague. In 1843 she married Octavius Friere Owen, who had earned an M.A. from Christ Church, Oxford, and was an Anglican priest, domestic chaplain to the Duke of Portland, translator, editor, and prolific writer. In addition to giving birth to ten children, Owen, who published as Mrs. Octavius Friere Owen, was a composer and published a number of books, including *The Heroines of History* (1854) and *The Heroines of Domestic Life* (1861).

The Heroines of History, as the title suggests, explores the subject of heroism as it relates to women. Owen's design in writing a history of female heroes was "to instruct by attraction." She identifies herself as a historian "wander[ing] through the garden of the Past, cull[ing] from each fairest plant the brightest hints, the richest odours, to stimulate the ambition or support the endurance of the young mothers of the future generation."[15] She divides history into three eras: Jewish, Classic, and Modern, including in the Jewish era only Jael, Judith, Salamona, and Marianne. Twenty other heroines are discussed in her book.

Owen's historical interests are apparent in her treatment of Jael. She stresses differences in education and circumstances between her own time, which she idealizes, and the world of Jael. At the same time, she wonders if Jael "may have been endowed with a heart as tender, a mental organization as delicate, to which the very name of violence, or a deed of bloodshed, was as repellent as to your own, or to that of any other sensitively nurtured daughter of our favoured land!" That being said, she refuses to interpret the story in light of her own assumptions about the nature of women.

Owen draws on historical and biblical scholarship to illumine the story and shows appreciation for Jewish tradition, introducing an alternative reading that further justifies Jael's act as it implies that Sisera expected sexual favors from Jael. She notes Charles Taylor's justifications of Jael's actions and, rather than engaging them one by one, states that her method is to stick to what is explicitly stated in the passage — a very Protestant hermeneutic.[16]

---

15. Mrs. Octavius Friere Owen, *The Heroines of History* (London: George Routledge & Sons, 1854), v.

16. Nonconformist Charles Taylor (1756-1823) produced an updated English version of Calmet's *Dictionaire historique et critique de la Bible* (1734). *Calmet's Dictionary of the Holy Bible* went through many editions in the nineteenth century.

Owen recognizes that this means the reader is left to interpret a text that contains obscurity about the motivations of Jael. This explicit acknowledgement of the ambiguity of the text and her decision to respect this characteristic make Owen an unusual commentator, as most smooth out the rough spots to bring them into conformity with their own convictions.

Owen discusses the reference to Jael as "blessed" in Deborah's song, claiming that it refers to the results of her actions rather than their innate goodness. Her conclusions are similar to Grandfather's claim in Eliza Smith's work that applause is often for the success of a project rather than its own virtue. Owen approaches the difficulties regarding the ethics of Jael's actions by considering other examples where God uses questionable characters and tactics to accomplish holy tasks. Owen also is the only interpreter to note the parallel between Jael and Judith in the Apocrypha. She undoubtedly chose Jael as her only Old Testament heroine on the basis of the epithet given to her by Deborah, lifting her up as "blessed above women."

Jael, or Jahel

B.C. 1296

"Blessed above women shall Jael, the wife of Heber the Kenite be." Do we ever reflect, in enumerating the ineffable blessings accruing to us from the gospel dispensation, that amongst them ranks the privilege of living in times when our faith is not likely to be tested by, nor our hope of heaven based upon, the performance of a duty at variance with every softer impulse of our woman's nature? Fenced around by refinement, carefully guarded from aught that can assail the feminine character in these happy days, we are apt to regard those of our sex like Jael, and the parallel case of Judith,[17] as possessing a wholly distinct temperament from our own; and to a certain extent we are right. Education and circumstances have operated to the last degree beneficially upon our existence, and perhaps the present age is one permitting the nearest approach to actual perfection as regards civilization, and due esteem to those who are to become the mothers of the next (and perhaps still more enlightened) generation. Yet start not, gentle reader; the heroic Israelite may

---

17. [Judith 13:16.]

have been endowed with a heart as tender, a mental organization as delicate, to which the very name of violence, or a deed of bloodshed, was as repellent as your own, or to that of any other sensitively-nurtured daughter of our favoured land! Let us gratefully acknowledge, therefore, the boon, that to us is intrusted the performance of religious duty, unfettered by persecution and untried by the ordeal of nature's most fearful conflict.

The history of Jael is brief: [Owen summarizes the story.] . . . Whatever difficulty may exist in the minds of commentators as to the subsequent conduct of Jael, the words quoted appear to imply that the Lord would overrule her acts for good to his people, as upon another occasion he made Balaam's cupidity a vehicle for assuring the promise of Messiah to the world,[18] and even converted the remorse of Judas into a method of vindicating the fulfillment of his word.[19] Much allowance must be made for the obscurity which envelops the motives of Jael as well as the circumstances which attended the presence of Sisera in the tent, his conduct towards her, and the exasperation, probably, his tyranny excited in the hearts of all the Jews, a people ever brave and patriotic. No cause except one of these last appears of sufficient power to incite a woman of the East, notoriously proverbial for its strictness in maintaining hospitality, to exhibit what must otherwise be deemed one of the most flagrant proofs of treachery and malice. By way of apology, the Rabbis say that the words "at her feet he bowed, he fell," signify that he offered violence to her, for which cause she put "her right hand to the workman's hammer"; but this seems very improbable in a man who was overpowered by sleep. Again, the difficulty is increased by the implied security of the food given by Jael to him, which is in the East of considerable importance. Taylor suggests, 1st, that Jael had felt herself the oppression of Israel by Sisera: 2nd, that she was moved by patriotism: 3rd, that the general character of Sisera was so bad, that his death was desirable at any rate.[20] However this may be, certain it is, that the whole history is exactly parallel to that of Judith, in the anxiety it evinces to deliver the people, and the use of artifice to accomplish the desire.

It is safer, on the whole, in matters of this kind, to adhere simply to what is known, without endeavouring to wrest the actions of others to our own rule of conduct, when we know little of the circumstances of the former.

As the narrative appears shorn of all explanatory relations, it strikes us

18. [Numbers 22–24.]
19. [Matthew 27:3.]
20. Augustin Calmet, Charles Taylor, Edward Robinson, *Calmet's Dictionary of the Holy Bible as published by the Late Mr. Charles Taylor with the Fragments incorporated,* revised by Edward Robinson (Boston: Crocker and Brewster, 1832), 543.

with horror that blood should be spilt by treachery, be the victim ever so hated or the motive ever so strong: indeed it is an anomaly to say, as many do, that a bad action can spring from a good motive, for the turpitude of the former casts back a reflective stain upon the latter. A person may moreover, be spoken of as "blessed," in reference to the *results* of a certain action, and not as to its inherent goodness; but knowing that God abhors a lie, and that he desires truth "in the inward parts,"[21] it is sufficient for us, "not to seek to be wise beyond what we are able,"[22] in cases which, like the present, are so stated as to render heroism doubtful, by the very questionable incidents which surround it. The history is given at full in the fourth and fifth chapters of Judges, so that to repeat it here would be superfluous, in the absence of other materials. The events occurred between B.C. 1316 and B.C. 1296.

Source: Mrs. Octavius Friere Owen, *The Heroines of History* (London: George Routledge & Co., 1854), 1–5.

Constance de Rothschild and Annie de Rothschild

A True Hebrew Woman at Heart

Baroness Constance de Rothschild (1843–1931) and her sister, Baroness Annie Henrietta de Rothschild (1844–1926), were the daughters of Sir Anthony Nathan de Rothschild, baronet, banker, and landowner, and Louisa Montefiore, a philanthropist. The sisters received a fine education from private tutors. Their mother taught them about their Jewish faith along with the New Testament, also encouraging them to visit the poor and to teach in a Jewish Free School in a poor East London Jewish community. In 1871 the sisters published an impressive two-volume work, *The History and Literature of the Israelites,* for a young but sophisticated readership. Their work shows considerable knowledge of contemporary biblical scholarship, including a surprising understanding of the idea of the dual authorship of Isaiah, a notion that was not popularized in Britain until the 1890s. Constance de Rothschild later questioned her Jewish faith and in 1877 married Cyril Flower, an

21. [Psalm 51:6.]
22. [Ecclesiastes 8:17.]

Anglican involved in politics. Annie de Rothschild married the Honorable Eliot Yorke in 1873.

The Rothschilds' account of the story of Jael in *The History and Literature of the Israelites* follows the biblical account closely. Unlike most interpreters, the sisters evaluated Jael primarily within her own context, claiming that although she is not a role model for those living "in our happier times and with our better experience," we are to understand how her treason "was accepted and even praised by an oppressed and struggling people in that early dawn of civilization." This judgment reflects their progressive view of history and use of situational ethics.

Unlike Sarah Hall and Mary Cornwallis, who absolve Jael by claiming that God was working through her, the Rothschilds rely on differing historical contexts to exonerate Jael. They cast Sisera as the enemy, "the representative of heathen might and hatred," and Jael as "a true Hebrew woman at heart, although she dwelt in friendship with the idolaters." They add to the story by making Jael's intentions, emotions, and actions explicit. They make no attempt to imagine a special relationship between the Kenites and the Israelites or to allow, like Eliza Smith through the voice of the Grandfather, that the Kenites worshiped the true God and kept the law of Moses. For the sisters, there can be only one true people of God: the Israelites. They also imagine that it is possible for an outsider, like Jael, to side with God's people. In the context of nineteenth-century England, which was renegotiating the place of the Jewish community in a Christian nation, this is instructive.

The Hebrew warriors, not numerous but singularly inspired by courage, assembled at Mount Tabor. When Sisera was informed of their advance, he felt that a great struggle for deliverance was imminent, and he determined to crush what he considered an audacious rebellion by the whole strength of his army assisted by his nine hundred iron war-chariots. He drew up his troops along the river Kishon, that was soon to become renowned as "the river of battles."[23]

But Deborah knew that the Lord's help was near; she exclaimed to Barak: "Up, for this is the day in which the Lord has delivered Sisera into thy hand; is not the Lord gone out before thee?" Barak with his 10,000 men hastened

23. [Judges 5:21; Psalm 83:9.]

Jael

promptly from the highlands of Tabor, and rushed valiantly onward against the horsemen of Sisera. A fearful carnage ensued: the corpses of the slain enemies filled the plain, or were swept away by the waters of the Kishon; the formidable chariots were of no avail; Sisera himself, seeing every chance lost and abandoning all hope, leapt from his chariot, and fled on foot for his life. He escaped probably northwards, wandering among his well-known mountain refuges, until he came to the settlement of Heber the Kenite, who had severed himself from the Hebrews, and lived in the plain of Zaanaim and Kadesh, like an independent chief. As Jabin the king of Hazor and Heber the Kenite were at peace, Sisera felt that he had at last found a safe retreat. He went to one of the tents, a worn-out fugitive. Jael, the wife of Heber, came out to meet him. She was a true Hebrew woman at heart, although she dwelt in friendship with the idolaters, and she exulted to find that the powerful general had fallen into her hands. Shrewdly dissembling her feelings, she said, "Turn in to me, my lord, turn in to me, fear not." When he had entered, she showed him the most studied attention. He was thirsty and asked for water, she offered him a draught of sweet milk. He was weary and desired to rest, she covered him with a mantle; but he cautiously bade her, "Stand in the door of the tent, and when anyone comes and enquires of thee and says, Is there any man here? thou shalt say, No." She promised to do as he had requested. Then she waited a while until she was certain that he was asleep. Now the moment for executing her design had arrived. She drew one of the large tent-nails from the ground, and took a hammer in her hand; then advancing softly to the sleeping man, she struck the nail into his temples, and without fear or mercy, she fastened it firmly to the ground!

In the meantime Barak had hotly continued his pursuit of Sisera. Following his traces, he breathlessly approached Heber's tent. Jael came out to meet him in all the flush of triumph, and exclaimed, "Come, and I will show thee the man whom thou seekest." She led Barak into the tent, and there lay the great captain murdered, with the nail in his temples.

In verse and in plain narrative the deed of Jael has been extolled as one of supreme merit. And yet, can we really admire that deceitful and relentless woman, who profaned and disgraced the sacredness of hospitality, knew of no pity or tenderness to a wearied soldier, a fallen enemy, and perfidiously lured him to a terrible death? Her contemporaries saw in her only the most patriotic lover of her people, and therefore revered her as a heroine. They looked upon Sisera not as a trembling fugitive, but as the representative of heathen might and hatred, and therefore glorified his destroyer as the great instrument that decided the destiny of the chosen people. Though we, in our happier times and with our better experience, justly revolt from an act of treason and ferocity, we can at least understand how it was accepted and even praised by an oppressed and struggling people in that early dawn of civilization.

Source: Constance de Rothschild and Annie Henrietta de Rothschild, *The History and Literature of the Israelites, according to the Old Testament and the Apocrypha,* vol. I: *The Historical Books,* 2nd edition (London: Longmans, Green & Co., 1871 [originally 1870]), 284–86.

Harriet Beecher Stowe

The Tiger, Tracked, Snared, and Caught

Harriet Beecher Stowe (1811–96), a renowned American writer and activist, was also a fine biblical interpreter.[24] In her 1873 work, *Woman in Sacred History,* Stowe expounds Judges 4–5, drawing on resources from the academy, nineteenth-century culture, and her experiences as a woman. Stowe contrasts Moses's ideals of a theocratic society and the lawlessness of the time of the judges, highlighting especially women's loss of dignity and self-respect. She regards Sisera as "the ravisher and brutal tyrant of helpless women" and extols Jael who entrapped "the ferocious beast." Like Eliza Steele, Stowe roots Deborah's blessing of Jael in her extreme anger against the "outrages on wives, mothers and little children, during twenty years of oppression." Unlike interpreters who felt compelled to draw specific spiritual lessons from Jael, Stowe exonerates her and reads the story as an episode within the larger story of salvation history.

The Book of Judges is the record of a period which may be called the Dark Ages of the Jewish Church. . . . Like all beautiful ideals, the theocratic republic of Moses suffered under the handling of coarse human fingers. Without printed books or printing, or any of the thousand modern means of perpetu-

---

24. For more details on Stowe's life, see "An Inspired Poet" in the Deborah chapter.

Jael

ating ideas, the Jews were constantly tempted to lapse into the customs of the heathen tribes around. [Stowe introduces the story of Deborah, describing "the class of prophetic and inspired women" to which Deborah belonged and "the condition of woman in those days, when under the heel of the oppressor."]

... The barriers and protections which the laws of Moses threw around the Jewish women inspired in them a sense of self-respect and personal dignity which rendered the brutal outrages inflicted upon captives yet more intolerable. The law of Moses commanded the Jewish warrior who took a captive woman to respect her person and her womanhood. If he desired her, it must be as a lawful wife; and even as a husband he must not force himself at once upon her. He must bring her to his house, and allow her a month to reconcile herself to her captivity, before he took her to himself.[25] But among the nations around, woman was the prey of whoever could seize and appropriate her.

The killing of Sisera by Jael has been exclaimed over by modern sentimentalists as something very shocking. But let us remember how the civilized world felt when, not long since, the Austrian tyrant Heynau outraged noble Hungarian and Italian women, subjecting them to brutal stripes and indignities. When the civilized world heard that he had been lynched by the brewers of London, — cuffed, and pommeled, and rolled in the dust, — shouts of universal applause went up, and the verdict of society was, "Served him right." Deborah saw, in the tyrant thus overthrown, the ravisher and brutal tyrant of helpless women, and she extolled the spirit by which Jael had entrapped the ferocious beast, when her woman's weakness could not otherwise have subdued. [Stowe continues with a discussion of the Song of Deborah.] ...

Then follows a burst of blessing on the woman who had slain the oppressor; in which we must remember, it is a woman driven to the last extreme of indignation at outrages practiced on her sex that thus rejoices. When the tiger who has slain helpless women and children is tracked to his lair, snared, and caught, a shout of exultation goes up; and there are men so cruel and brutal that even humanity rejoices in their destruction. There is something repulsive in the thought of the artifice and treachery that beguiled and betrayed the brigand chief. But woman cannot meet her destroyer in open, hand-to-hand conflict. She is thrown perforce on the weapons of physical weakness; and Deborah exults in the success of the artifice with all the warmth of her indignant soul.

25. [Deuteronomy 21:10–14.]

> "Blessed above women be Jael, the wife of Heber the Kenite!
> Blessed shall she be above women in the tent!
> He asked water and she gave him milk;
> She brought forth butter in a lordly dish,
> She put her hand to the nail,
> Her right hand to the workman's hammer.
> With the hammer she smote Sisera,
> She smote off his head.
> When she had stricken through his temple,
> At her feet he bowed, he fell, he lay prostrate,
> At her feet he bowed, he fell.
> Where he bowed, there he fell down dead!"

The outrages on wives, mothers, and little children, during twenty years of oppression, gives energy to this blessing on the woman who dared to deliver.

By an exquisite touch of the poetess, we are reminded what must have been the fate of all Judean women except for this nail of Jael.

> "The mother of Sisera looked out at a window,
> She cried through the lattice,
> Why delay the wheels of his chariot?
> Why tarries the rattle of his horse-hoofs?
> Her wise ladies answered: yea, she spake herself,
> Have they not won? Have they not divided the prey?
> To every man a virgin or two;
> To Sisera a prey of divers colors, of divers colors and gold embroidery,
> Meet for the necks of them that take the spoil."

In the reckoning of this haughty princess, a noble Judean lady, with her gold embroideries and raiment of needle-work, is only an ornament meet for the neck of the conqueror, — a toy, to be paraded in triumph. The song now rises with one grand, solemn swell, like the roll of waves on the sea-shore: —

> "So let all thine enemies perish, O Jehovah!
> But let them that love thee shine forth as the sun in his strength."

Source: Harriet Beecher Stowe, *Woman in Sacred History* (New York: Ford, Howard & Hulbert, 1873), 83–90.

Jael

Elizabeth Jane Whately

God's Executioner

Elizabeth Jane Whately (1822–93) was the eldest daughter of Elizabeth Pope and Reverend Richard Whately, principal of St. Alban Hall Oxford (1825–31) and Anglican archbishop in Dublin (1831–63). Whately was educated by her parents, a governess, and the finest private tutors. She became involved in various missional and philanthropic endeavors and published almost forty works in the areas of Christian missions, apologetics, religious education, biography, biblical interpretation, theology, and history. The death of her father in 1863 marked the end of many of her family and church-related obligations and the beginning of her more extensive involvement in missions and writing, including her father's biography, a collection of his sermons, writings, and abridged versions of several of his books. Whately was an ardent evangelical, and many of her writings have an apologetic and anti-Roman Catholic focus, including *Maude; or, The Anglican Sister of Mercy* (1869) and *Romanism in the Light of the Gospel* (1882).

Whately's apologetic book, *How to Answer Objections to Revealed Religion* (1875), was written to help "the inexperienced and young" use their reason and common sense to respond to objections being "continually brought forward in one shape or another" by "enemies" inside and outside the church. Whately organized her book into three parts: objections to the Old Testament, objections to the New Testament, and objections to Christianity generally, with each part containing several sections that are organized topically. The excerpt below comes from the part of her book on apparent moral difficulties in the Old Testament history.

In Whately's apologetic treatment the actions of Jael are discussed together with the revolt of Jeroboam and the massacre of Jehu as instances in which cruel, base, and treacherous behavior is seemingly sanctioned by the God of Israel. Her answer responds to the charge, made by enlightened nineteenth-century atheists, that God instigates and applauds morally repugnant behavior. One such atheist was Whately's American contemporary, Elmina Slenker, who used the story of God's approval of Jael's "mean, unjustifiable treachery towards a poor fugitive" in her attempt to undermine the Bible's credibility and authority.[26] Whately replied to

---

26. Elmina Drake Slenker wrote rather tongue in cheek: "As God allowed this deed of mean, unjustifiable treachery towards a poor fugitive to be accomplished, of course it was a merito-

critics like Slenker by introducing a distinction between action that God deems necessary in order to achieve a holy end and behavior approved by God. In this case God uses Jael's execution of Sisera to bring about a good end. Further, like Emily Owen, Whately mentions the possibility of a translation of the Hebrew text that suggests that Jael executed an alert rather than a sleeping criminal.

OBJECTION 3. That the conduct of many who commit actions which in our day would be looked on, not only as cruel, but as base and treacherous, is sometimes recorded in such a manner that the reader might be led to think God approved of and sanctioned such conduct. Under this head may be classed the act of Jael to Sisera,[27] the revolt of Jeroboam,[28] the massacre perpetrated by Jehu,[29] etc.

ANSWER. A good deal of confusion is caused, both in this and other cases, by confounding prophecy or history with precept. The warnings and threats of Scripture have often been fulfilled by men who were very far from serving and obeying God. In the Old Testament we meet with frequent instances in which God made use of wicked men and wicked nations to fulfil His own purposes — as in the case of Pharaoh, in Egypt, of whom He says, "For this cause have I raised thee up";[30] and again when He made Assyria, Babylon, and finally Rome, His instruments of executing judgments on His rebellious people of Israel, on the one hand, and on wicked heathen nations who had contended against them, on the other.

But using men as instruments is not the same thing as sanctioning or approving their conduct; it merely shows that His power can turn "the wrath of man to praise Him."[31] . . .

In the case of Jael, it is a matter of discussion among learned commentators whether the passage describing her action may not have been incorrectly

---

rious one; yet who of *us* could so betray the confidence of one who trusted in our promises, and turned to us for help in the hour of need?" *Studying the Bible; or, Brief Criticism of Some of the Principle Scriptural Texts* (Boston: Josiah P. Mendum, 1870), 26.

27. Judges iv and v. [Original note marked with asterisk.]
28. [1 Kings 11:26–14:20.]
29. [2 Kings 9:25–10:17.]
30. [Exodus 9:16.]
31. [Psalm 76:10.]

Jael

translated, and whether she may not have struck down Sisera (instead of killing him in his sleep) acting from a Divine commission.[32]

But it is not needful for ordinary students to enter into this question; all we need reply to objectors, is, that if she acted by Divine command, she was as truly God's executioner as Joshua and others like him; and if not, she must be looked on as one of those instruments whom He is pleased to make use of, without sanctioning or approving their conduct; and Deborah's praise of her must be regarded as an enthusiastic outpouring of the patriotic exultation of a Hebrew, and not as the authorised expression of God's approval.

No one can study history, ancient or modern, without seeing how often the providence of God has so turned the evil designs of wicked men as to lead to consequences ultimately beneficial to the world at large. And this overruling power of God's providence, which we are enabled to trace in the study of profane history, by watching the course of events, is pointed out to us, in sacred history, by the express statements of Scripture.

Source: Elizabeth Jane Whately, "Objections to the Old Testament," in *How to Answer Objections to Revealed Religion* (London: Religious Tract Society, 1875), 41–43.

Etty Woosnam

Unsexing Jael and Fighting Demon Drink

The two published volumes on women of the Bible authored by Anglican Etty Woosnam (1849–ca. 1883) grew out of a series of studies of women in Scripture for privileged young women intended to teach them how to study Scripture, to deepen their understanding of the Christian life, and to prepare them for marriage and motherhood.[33] In her essay on Jael from her work *Women of the Old Testament* (1881), Woosnam sets out a classic interpretive approach to difficult Old Testament texts and reveals her theology as well as her own life and times. She draws on the works of contemporary poets and essayists to strengthen her arguments.

---

32. See Bishop Wordsworth's "Commentary on the Book of Judges."
33. For more information on Woosnam, see "Rahab: True Conversion" in the Rahab chapter.

Woosnam's essay on Jael is built around the commonplace metaphor of battle to describe the Christian life. She grounds her figural reading of the story on 1 Corinthians 10, where Paul argues that some Old Testament events occurred in order to provide examples through the ages. Woosnam moves quickly from an exposition of the literal sense of the story to explore its spiritual sense: King Jabin is a type of sin, his officers symbolize worldliness, Sisera is the antitype and archenemy of the church, and Jael is a type of the Christian. She calls her audience to be "a spiritual Jael and nail down to the ground her Sisera." She notes that we should identify and kill our "Siseras," whatever they might be, suggesting "hardness of heart" as one example and "love of drink" as another. In her discussion of demon drink, Woosnam advocates total abstinence and parallels drinking in moderation with allowing Sisera to remain sleeping. The place where the nail entered into Sisera's body also holds significance for Woosnam as she argues that, while both the head and the heart must be "subdued," it is the will that must first be "brought into subjection to God's will." She concludes with further comments about the nature of Christian warfare and calls readers to be "conquerors through Him that loved us."

Jael

The Spiritual Campaign

The children of God on earth are marching through an enemy's land, and, unless they are deserting their colours, life is to them a battle-field. . . . the Christian warfare is not a series of blunders, reverses, and defeats. It is a triumphant campaign, and ends in glory. The great Captain is responsible for the provisions, armour, and generalship of the whole undertaking from first to last.

[Woosnam summarizes the conquest narratives, comparing the historical battles with spiritual battles faced by the church.] . . .

And now, under the judgeship of the prophetess Deborah, Jabin, king of Canaan, mightily oppressed Israel for twenty years. Every true-hearted Israelite must have blushed for shame; and chafed with impatience to drive back this hostile power. The men had been so neglectful of their duty, that the women had to act the part of champions and warriors, *which ill becomes*

Jael

them. As a rule, whenever women have been obliged to head the forces, as in Joan of Arc's time, and as in the time of Jael and Deborah, it has been because so few men were found to take an aggressive part. In Judges iv. we find Deborah accompanying Barak to the war, and defeating the Canaanites. But the Canaanite general escaped, and it was incumbent upon every Israelite who had an opportunity to slay Sisera. Was there no fighting man of Zebulon or Naphthali of all the 10,000 whom Barak had marshalled at Kedesh to pursue after Sisera in his flight, that he must die by foul means, and by the hand of a woman? Perhaps God's design was to humble in a more marked manner the pride of Jabin, and pour contempt on the confidence which Sisera had had in his 900 chariots of iron. Perhaps to shame the selfish and slothful men of Meroz, Dan, and Asher, because they remained in their ships and sheepfolds, and gave no helping hand in the Lord's battle, a woman was permitted to unsex herself by performing a cruel deed which would have been a grand feat for a victorious soldier in the open field.

One thing is clear, viz.: "All these things happened unto them for examples (or by way of figure), and they are written for our admonition."[34] It is for our admonition we are told that there is a King Jabin mightily oppressing us, whose name is Sin; and his officers are worldliness, avarice, love of drink, and infidelity. Probably Sisera's great antitype and the archenemy of God's Church now is a lack of warm interest in heavenly things, a general indifference to God's glory. Let every woman among us be a spiritual Jael and nail down to the ground her Sisera. For sin will ever continue to tempt and harass a Christian, even when it does not *reign* in him. Shall we leave all the hardships and all the success to the brave vanguard of Judah? or keep Sisera asleep on the chance that some good soldier may perhaps come in before he wakes and slay him for us? We recognize Siseras easily enough — our coldness and hardness of heart and our grievous besetting sins. Let us destroy them without delay. To pause is ruin. Wherever there is earnestness, there is decision. . . .

There are thousands of men and women in England who resolve every day to give up strong drink gradually, and become very moderate drinkers — poor misguided creatures! They do not know that Satan is perfectly satisfied with such an arrangement; they do not understand the energy and promptitude with which sin must be overcome. "Webb, the celebrated walker, who was remarkable for vigour both of body and mind, drank nothing but water. He was one day recommending his regimen to a friend who loved wine,

---

34. [1 Corinthians 10:11.]

and urged him with great earnestness to quit a course of luxury by which his health and talent would be equally destroyed. The gentleman was quite convinced, and told him that though he thought he could not change his course of life all at once, he would leave off strong liquors by degrees." "By degrees!" exclaimed Webb with indignation; "if you should unhappily fall into the fire, would you caution your servants to pull you out by degrees?"[35] [Woosnam quotes Adelaide Procter's poem "Now," which calls readers to rise up and embrace life's battles "for the day is passing."[36]] . . .

Did Jael use over-strong measures when she took one of the long pins or stakes with which the tent was fastened? and yet it was the only available one which was effectual. Are we thought to be stretching a point too far if we advocate total abstinence in an age in which fearful ravages are being made by the demon drink? It is the only available means of crushing it that we know of which is effectual; and God works by means.

In the conflict against sin in our own hearts, let us get a hint from Jael's example. She hammered the nail "into his temples." The mind of man is the seat of authority and power. If she had strapped him down, or wounded, without killing him, his men might have come up and released him, and the battle might have turned against Jael after all. But she touched the vital point! and we must have the evil principles of our minds and hearts subdued — our *will* must first be brought into subjection to God's will, or it will be useless for us to be watchful over our footsteps, hands, eyes, and tongues. If some old latent self-love or worldly desire remains upper-most in our thoughts, the love of God cannot abide and grow there too. But if we strictly guard our minds and ask for the Holy Spirit to purify and cleanse them, the words and actions which proceed from them will grow purer. It is said: "A man does harm to his neighbour by his words and deeds, but to himself by his thoughts," and Solomon says: "As he thinketh in his heart, *so is he*."[37] St. Paul knew what it was to fight against his thoughts, and he encourages, others by the words: "The weapons of our warfare are not carnal, but mighty through God to the pulling down of strongholds; casting down imaginations and every high thing that exalteth itself against the knowledge of God, and bringing into captivity every thought to the obedience of Christ."[38] . . .

Lastly, let us remember . . . [the] holy warfare between good and evil is

---

35. From the *Quarterly Review*, volume 27, page 121. "Reid on Nervous Affections."

36. Adelaide Ann Procter (1825–64) was a famous British poet and philanthropist who advocated for the rights of women.

37. [Proverbs 23:7.]

38. [2 Corinthians 10:4–5.]

not carried on by the carnal weapons of bloodshed and violence, nor by arguments and high words, like the battles of this world; but by the loving hearts of men and women set on fire by the love of God to them. Love overcometh all things. The Captain of our salvation is the Prince of Peace; and the peace-makers shall be called the children of God. One of our British Kings[39] usually began the terms of any treaty with these pacific words: — "When Christ came into the world, peace was sung; and when He went out of the world, peace was bequeathed." This is not inconsistent with these words of the meek and lowly Jesus: "Think not that I am come to send peace on earth; I came not to send peace, but a sword."[40] His life and death made peace between God and man; but it established an open opposition against the Prince of this world. There is such a thing as a war for peace — a war which tends to make all warfare cease.

To be at peace with God is to be at war with Satan; to make no truce with our evil desires and habits; but to be filled with the Spirit, of which the first fruits are love, joy, and peace.[41] "In all these things we are more than conquerors through Him that loved us."[42]

Source: Etty Woosnam, *The Women of the Bible: Old Testament*, 4th edition (London: S. W. Partridge & Co., 1881), 97–109.

Anne Mercier

Deborah Was Wrong about Jael

Anne Mercier (1843–1917) was married to Jerome Mercier, the Anglican rector of Kemerton. She was a teacher and a prolific author of religious works, including a very popular book for girls on English church history, doctrine, and ritual; a history of Christianity in England; and many works of religious fiction. In 1887 Mercier published *The Story of Salvation: Thoughts on the Historic Study of Scripture,* one of many books written for young readers

---

39. Henry VII.
40. [Matthew 10:34.]
41. [Galatians 5:22–23.]
42. [Romans 8:37.]

at the close of the nineteenth century intending to correct "the old ways" of teaching the Bible by introducing critical methods and ideas as well as presenting a revised understanding of inspiration and revelation. In a series of conversations between a well-read Anglican named Mrs. Askell and her two nieces, Mercier presents an overview of the Bible and introduces various Bible study methods and such resources as chronological charts, a harmonization of the Gospels, an appendix on Bible versions, and a list of reference books.

Mercier's commentary on Jael addresses the story's interpretive challenges directly. Mercier contemporizes Jael's violent act by drawing parallels between Jael and Charlotte Corday (1768–93), a French revolutionary hero, who murdered the Jacobin leader Jean-Paul Marat in his bathtub with a kitchen knife that had a six-inch blade. She calls both women heroines, but judges their acts as being unworthy of imitation. Like Eliza Smith and Emily Owen, Mercier attempts to reconcile her understanding of woman's nature and Jael's act by filling in the text's silences about Jael's inner feelings, imagining Jael's "bitter struggle" within before "she could quell her womanly timidity and her sense of shame" and commit murder. To solve the puzzle of Deborah's praise of Jael, Mercier suggests that Deborah's song is "a poetic rather than a Divine inspiration." Like Elizabeth Whately, Mercier suggests that, with a proper understanding of the nature of the Old Testament as history, many of the moral puzzles in Old Testament narratives could be solved.

[The excerpt follows Mrs. Askell's summary of the story of Deborah, Barak, and Jael.]

"We know how [Jael] belied her Oriental creed of hospitality, and slew Sisera with a hammer and one of the tent pins when he was sleeping in faith in her protection. No one can defend the act as such, but we must allow for the fierce times she lived in, for her belief that her first duty was loyalty to the sacred race she was allied with; and perhaps as bitter a struggle arose in her heart, before she could quell her womanly timidity and her sense of shame, as raged in the heart of Charlotte Corday. We would imitate neither, but we must call each a heroine."

"The difficulty is, that Jael's act is praised by Deborah. Was she not inspired to do so?" asked May.

Jael

"I think the splendid ode in chapter v. is rather a poetic than a Divine inspiration. Even St. Paul had moments when he was not inspired, as we know, from his careful guarding of his advice in 2 Cor. viii.8 and 1 Cor. vii.6. The treble character of judge, prophetess, and poetess united in Deborah makes it hard to distinguish this; but reason would tell us that though our God is *one Lord,* and His counsels are ever the same, yet ages differ, and in the joy of conquest the woman judge and poet would fain give praise to the woman-deliverer. Remember the Bible in its historical parts is a narrative and not a series of moral essays. For lack of freely owning this, persons are sorely puzzled when no puzzle exists, if we would but study the history as such."

Source: Anne Mercier, *The Story of Salvation: Thoughts on the Historic Study of Scripture* (London: Rivingtons, 1887), 111–12.

M.G.

Nailing Sin to the Cross

Little is known about the English writer M.G., who published *Women Like Ourselves: Short Addresses for Mothers' Meetings, Bible Classes, etc.* (1893). M.G. delivered the addresses on women to various gatherings of women, probably in an Anglo-Catholic parish, and later wrote them down from memory and published them for the benefit of inexperienced teachers. In another day, M.G.'s addresses might be called sermons. M.G. approaches biblical characters as real people who acted "exactly as we ourselves would be likely to act under the same circumstances."

The story of Jael presents a challenge to M.G.'s interpretive approach, as finding a connection between "the unwomanly, deceitful and dishonourable" Jael and her audience was difficult. She explains the difference using the notion of distinctive Old and New Testament dispensations, contrasting the principle "love thy neighbour and hate thine enemy" with Jesus's commandment to "love thine enemy." Like Etty Woosnam, M.G. uses a figural approach to discern the story's spiritual meaning. The warfare between Israel and the heathen nations around them is read as a "type of the ceaseless warfare [that Christians] have to carry out against Satan and his army." Jael's actions more specially reveal that "women and girls are attacked and have to fight as bravely as men." Unlike many interpreters, M.G. applauds Jael's treatment of the enemy in her tent and calls women to take out their hammers and to nail their "Siseras" to the ground.

Jael

And now we come to the part taken by another woman, named Jael, in this victory. Mind, I am not going to say that what Jael did was right. The Bible does not give her praise or blame; it simply gives us a truthful account of what Jael did, and what Deborah said about it.

Jael was not an Israelite, and therefore Sisera hoped and expected to find refuge in her tent, and there, surely enough, he received a hearty welcome. He gasped out a request for water, and she brought him milk and curds, the best she had at hand, and then encouraged him to lie down to rest after the fatigues he had been through. Carefully she covered him over and watched till he was sound asleep, and then came her time. Snatching up the heavy hammer in one hand, and one of the long tent pins in the other, Jael stole to the side of the sleeping man, and with steady blows drove the cruel nail right through his temples till it was fixed into the ground beneath — and the enemy of God's people lay dead at her feet. To us it sounds not only unwomanly, but deceitful and dishonourable — a breach of all the laws of hospitality. But it is not for us to condemn. We have been taught lessons of charity and forgiveness and truth from our cradles, which Jael and Deborah never knew. It was not until Christ came that the commandment "Love thine enemy" was given. Till then the principle had been "Love thy neighbour and hate thine enemy," and Jael by her cunning and cruelty was only proving her intense hatred.

This history teaches us in parable a great spiritual lesson. The constant struggle between God's chosen people and the heathen nations around, is to us a type of the ceaseless warfare we have to carry on against Satan and his armies, and in this warfare women and girls are attacked and have to fight as bravely as men. Do not our spiritual enemies seize us just when we least expect them, when we are going quietly about our daily work, when we are talking to our friends, even when we come to draw water out of the wells of salvation? At any moment the arrows of Satan may strike us unseen, and more often than not they leave us vexed and wounded. Our only hope is

Jael

in resolute fight. We have all, women and children too, been marked "with the sign of the Cross, in token that we should fight manfully" against those three captains, "the World, the Flesh, and the Devil,"[43] and continue faithful soldiers unto our lives' end. So it is for us to join, and to encourage others to join, in this warfare. . . .

A special teaching lies, too, in the action of Jael. By the time Sisera reached her tent the battle was practically over; the Canaanites were slain or drowned or put to flight. But *there was still one of them left*. Only one! Might not his life have been spared? Could one do much harm alone, when the rest of the army was destroyed? Jael did not stay to reason thus. It was enough to know that one of the enemy was in her tent, and at all costs he must be slain. All the maxims of hospitality were as nothing compared to the danger. She had sinned in inviting him to come in — she must not sin further by allowing him to stay there alive. Not one of the accursed Canaanites must be spared — least of all their captain — so with determined blows Jael hammered till she knew that life was for ever gone.

It often happens that when we have been fighting bravely against temptation, and have put Satan and his host to flight, some one sin remains hidden away in our heart, and would persuade us to lull it to sleep there without further opposition. For instance, when you have fought down the temptation to quarrel with a neighbour, and done some kind action to prove your forgiveness, don't you often find the inclination very strong to say something cutting about her to your friends, as your one little bit of revenge? Oh, that is your Sisera still left in your heart. Out with the hammer, and nail that ill-natured speech tight down before it has had time to cross your lips. Or you have successfully resisted all the assaults Satan may have made upon your purity, you may have had a very hard fight, but by God's grace you have been victorious. But though you have conquered the temptation to sinful deeds, is there ever such a little thought about it left in your mind, begging you to let it rest there, and trying to persuade you that one little impure thought can't do much harm? Don't listen to it, crush it to death, or it may yet bring back all the hosts of the devil. Or, when you have overcome all your other sins, that dangerous captain called Pride will be sure to want to creep in and hide himself. He can do this so cleverly that we may not ourselves know that he is there; but if he is allowed to come in he will do more harm than any of the others. . . .

And what must we do with our enemies to insure their never returning?

---

43. Quotation from the Anglican Baptismal service in the Book of Common Prayer.

When I was a child I was sometimes taken to have tea at a gamekeeper's cottage, and in the wood close by I often saw the dead bodies of weasels and wild cats and other vermin nailed up to the trees to scare their fellows away. That is what we must do with our sins. Nail them firmly to *the* Tree, on which our dear Lord was nailed for us. In the light which streams from the Cross we shall see them as they really are, and once nailed there, with the nails of penitence and love, of prayer and of fasting, they will hurt us no more.

After the death of Sisera the land had rest forty years (Judges v.31). And hereafter, when all our enemies have been finally conquered, will come rest for you and for me and for all the people of God. Rest not only for forty years, but for ever and ever — when the great army of God will no longer be called "the Church Militant," i.e. "fighting," but "the Church Triumphant."

"And the great Church victorious
Shall be the Church at rest."[44]

Source: M.G., *Women Like Ourselves: Short Addresses for Mothers' Meetings, Bible Classes, etc.* (London: Society for the Promotion of Christian Knowledge, 1893), 60–66.

Elizabeth Cady Stanton

Cold-Blooded Fiend

Elizabeth Cady Stanton (1815–1902), a renowned American women's rights activist, published *The Woman's Bible*, a two-part commentary on the passages of the Bible dealing with women in 1895 and 1898.[45] Stanton's exposition on the Jael narrative is very brief and highly critical. Stanton is "revolted" by Jael's deceitful and inhospitable actions toward Sisera, whom she views not as an enemy but as a "luckless general." She assesses Jael's cold-blooded murder as "more like the work of a fiend than of a woman" and implicitly criticizes the church for glorifying the "heroism" of Jael. Stanton uses the story as a platform for criticizing Israel's God as well as the biblical story, which she

---

44. Quotation from Samuel John Stone's hymn from the 1860s, "The Church's One Foundation."

45. For additional biographical details, see "The Question of Motives" in the Rahab chapter.

Jael

views as the work of "the sacred fabulist." She adapts a traditional typological reading of war in the Old Testament, seeing little difference between tribal warfare in the Old Testament and contemporary "warfare" between "saints and sinners, orthodox and heterodox, persecuting each other" today. Stanton does not hide her contempt for the story and the interpretations presented by those within communities of faith.

The deception and the cruelty practised on Sisera by Jael under the guise of hospitality is revolting under our code of morality. To decoy the luckless general fleeing before his enemy into her tent, pledging him safety, and with seeming tenderness ministering to his wants, with such words of sympathy and consolation lulling him to sleep, and then in cold blood driving a nail through his temples, seems more like the work of a fiend than of a woman.

The song of Deborah and Barak, in their triumph over Sisera, has been sung in cathedrals and oratorios and celebrated in all time for its beauty and pathos. The great generals did not forget in the hour of victory to place the crown of honor on the brow of Jael for what they considered a great deed of heroism. Jael imagined herself in the line of her duty and specially called by the Lord to do this service for his people.

Nations make their ideal gods like unto themselves. At this period He was the God of battles. Though He had made all the tribes, we hope, to the best of His ability; yet He hated all, the sacred fabulist tells us, but the tribe of Israel, and even they were objects of His vengeance half the time. Instead of Midianites and Philistines, in our day we have saints and sinners, orthodox and heterodox, persecuting each other, although you cannot distinguish them in the ordinary walks of life. They are governed by the same principles in the exchanges and the marts of trade.

Source: Elizabeth Cady Stanton, "The Book of Judges, Chapter II," in *The Woman's Bible, Part II: Joshua to Revelation*, ed. Elizabeth Cady Stanton (Boston: Northeastern University Press, 1898), 20–21.

STUDY QUESTIONS

1. All of the commentators struggle with the deception and gruesome slaying that Jael perpetrated against Sisera. What made you uncomfortable with this story and why? How did the commentators deal with biblical passages that challenged their understanding of God and the character of women? Did any commentator help you address your discomfort?
2. What are the ethical issues involved in Jael's decision to kill the enemy? Does the narrator condemn her? Is killing ever right? Are ethical demands different in times of war?
3. In Eliza Smith's commentary, "Marianne" does not want to hear about the battles, but her grandfather insists on her listening to the entire text. Are there parts of the Bible people prefer not to hear? What might be the consequences of avoiding difficult scriptural texts?
4. Deborah called Jael "most blessed of women." How did nineteenth-century women interpret Deborah's praise? How do you?

5

Jephthah's Daughter

The story of Jephthah[1] and his daughter, with its troubling silences, religious enigmas, and theatrical potential, has intrigued readers throughout history.[2] Forming part of the larger story found in Judges 10:6–12:7, Jephthah is introduced as a valiant warrior, driven from his home by half-brothers who denied him a share in the family inheritance because his mother, a prostitute, is not their own. Fleeing to Tob, he surrounds himself with outlaws until sometime later when the elders of his hometown, Gilead, ask Jephthah to lead them against Israel's enemies, the Ammonites. After sincere but ultimately unsuccessful diplomatic attempts to negotiate peace, Jephthah leads a traditional campaign against the Ammonites. The Spirit of the Lord comes upon him, and, before the actual battle, Jephthah vows that if he is victorious,

---

1. Note the alternative spellings: Jepthah (Steele) and Jephtha (Cooke).

2. This is seen most clearly in Wilbur Owen Sypherd's comprehensive *Jephthah and His Daughter: A Study in Comparative Literature* (University of Delaware, 1948). Part 2 of Sypherd's book consists of a chronological list with bibliographical and critical notes on the hundreds of literary treatments, musical compositions, and other art forms used to interpret Judges 11 from the Middle Ages to the middle of the twentieth century from various culture and language groups. In *Writing the Wrongs: Women of the Old Testament among Bible Commentators from Philo through the Reformation* (Oxford: Oxford University Press, 2001) and *Reading the Bible with the Dead: What You Can Learn from the History of Exegesis That You Can't Learn From Exegesis Alone* (Grand Rapids: Eerdmans, 2007), 33–48, John Thompson focuses on the reception history of the story of Jephthah's daughter among Bible commentators from Philo through the Reformation. David Gunn's commentary on Judges 11 in the Blackwell Bible Commentary also presents a wide sampling of the interpretations by male and female writers and artists throughout history; *Judges* (Oxford: Blackwell, 2005). See also Maricn Ann Taylor, "The Resurrection of Jephthah's Daughter: Reading Judges 11 with Nineteenth-Century Women," in *Strangely Familiar: Protofeminist Interpretations of Patriarchal Biblical Texts*, ed. Nancy Calvert-Koyzis and Heather E. Weir (Atlanta: Society of Biblical Literature, 2009), 57–73.

whatever comes out of the doors of his house after the great triumph would be sacrificed to the Lord. Returning home after defeating the Ammonites, Jephthah is greeted by his beloved daughter dancing, accompanied by the sound of tambourines. Shocked that his only child was to be the object of sacrifice, Jephthah tears his clothes, blames his daughter, and claims that his vow must be kept. After acknowledging her father's vow, Jephthah's daughter asks for a two-month reprieve to spend with her friends in the mountains to mourn her loss. Upon her return, her father fulfills his vow, and the text says Israelite women commemorated her sacrifice yearly. The final scenes of Jephthah's life involve internecine warfare that resulted in the slaughter of forty-two thousand Ephraimites, and the story concludes by noting that he led Israel for six years before his death and burial in Gilead.

This disturbing story of "the atrocious vow of Jephthah, and its atrocious accomplishment"[3] elicited the comments of many nineteenth-century women, who used a variety of literary genres to explore its meaning for their disparate audiences. Using a selection of tools to aid interpretation, such as other biblical texts, traditional and contemporary biblical scholarship, and distinctively feminine lenses, shaped by their experiences as daughters, wives, and mothers, they produced widely varying results, although patterns do emerge. Interpreters were deeply perplexed by the details and gaps in the story, and they questioned the character of Jephthah, whom Hebrews 11:32 names as a hero of faith. Interpreters pondered the nature of his vow: why did he make it, and why did he keep it? The story of Jephthah's unnamed daughter was the catalyst for many nineteenth-century discussions about moral, theological, pastoral, and ideological issues relating to contemporary debates about women's nature and duty before God and others, in addition to moral questions about killing and war. Caroline Gilman, a young poet, sees Jephthah's daughter as a model for women whose lot in life involves sacrifices of various kinds. Adelia Graves, a woman who had lost a son in the American Civil War, also stresses the importance of patriotic sacrifice.[4] Cecil Frances Alexander reads the story through an Anglo-Catholic lens, seeing the daughter's sacrifice as a "whisper" or type of a greater sacrifice yet

---

3. Lady Sydney Morgan, *Woman and Her Master* (Philadelphia: Carey & Hart, 1840), 1.73.

4. Susie Silsby's long poem "Jephtha's Vow" also interprets the daughter's sacrifice as a patriotic act: "Though dark is the future that waiteth for me, / Yet the vow of my father unbroken must be; / My love for the world shall not stand in the way, / When the good of our country forbids me to stay." Albert J. Sanborn, ed., *Green Mountain Poets: A Collection of Poems from the Best Talent in the Green Mountain State (Vermont)* (Claremont: Claremont Manufacturing Co., 1872), 129–36.

to come. American political rights' activist Elizabeth Cady Stanton wishes Jephthah's daughter had recognized her own rights and defied her father.

Many interpreters, such as Mary Schimmelpenninck, adopt the less abhorrent reading of the Hebrew text that suggests that the daughter was not killed but sacrificed to a life of virginity and isolation. Yet even this reading raises questions about human rights and the nature of religious vocation. Some interpreters focus attention on particular scenes within the story; they all fill in gaps in the story using various cultural, social, political, and religious lenses. Many women give voice to the daughter; they explore her inner feelings and her struggles to espouse the values of self-sacrifice and honor, and the forsaking of the dreams of marriage and children.

A number of nineteenth-century interpreters of the story of Jephthah's daughter anticipate later feminist approaches. Specifically, the naming and developing of Jephthah's daughter's character in such a way that her personal pain and sacrifice is recognized and valued, acknowledging the horror of the act, and calling for this redemptive act to be remembered and memorialized by the world.[5]

Caroline Howard Gilman

Obedient unto Death

Caroline Howard Gilman (1794–1888) was born into a wealthy and well-connected family in Boston and raised by an older sister after her parents died. Although her formal education was limited, she was drawn to good literature from an early age. To her dismay, one of her early poems, "Jephthah's Rash Vow," was published without her permission when she was sixteen. In 1819 she married Samuel Gilman, a Unitarian minister in Charleston, South Carolina. The Gilmans had a fairly traditional southern marriage, owned household slaves, and lived at the center of Charleston's city and literary life. Gilman's literary career blossomed in 1832, after the death of her sixth child, when she founded a widely read weekly journal for children and, later, adults. Her journal included stories, poetry, and three serialized novels that

---

5. Compare, for example, Phyllis Trible's memorializing of Jephthah's daughter in her *Texts of Terror* (Philadelphia: Fortress, 1984), 92.

were later published as books.[6] The death of her seventh baby in 1839 marked the virtual end of her creative writing, though she republished some of her earlier works. She outlived all but one of her children, dying in Washington at the age of 94.

Gilman's 96-line poem opened up the question of woman's nature and duty by setting natural human emotion and duty in tension with one another. Gilman presents Jephthath's daughter as a loving child whose tender relationship with her father is hardly strained by his rash vow as she rushes into his arms to find comfort and protection, "as a flower when chill'd by the blast, / Reclines on an oak while its fury may last." Readers feel the pathos of that moment as father, daughter, and even onlookers shed tears of sorrow. But like a saint,[7] Gilman's daughter figure rises above her expected response of "weakness" and prays for the well-being of the man whose vow cost her life, declaring "My Father, for thee I can die." She does not include the daughter's request for time to mourn or the yearly remembrance of her life, but concludes her poem by focusing on the "old chieftain's grief-stricken eye."

The young Gilman, identifying with the plight of Jephthah's daughter, portrays her as a particular female type who submits to a life of subordination and self-sacrifice. Wrestling throughout her life with questions about the nature and place of women, Gilman typically supported a traditional position on the Woman Question but recognized the cost of such submission. In her poem "Household Woman," for example, Gilman encouraged women to carry out their household tasks "with cheerful duty in her eyes," looking "meekly upward to her God."[8]

Jephthah's Rash Vow

The battle had ceas'd, and the victory was won,
   The wild cry of horror was o'er. —

---

6. For a full treatment of Gilman's literary work, see Cindy Ann Stiles, "Windows into Antebellum Charleston: Caroline Gilman and the *Southern Rose* Magazine" (diss., University of South Carolina, 1994).

7. Harriet Beecher Stowe also idealized Jephthah's daughter's response to tragic adversity. She was a heroic soul "that could meet so sudden a reverse with so unmoved a spirit!" *Woman in Sacred History* (New York: Fords, Howard & Hulbert, 1873), 98–99.

8. Gilman, "Household Woman," *Verses of a Lifetime*, 225.

Jephthah's Daughter

Now arose in his glory the bright beaming sun,
And with him, his journey the war-chief begun,
   With a soul breathing vengeance no more.

The foes of his country lay strew'd on the plain —
   A tear stole its course to his eye,
But the warrior disdain'd every semblance of pain,
He thought of his child, of his country again,
   And suppress'd, while 'twas forming, a sigh.

"Oh, Father of light!" said the conquering chief,
   "The vow which I made, I renew;
'Twas thy powerful arm gave the welcome relief,
When I call'd on thy name in the fulness of grief,
   And my hopes were but cheerless and few.

"An off'ring of love will I pay at thy fane,
   An off'ring thou canst not despise:
The first being I meet, when I welcome again
The land of my fathers, I left not in vain,
   With the flames on thy altar shall rise."

Now hush'd were his words, thro' the far spreading bands,
   Nought was heard but the foot-fall around —
Till his feet in glad tread press his own native lands,
And to heav'n are uplifted his conquering hands;
   Not a voice breaks the silence profound.

O, listen! at distance what harmonies sound,
   And at distance, what maiden appears?
See, forward she comes with a light springing bound,
And casts her mild eye in fond ecstasy round
   For a parent is seen through her tears!

Her harp's wildest chord gives a strain of delight;
   A moment — she springs to his arms!
"My daughter, Oh God!" — Not the horrors of fight,
While legion on legion against him unite,
   Could bring to his soul such alarms.

In horror he starts, as a fiend had appear'd,
    His eyes in mute agony close;
His sword o'er his age-frosted forehead is rear'd,
Which with scars from his many fought battles is sear'd;
    Nor country nor daughter he knows.

But sudden conviction in quick flashes told,
    That *that* daughter was destined to die;
No longer could nature the hard struggle hold,
His grief issued forth unrestrain'd, uncontroll'd
    And glaz'd was his time-sunken eye.

His daughter is kneeling, and clasping that form
    She ne'er touch'd but with transport before;
His daughter is watching the thundering storm,
Whose quick flashing lightnings so madly deform
    A face, beaming sunshine no more.

But how did that daughter, so gentle and fair,
    Hear the sentence that doom'd her to die?
For a moment was heard a shrill cry of despair —
For a moment her eye gave a heart-moving glare —
    For a moment her bosom heav'd high.

It was but a moment — the frenzy was past,
    She trustingly rush'd to his arms,
And there, as a flower when chill'd by the blast,
Reclines on an oak while its fury may last,
    On his bosom she hush'd her alarms.

Not an eye saw that scene but was moistened in woe,
    Not a voice could a sentence command;
Down the soldier's rough cheek tears of agony flow,
The sobs of the maidens rose mournful and low,
    Sad pity wept over the band.

But fled was the hope in the fair maiden's breast,
    From her father's fond bosom she rose;
Stern virtue appear'd in her manner confest,

Jephthah's Daughter

She look'd like a saint from the realms of the blest,
    Not a mortal encircled with woes.

She turn'd from the group and can I declare
    The hope and the fortitude given,
As she sunk on her knees with a soul breathing prayer,
That her father might flourish, of angels the care,
    Till with glory he blossom'd in heaven?

"Oh, comfort him, heaven, when low in the dust
    My limbs are inactively laid!
Oh, comfort him, heaven, and let him then trust,
That free and immortal the souls of the just
    Are in beauty and glory array'd."

The maiden arose, — oh! I cannot portray
    The devotion that glow'd in her eye;
Religion's sweet self in its light seem'd to play
With the mildness of night, with the glory of day —
    But 'twas pity that prompted her sigh.

"My father!" — the chief rais'd his agoniz'd head
    With a gesture of settled despair —
"My father!" — the words she would utter had fled,
But the sobs that she heav'd, and the tears that she shed,
    Told more than those words could declare.

That weakness past o'er, and the maiden could say,
    "My father, for thee I can die."
The hands slowly mov'd on their sorrowful way,
But never again from that heart-breaking day,
Was a smile known to force its enlivening ray
    On the old chieftain's grief-stricken eye.

                                            Watertown, Mass., 1810.

Source: Caroline Howard Gilman, *Verses of a Lifetime* (Boston: James Munroe & Co., 1848), 127–31.

Sarah Ewing Hall

A Child Protests: A Mother Listens

Sarah Hall (1761-1830) was an American author whose major publication, *Conversations on the Bible* (1818), retells the stories of the Old Testament in the form of a conversation between a mother and her three children.[9] The children raise the story's difficult moral and theological issues while the wise mother figure answers their questions.

Hall's treatment of Judges 11 in this work is both typical and extraordinary. Hall initially presents Jephthah's daughter as a model child: sensitive, patriotic, submissive, and respectful. She is "full of pity for her father," who was distressed when he realized the implications of his vow. Mother praises the daughter's patriotism and commends her submission, "the amiable maiden submitted" — thus providing the lesson that submission is something maidens should do. Indeed she is held out as a further example for children in that she asked for "permission" to retire with her female companions to lament her "hard destiny."

Hall then challenges the very reading of the story that she initially endorsed by including a child's voice of protest: "Dear Mother! do not tell that Jephthah sacrificed his only child!" At this point, Hall introduces the "survivalist" reading of the story according to which Jephthah does not kill his daughter but rather condemns her to a single life.[10] This reading evokes yet another voice of protest regarding a child's rights: does a father have the right to make his daughter "live a single life"? Anticipating the child's next question, Mother continues: "Had she resisted the execution of his inconsiderate vow, he would nevertheless have been guiltless." Later American authors Elizabeth Cady Stanton and Louisa Southworth would take up the discussion about rights and justice raised in this story to a higher level. Hall's interactive commentary models an approach to studying Scripture involving questions, challenges, and debate between a parent

---

9. For a fuller biography of Hall, see "A Sanitized Rahab" in the Rahab chapter.

10. Mary Anne Schimmelpenninck fleshes out the grammatical argument that Hall assumes based on the Hebrew text in *Biblical Fragments* (London: Ogle, Duncan & Co., 1821), 215-17. See "Schimmelpenninck: It's All about Translation." David Gunn suggests that more space was devoted to the question of the daughter's fate than any other interpretive issue in commentaries and dictionaries on Judges during this period. Those who argued that Jephthah condemned his daughter to celibacy follow "the survivalist position," first defended by David Kimchi in the twelfth century (Gunn, *Judges*, 149).

Jephthah's Daughter

and child that permitted rethinking of the typical reading of the story that encourages submission.

MOTHER. About the same period in which the transactions I have been relating occurred [Mother has just told the story of the Levite's concubine and the carnage that followed it], we find a man sacrificing his own daughter, or otherwise disposing of her, to perform a rash vow, in direct opposition to the law and custom of his country. [Hall rehearses the biblical narrative, painting Jephthah as a "gallant" man and an "enterprising spirit."] . . .

The war was successful, and Jephthah returned in triumph to his dwelling. But short-lived are the triumphs of mortals! — The door of his house is opened, and a beloved daughter comes forth with instruments of music to welcome his return! His daughter — the *only child* of his affection, the innocent victim of his unlawful oath — Jephthah could not conceal his distress! He told her his engagement, adding, "I have opened my mouth to the Lord, and I cannot go back!" Full of pity for her father, and pious gratitude for the deliverance of her country, the amiable maiden submitted; requiring only permission to retire with her female companions for a time, to lament her hard destiny!

CHARLES. Dear mother! do not tell us that Jephthah sacrificed his only child!

MOTHER. Alas, my son! — there is the difficulty which I am not able to solve to my own perfect satisfaction. The act was so unnatural, human sacrifices were so strictly forbidden, that some commentators have embraced a construction of the words — "he did according to his vow," less revolting than your apprehension. We are told in the conclusion of the story, that it became a custom for the daughters of Israel to go four days in the year, to lament, or *to talk with* the daughter of Jephthah; from which they suppose she retired to a solitude in the mountains, and was condemned to a single life.

CATHERINE: To relinquish altogether the society of his daughter — that daughter too his only child, might indeed fill the heart of Jephthah with sorrow: but a *burnt-offering* implies the death of the victim.

MOTHER. The advocates for the more favourable construction of Jephthah's vow, make it convertible to the case as it might happen, by rendering the words, *and* offer it, into a conditional promise — *or* offer it, as might be suitable, when the thing devoted should be seen. Unclean animals no more than human creatures, might be offered in sacrifice — but they might be vowed and afterwards redeemed. It is reasonable to suppose that Jephthah having this alternative would not hesitate to save his only daughter.

FANNY. Had he a right to oblige her to live a single life?

MOTHER. Perhaps not; yet the law of Moses invested parents with a very extensive authority over their children. Had she resisted the execution or his inconsiderate vow, he would nevertheless have been guiltless.

Source: Sarah Hall, *Conversations on the Bible* (Philadelphia: Harrison Hall, 1818, taken from the fourth edition, 1827), 167–71.

Mary Anne Schimmelpenninck

It's All about Translation

Mary Anne Schimmelpenninck (1778–1856) was raised in a wealthy family in Bristol, England, where she met such leading intellectuals as Joseph Priestley, Benjamin Franklin, and Erasmus Darwin.[11] She was also exposed to a variety of Christian traditions, including Quaker, Roman Catholic, Church of England, Wesleyan Methodist, and Moravian. She associated herself with a number of different churches before joining the Moravian church in 1818. Her publications reflected her wide-ranging interests, which included a work on Christian esthetics: *Theory on the Classification of Beauty and Deformity* (1815), *Psalms according to the Authorized Version* (1825), and *Biblical Fragments* (1821–22), which contains her comments on what she views as the interpretive crux of the story of Jephthah's daughter.

The well-educated Schimmelpenninck applies her linguistic skills to the story and argues for the "survivalist position."[12] She follows the twelfth-century Kimchi, who translated the Hebrew conjunction *waw* (usually rendered as "and" in Judges 11:31) as "or." This translation meant that Jephthah's vow allowed him the option of either dedicating *or* sacrificing what came out of his house to the Lord. Schimmelpenninck explains the significance of

---

11. For a fuller discussion of Schimmelpenninck, see Lissa M. Wray Beal, "Schimmelpenninck, Mary Anne (1778–1856)," in *Handbook of Women Biblical Interpreters: A Historical and Biographical Guide*, ed. Marion A. Taylor and Agnes Choi (Grand Rapids: Baker, 2012), 436–40.

12. See Hall's discussion of the story, which also presents an argument for the "survivalist position."

this small change: "If it be a person, therefore not a fit subject for sacrifice, that person shall be yet dedicated to GOD; but if it be a beast, I will then offer it up in sacrifice." She defends this reading, suggesting that this change in translation solves the moral problem of a father killing his daughter.

[Schimmelpenninck's discussion follows the text of Judges 11:30–40.]

This passage has often been misunderstood.

It has been supposed that Jephthah actually slew his daughter in sacrifice, instead of having devoted her to a single life, in the service of the Lord; which is the true sense.

This mistake has arisen from our translators having rendered the ü, *vwaff* [sic] in the latter clause of verse 31, *conjunctively*, instead of *disjunctively*.

Thus the passage stands in our English version: *Whatsoever cometh forth of the doors of my house to meet me when I return in peace from the children of Ammon*[13] *shall surely be the Lord's,* AND *I will offer it up for a burnt-offering.* Whereas it ought to stand, *Whatsoever cometh forth of the doors of my house to meet me when I return in peace from the children of Ammon shall surely be the Lord's,* OR *I will offer it up for a burnt offering.* That is, if it be a person, therefore not a fit subject for sacrifice, that person shall be yet dedicated to GOD; but if it be a beast, I will then offer it up in sacrifice.

The sense of the passage is perfectly obvious, with this correction, to any one reading the whole story.

Jephthah had this one only daughter, and had no other successor. But on her being thus unexpectedly devoted to a single life, her father's family became extinct.

Hence the grief exhibited both by Jephthah and his daughter. Nevertheless, that the name of this great chief, who had wrought so signal a deliverance, might be held in everlasting remembrance, the daughters of Israel established a festival four days in the year, in commemoration of Jephthah and his daughter.

Source: Mary Anne Schimmelpenninck, *Biblical Fragments* (London: Ogle, Duncan & Co., 1821), 214–17.

---

13. The words are in Hebrew: *wᵉhāyâ laYHWH wᵉhaᶜᵃlîtihû ᶜôlâ*, and it shall be to Jehovah, or I will offer it up a burnt-offering.

Susanna Rowson

The American Dream Sacrificed

Susanna Rowson (1762–1824), an actress, writer, editor, and educator who lived in England and America, published her most explicit work of biblical interpretation, *Biblical Dialogues*,[14] in 1822 after retiring from teaching.[15] She intended her lengthy two-volume work to be used as a textbook in schools.

Like Sarah Hall,[16] Rowson interprets this difficult story by employing a familiar catechetical format and opens the discussion by sketching Jephthah in an extremely sympathetic light. Depicting him as an ancient example of a man who lived the American dream, Rowson applauds the hard work that allowed him to "inherit a share of God's blessing." Refusing the suggestion that Jephthah's actions (making the vow and/or dedicating his daughter) were sinful, Rowson asserts that the moral of the text is about "the sin and folly of making vows without due consideration." Rowson, reminding us of Hall's work, raises the question of the daughter's fate in the voice of a child. Charilea asks: "Do you think, sir, that Jephthah really slew her?" Using scholarly debate over the translation of the Hebrew text and adding the evidence from Leviticus 27:5, indicating Jephthah could have paid ten shekels to buy his daughter's release, Rowson supports the "survivalist position" and contends that he could have got out of his vow. Father argues that Jephthah "consecrated her to God and devoted her to a single life, and to live in retirement all her days." Amy opines that this reading does not justify the amount of grief exhibited by the father and daughter: "Why was her father so sorry? He could go and see her." In the end, Rowson is much more concerned about the father than the daughter. She shows little sensitivity to the plight of the "dutiful and submissive" daughter, who was not able to fulfill the dreams her father had for her.

---

14. The full title of Rowson's book was *Biblical Dialogues between a Father and His Family: Comprising Sacred History from the Creation to the Death of Our Saviour Christ. The Lives of the Apostles and the Promulgation of the Gospel; with a Sketch of the History of the Church down to the Reformation. The Whole Carried on in Conjunction with Profane History*, 2 vols. (Boston: Richardson & Lord, 1822), 416, 395.

15. For a fuller discussion of Rowson, see "Is Lying Always Wrong?" in the Rahab chapter.

16. Compare also the interpretation of Eliza Smith, who published under the pseudonym A Clergyman's Daughter in *The Battles of the Bible* (Edinburgh: Paton & Ritchie, 1852), 134–39. She also argues for the survivalist option, and her female character Marianne protests that it was unfair that Jephthah's daughter was "obliged to live like a nun, spending all her life in seclusion" (138).

Jephthah's Daughter

FATHER. As we are now entering on the life of Jephthah, I wish you all to make two observations; first, that it is cruel and unjust to despise a man on account of his birth, as it is a blemish for which he is by no means accountable; and if he is virtuous, brave, of strict integrity, and good understanding, he is as likely to rise in the world, and make a name for himself, as the noblest born, and will inherit as large a share of God's blessings. Secondly, you will perceive by the subsequent part of the story, the sin and folly of making vows without due consideration.

AMY. Oh! I know what you mean — Jephthah's poor daughter.

FATHER . . . But before he [Jephthah] took the field, he made a vow, that if he returned with victory, the first thing that came forth from his house to meet him he would sacrifice to the Lord.

JOHN. That was both wicked and foolish.

FATHER. No, to make a vow was not in itself culpable; the error lay in not considering before he took the vow the consequences that might follow. Jephthah having delivered his country from foreign enemies, and quelled a dangerous insurrection among the Ephraimites, returned home in triumph; when, as he approached his own house, his only child, a lovely and beloved daughter, at the head of a company of virgins, with garlands and musical instruments, came forth to meet him, and congratulate him on his victories. What a sight was this! the exultation of the general and conqueror was lost in the grief of the father. He covered his face with his mantle, and cried, "Alas! my daughter." The astonishment of his daughter was soon changed into grief, when she understood the vow her father had taken; but dutiful and submissive, she said, "My father, lament not, but if thou hast made a vow unto the Lord, perform it."

CHARILEA. Do you think, sir, that Jephthah really slew her?

FATHER. It is a question, my dear, which has employed the pens of many learned men; many think, (and I must own that I am of that opinion myself) that she was not sacrificed; for it appears altogether improbable that so tender a father as Jephthah is represented to be, would sacrifice an innocent dutiful child, in discharge of a rash vow; when according to the prescription of the law, (as you may see by consulting Leviticus twenty-seventh chapter, fifth verse) he might have redeemed her for ten shekels of silver. It is therefore natural to infer, that he consecrated her to God, and devoted her to a single life, and to live in retirement all her days; secluded from any society but that of the young maidens, her companions, who went once every year to condole with her on her solitary state. For as she never could marry, her father's family, (she being his only child,) would become extinct at her death, and this solitary state they lamented the more as all the Israelitish women were ambitious of becoming mothers; each one hoping that she might be the mother of the promised Messiah.

AMY. But why was her father so sorry? he could go and see her.

FATHER. Most probably, when she was devoted to a life of austerity and seclusion, her father bade her an eternal farewell; and surely it was a great affliction, to see a lovely, and beloved child, thus cut off from all intercourse with the world; a child whom he had once, perhaps, fondly hoped to have seen wedded to some great and powerful man, endowed with wealth, and raised to honour, whose children might have perpetuated his name, and to whom his wealth might have descended for many generations; this, surely, was sorrow and disappointment sufficient, to make him rend his clothes, and refuse comfort.

Source: Susanna Rowson, *Biblical Dialogues between a Father and His Family Comprising Sacred History from the Creation to the Death of Our Saviour Christ* (Boston: Richardson & Lord, 1822), 1.284–86.

Eliza R. Stansbury Steele

Maid of Gilead, Fare Thee Well

Little is known about the life of the American author Eliza R. Stansbury Steele (fl. 1840–50s).[17] The story of Jephthah's daughter is one of the seven stories of biblical heroines that Steele tries to "render more attractive," by portraying them with "the costumes, scenery, and manners" of the times in which they lived in her *Heroines of Sacred History*.[18] Steele playfully rewrites the story of Jephthah's daughter, using Scripture, scholarly resources, along with her imagination to fill in the gaps. Her lengthy embellishments are

---

17. For further information on Steele, see "A Mother's Love" in the Jael chapter.
18. Eliza Steele, *Heroines of Sacred History* (4th ed.; New York: John S. Taylor & M. W. Dodd, 1851), vi.

often rooted in Scripture; she invokes, for example, legal texts on vows (e.g., Leviticus 27:5), moral teachings on shunning evil influences (1 Corinthians 15:33), and social customs regarding the use of sackcloth and ashes as signs of repentance. Using such techniques allows Steele to suggest that Jephthah made a "grievous error" of judgment because he had been negatively influenced by the "sons of Baal" who regularly sacrificed humans to their gods. Similarly, Steele explains why the community allowed Jephthah to carry out his foolish vow. In her fictionalized account, the elders consult with Israel's high priest, who judges that God punished Jephthah's rashness by "sending [his] daughter forth" and rules that she "be taken to Shiloh, where in perpetual virgin seclusion" she would serve the Lord in the tabernacle. Although Steele's daughter figure yields to the high priest's will, she "bewails her hapless lot," and her friends also find little meaning in her sad sacrifice.

[The excerpt begins at the end of part III, "the Vow."]

In the whirlwind of battle, Jepthah for one moment forgot his trust in God, and tempted him to fight upon his side; he vowed a vow before the Lord.... A rash vow which Jepthah ever after deplored, and, which if he had reflected one moment, he would not have made. Jepthah suffered from his first error, *evil communication*, he had "stricken hands,"[19] with idolaters, and while residing with them, had witnessed their frequent sacrifices to their gods, and forgot he spoke to a God who delighted not in such vows. Into this grievous error he had not fallen, if he had shunned instead of making friends, of the sons of Baal. The children of Ammon fled before the host of Jepthah. They were pursued into the heart of their country, and twenty cities conquered, and the whole land completely subdued.

Part IV: The Sacrifice

The city of Gilead was filled with rejoicing that their enemy was repelled, and its streets were crowded with the citizens, eager to behold the triumphant entry of their victorious leader. Jepthah approached, seated in a brazen chariot surrounded by his steel clad warriors. His robe of blue embroidered with

19. [Proverbs 6:1.]

gold, was bound by a broad girdle of golden mail, a sword hung in chains from his side, and shoes of brass defended his feet, a scarlet mantle fell from his shoulders, and around his head was a band of steel chain-work, from which, projected in front, a horn of gold, giving him a fierce and terrible appearance. When the procession arrived before the house of Jepthah the gate was thrown open, and a group of young girls came dancing forth, mingling their jocund music with the cheers of the populace. What saw the conqueror in yon joyous train, that he started as if a shot from the enemy's archers had stricken him! — why bowed his lofty head unto his bosom? At the head of the youthful train came the hero's daughter, his only child, holding aloft the sweet sounding timbrel, and attired as became a rulers daughter, in a robe of divers colours, richly embroidered with gorgeous feather-work, and gold, and silk of varied dies. A fillet of white roses bound her dark tresses, and her tiny feet were strapped in scarlet sandals. Smiles lighted up her fair face, and her soft doves eyes beamed with filial tenderness when raised to her lordly father.

Behind her, were the maidens of Gilead, clad in white, with chaplets of red roses; their slender ancles [sic] circled with silver bells. Like leaves from a gay parterre swept onward by a summer breeze, these lovely flowrets floated in mazy whirls until beside the chariot of the conqueror. The daughter of Jepthah approached her father, and when the people looked to see him fold her in his embrace, with a frantic start, he rent the bosom of his gilded robe, and covering his head with his mantle he groaned with anguish. "My father!" said a gentle voice beside him. "Alas, my daughter!" cried the conquerer, with a burst of agony — "From my high estate of joy thou hast brought me low down in the dust!" There was deep silence while he spoke — "O God, forgive me! my child, forgive me! When I faced the children of Ammon in battle, I vowed, if the Lord would deliver them into my hands, I would offer up, as sacrifice unto him, the first that came forth from my house to meet me! Thou art the first — my child! my only one!"

A deep consternation fell upon the hearts of all, when this rash vow was heard — on all, save upon that fair and gentle creature who was the victim. With brow unblanched, and with a glow of generous self-devotion, she said to Jepthah — "My father, if thou hast opened thy mouth to the Lord, do unto me as thou hast vowed. Thy God hath made thee conqueror over thy enemies — the children of Ammon have fallen before thee, and if I am to be the price of victory, take me and do unto me according to thy vow. I die for my country and for my father — in that death there is no bitterness." At the request of the Elders who now approached, Jepthah descended from his

Jephthah's Daughter

chariot, and, accompanied by them and his daughter, he entered his habitation. Here he threw himself upon the ground, covered his head with dust, and refused all his child's endeavors to comfort him.

Meanwhile the Elders consulted aside, upon the best measures to be pursued in this sorrowful and unexpected emergency. That Jepthah should sacrifice his daughter, was not to be thought of, since, to offer her as a burnt offering would be worthy only of an idolater — it was an impossible, unheard of, detestable crime. But on the other side, it was urged, he had made a solemn vow to the Lord, and perhaps in consequence of that vow he had received the victory — must he now refuse to perform his vow? What evils might not the Lord, in anger, inflict upon them, if that were so.

Many days were passed in sorrow, and in deep perplexity by the people of Gilead. At last, it was determined by a council of Elders, that a deputation of their number should be sent to Shiloh, in order to obtain the advice of the priests of the tabernacle upon this difficult and unhappy matter. The time of their absence was passed in great anxiety by the people, and in deep humiliation and anguish by Jepthah. Their approach was at length descried from the watch-tower — they entered the city, and, followed by a train of eager citizens, sought the unhappy Jepthah, who still remained upon the ground as they had left him, clothed with sackcloth, and covered with ashes.

"Hear, O Jepthah, the message of the High Priest of Israel!" — said the chief of the Elders — "Unlike a worshipper of Israel's God, thou hast vowed to offer in burnt-sacrifice the first that came to meet thee from thy house — such offerings are an abomination to the Lord, and to punish thee for thy rashness, he hath sent thy daughter forth." Jepthah answered with a groan of anguish.

"This sacrifice being forbidden by our laws, the person offered can be redeemed with money, and for a youthful female the priests demand ten shekels."[20]

She may then be saved! and the people were preparing to shout with joy, at her deliverance, when, a wave from the Elders hand restrained them.

"Thou hast said, such, coming forth to meet thee, shall *surely be the Lord's,* and by the laws of our holy Moses, things thus devoted, *cannot be redeemed.*" A sigh burst from many a bosom when they heard this cruel sentence. "Listen Jepthah to thy daughter's destiny — thou hast devoted her to be the Lord's, and as the Lord's her days must be spent in his service. She is henceforth forever dead to the world and dead to thee! She must be taken to Shiloh, where in perpetual virgin seclusion, her days must pass in the

---

20. [Leviticus 27:1-5.]

service of the tabernacle. She belongs no more to man, but must be kept as holy to the Lord." With this decree, the people were satisfied, and Jepthah was relieved. Still, his daughter was lost to him forever, and if not called upon to die, was doomed to a lonely life. How bitterly was his rash vow now repented! His cherished child, she whom he looked upon as the light and comfort of his declining years, must be to him as dead! To her, this destiny was worse than death. She had wrought her soul up to the great sacrifice of her life, but thus to lose home, and all held dear — to see none else but strangers near her — to surrender that fond hope, so cherished by her country women, of being the Saviour's mother,[21] brought to her young bosom, a chill as if from the tomb. Her fair brow was but a moment clouded. No reproachful word came from her lip, but with a smile of heroic fortitude she turned to Jepthah. — "Cheer thee, my father! I am raised from death," she said. "My life, devoted to my God, and given for my country, must be a happy one, for God will not willingly afflict his child." Jepthah threw his arms around his daughter, wetting her glossy locks with bitter tears. "Remember, thou hast many duties, and many honors father! Thou art a Judge of Israel. Thy brow is surrounded by a halo of glory, and thou hast much to render life dear to thee. Thou wilt forget this anguish soon, and, in worshipping thy God, and in thy country's service, will find peace at last."

Jepthah strained her to his heart in speechless sorrow. How could he part with this sweet child so lately restored to him! now become far dearer as her filial tenderness, her heroism and her religious faith became thus known to him. The maiden turned towards the Elders.

"I bow to the High Priest's decree, as a most righteous one," she said, "and I will yield me to his will. This only I would ask — give me some little time for preparation; to take farewell of all the friends and scenes so dear, — after this, I will accompany ye to Shiloh."

The Elders willingly acceded to her request, and then departed.

Some time was passed in preparation and in endeavors to soothe the sadness of her father, and then the daughter of Jepthah, accompanied by her young female companions, her friends and attendants, set out upon a pilgrimage among the city's environs, to bid farewell to all those friends and places, among whom her childhood's happy days were spent. She passed from one spot to another among the beautiful mountain scenery of Gilead, bidding a weeping adieu to every cherished scene.

---

21. An allusion to the commonly held view that all Israelite women looked forward to bearing the long-promised redeemer (Genesis 3:15), a hope denied Jephthah's daughter.

Jephthah's Daughter

With her companions, she bewailed her hapless lot, and mourned that she must lose the hope of seeing the promised Saviour among her descendants. She then returned to her father's house, who solemnly surrendered her into the hands of the Elders, and by them she was taken to Shiloh.

The loss of Jepthah's daughter was annually commemorated by the daughters of Israel at Gilead. Every year, upon the anniversary of this sad event, they walked in procession through the same paths she had trod with them, when bidding her early home adieu. Solemnly they wound among the hills, their fair hair hanging neglected upon their shoulders, and as they passed along, their silvery voices filled the groves while singing the following mourning hymn.

A Lament for Jepthah's Daughter

Maid of Gilead, fare thee well!
Hear our mournful chorus swell,
While among these valleys lone,
We, for thee, are making moan.
Breezes of her natal sky,
Waft to her our pitying sigh.
    Farewell Jepthah's daughter!

No mother watches o'er her bed —
No father blesses her young head —
Guarding her, no brothers stand —
Nor gentle smiling sister band —
Never may she, as a bride,
Grace a happy lover's side.
    Farewell Jepthah's daughter!

Lonely virgin, not for thee
A parent's sweet anxiety;
No 'olive buds' around thee twine,
No voices singing infant chime;
And that bright hope is lost to thee,
Head of Messiah's line to be.
    Farewell Jepthah's daughter!

Maid of Gilead, fare thee well!
Yearly shall this shady dell,
Mountain path, and verdant plain,
Echo our lamenting strain.
May our mournful chorus swelling,
Reach thee in thy lonely dwelling.
    Farewell Jepthah's daughter!

Source: Eliza Steele, *Heroines of Sacred History* (New York: John S. Taylor & M. W. Dodd, 1841), 188–98.

Adelia C. Graves

Her Life Bought Our Freedom

Adelia C. Graves (1821–95) was born in Kingsville, Ohio, and married Z. C. Graves, an ordained Baptist preacher and a pioneer of higher education for women.[22] They moved to Tennessee in 1850 when Z. C. Graves became president of Mary Sharp College, and Adelia Graves became the professor of literature and college matron. They shared the college's vision to give women the same education as men, believing that God designed a woman to be "a thinking, reflecting, reasoning being, capable of comparing and judging for herself, and dependent upon none other for her free, unbiased opinion."[23] Graves authored twelve volumes of Sunday school material under her pseudonym "Aunt Alice" and several other books, including a 659-page book on romanticism and her popular five-act drama *Jephthah's Daughter*.

Graves develops the biblical story of Jephthah's daughter into a five-act play for a female audience, replete with full character development, foreshadowing, suspense, drama, dialogue, song, theological reflection, and moralization.[24] Like Eliza Steele, she weaves other biblical figures such as Cain,

---

22. William S. Speer, *Sketches of Prominent Tennesseans* (Nashville: Albert B. Travel, 1888), 335–36.

23. J. J. Burnett, *Sketches of Tennessee's Pioneer Baptist Preachers* (Nashville: Press of Marshall & Bruce Co., 1919), 200.

24. Graves writes: "To the Pupils of the Mary Sharp College, with whom I have spent

Jephthah's Daughter

Abraham, Isaac, and Job into her embellished retelling. She interprets the story from a female perspective; she was both a mother who had sacrificed her own "self-sacrificing" son to the Civil War, a college administrator, and teacher of young women.[25] Graves fully develops the biblical characters and adds several figures to the biblical story, including a brokenhearted and spiritually confused fiancé and a mother. Graves's Jephthah's daughter, Adah, models the virtues of courage, heroism, patriotism, self-sacrifice, and filial obedience. Graves invites readers to empathize with Adah as she internalizes the consequences of her father's sin. Her thoughts of impending death are quite morbid as she ponders her personal losses and, like Job, reflects on the "greedy, gloating worm" that will devour her flesh. Adah is also a spiritually astute lay theologian, preacher, and wise woman. She addresses the question of God's role in the tragedy, alluding to the Deuteronomic teaching that God jealously visits the iniquity of the fathers on the children (Deuteronomy 5:9–10). She raises the question of alternatives, concluding that escaping the consequences of her father's wrong was not an option. Adah rebukes her father for his self-centered melodramatic bewailing of his punishment, contrasting him to Job, who did not bewail his fate, and Abraham, who trusted God to provide.

The play's final scene commemorates the life of Jephthah's daughter. Her maidens laud her strength, beauty, meekness, and filial devotion; "the crown of virgin womanhood" is unlike any "son of Judea." They pray that God will make them like her, for they judge Jephthah's vow to be foolish, suggesting that his daughter's life was too high a price to pay for military victory and prestige. Nevertheless, they honor Adah's Christ-like sacrifice and call "all the world" to claim her "Israel's and ours." The preface and scenes four and five are excerpted below.

---

many of the pleasantest hours of my life, this little work is most affectionately inscribed. May they be stimulated to all deeds worthy of Woman; then will each be worthy of self and her Alma Mater"; *Jephthah's Daughter: A Drama in Five Acts* (Memphis: South-Western Publishing House, 1897), 3.

25. The eldest of their four children, James (1843–63) left Dartmouth to serve in the Confederate army and was killed accidentally when his horse crushed him. His seemingly senseless death became a lens for Graves's reading of the story of Judges 11.

Preface

From my earliest girlhood, the history of Jephthah's Daughter, told as it is in so few words, and yet those few beautifully revealing to us a character perfect in its simplicity, and uniting, without the slightest ostentation, every element of feminine excellence, has had a peculiar charm for me.

The coolest courage, the most undaunted heroism, the loftiest patriotism, consummated in the extremest act of self-sacrifice humanity can perform, were all present in her ready concurrence in her father's dreadful vow; and yet the simple Israelitish maiden seems to have thought only of filial obedience and right.

And the stern majesty of Jephthah, outcast and insulted; feeling keenly the wrongs he suffered, yet, by his determination and energy, aided by the blessing of the God he served, patiently working out a reputation which finally triumphed, and brought him the honor for which he toiled so long and faithfully, has been a favorite subject for study. The master-passion of his nature I have made pride; fostered by the unfortunate circumstances of his life, and which, from his feeling his own worthiness, made him esteem himself just in proportion to the disesteem, or contempt of others; and which, so long as it led only to a just appreciation of himself, was right; but in excess became a wrong, as spoken by Telah, in scene first:

What was
Humility and faith at first,
May grow into self-confidence
And pride; and right, pursued too far
Or with unholy motive, grow
Into a wrong, —

inculcating the doctrine that all vices are but excesses of some virtue.

If I have preserved the unity of my plot and exhibited the character of Jephthah throughout, as it naturally would exhibit itself under the influence of this predominant passion, I have accomplished all I expected.

Mary Sharp College,
Winchester, Tenn.,
May 1, 1867.

Jephthah's Daughter

Characters in Jephthah's Daughter

JEPHTHAH — *The Gileadite.*
TELAH — His Wife.
ADAH — His daughter.
EBER — Betrothed of Adah.
MICAH — First captain of the guard.
HEZRON — Officer in charge of sick and wounded.
MIRIAM — Servant maid.
Men of Gilead.
Followers of Jephthah.
Musicians, attendants, and chorus of young girls, in scene fifth.

Scene Fourth

Jephthah, a few followers with him, approaching his home in Mizpeh. He dismisses them.

JEPHTHAH.
Go, now, my tried and trusty followers,
And as each one shall take his homeward way,
May ye, arrived, in mercy find 't is well
With those ye left behind. E'en so, with me,
That I find, too, all's well within the walls
That hold my heart's most precious ones.
Farewell.
(*They disappear in different directions, and he soliloquizes.*)
Why sinks my heart with such chill weight of dread?
Why shake my knees, as if no strength were left
In this strong, stalwart frame, as I do look
Upon the sheltering boughs above the roof
Where dwell my treasures all? My eyes are dim;
They have no power to look at those gray walls
That pen my little fold — the youngling and
Its dam. — Home! sweetest spot of all the earth.
A few more eager steps, and I am there;
Yet something still those longing steps restrains.
What if she haste to meet me here? — or that
Dear one, my other self? Oh! would 't were past

That I might know the worst, and knowing, fear
No more. Uncertainty! how dread the thought
Of what this hand may be compelled to do.
(*Music is heard, and Adah, comes with tabrets and dances to meet him.*)
'T is she! 't is she! My one ewe lamb! Oh, this
Is more than I can bear! Most dutiful
And loving child of all Judea's maids,
She comes, with signs of overmastering joy,
To greet her sire, who dooms his child to death
In all her virgin innocence! Punished!
And more, for all my wild ambition now.
(*Adah, seeing his wild, disordered looks and torn garments, stops.*)

ADAH.

O! Father, speak to me.
(*Jephthah, having covered his face with his hands, as if to shut her from his sight, stands motionless.*)
He will not speak,
He will not look at me!

JEPHTHAH.

I can not, for
My heart is burst with grief.

ADAH.

Who speaks of grief,
Returning from such signal victory?
Leader of Gilead —

JEPHTHAH.

O! name it not —
Most hateful thought that ever crossed my brain.

ADAH.

Greatly rejoiced my mother dear and I
To hear the tidings of thy messenger,
And scarce have slept for very joy, that thou
Wast safe from all the dangers that beset
Thy path among such deadly foes. Thou com'st,
And with a daughter's loving tenderness
And overflowing sympathy, with what
I deemed thy great, full joy at this that shall
Exalt thee over Gilead, I haste
To meet thee with a gladdened step. Not one

Jephthah's Daughter

Embrace! no father's fond, warm kiss! nor one
Sweet word of loving welcome! O! not e'en
A look! O! father, what means this? When thou
Hast come from off the hills with all thine armed
Men proudly at thy back, with valor flushed,
Thou'st bade me to thy arms, as if 't were joy
Beyond the battle's victory, to clasp
Thy child again. But now, thou heed'st me not!
    JEPHTHAH
My daughter, thou hast brought me very low.
    ADAH.
I, father!
    JEPHTHAH.
Thou'rt one of them that trouble me.
    ADAH.
What have I done? Thou dost not hate me now?
It can not be! Thou lov'st me, father? Say
But that, and I can bear it all!
    JEPHTHAH.
Love thee,
My precious child! — yea, better than my life.
    ADAH.
I knew 't was so, yet thou didst look so cold;
Had no kind word of greeting for mine ear —
I have done naught to anger thee?
    JEPHTHAH.
Nay, nay —
Thou never didst, my own sweet child. Thou gav'st
Me never slightest cause for grief, till now.
    ADAH.
Why now? Pray tell me all. Strong in thy love,
And in the sweet assurance of such cheering words,
I'm ready for the worst. Fear not for me.
'T were better over. Let the pang, I pray, be short.
    JEPHTHAH.
I've opened to the Lord my mouth; I can
Not now go back —
    ADAH.
My father, if unto the Lord, thy God,

Thou'st opened thy mouth, do unto me
According to the vow thy lips have made,
For on our enemies, the Ammonites,
His vengeance hath he taken by thy hand.
    JEPHTHAH.
My child, thou break'st my heart!
    ADAH.
Nay, father, nay —
My disobedience and disregard
Of all Jehovah's laws *would* break thy heart.
Do I not owe to thee my life? And should
That life be dearer to me than the right?
Than Jephthah's full approval of his God?
I'm Jephthah's child, his only one, and should
Men say in Israel: "She did defy
The law, mocked at her father's words; set them
At naught?" That were far worse than death, for God,
Thy God, hath armed thy right hand with *His* power; —
Hath smote thine enemies before thy face,
E'en as thou asked. And now, shall we withhold
That which thy lips did promise unto *Him?*
We *dare* not mock Him thus: a jealous God
He is, and the iniquity of him
That doeth wrong shall be (thou know'st the law)
Upon his children surely visited.
I could not then escape. 'T is not so great
A sacrifice.
    JEPHTHAH.
O! say not so! My all,
And nothing else. O, reckless vow! O, wild
Ambition to be first, where I have been
Spurned and insulted! Mad desire to show
Jehovah's power in me; that *He* approved
The banished brother, unacknowledged son!
Pride! pride! the great archangel's damning sin,
That drove him out of Paradise! Ah, me!
My punishment, like Cain's, is more than I
Can bear. He slew his brother, only; I
Must kill my child.

Jephthah's Daughter

ADAH.
Not thus did Job bewail
His children slain, his wealth all rifled in
An hour. Not thus did faithful Abraham,
When God, to try his faith, commanded him
To take his only son, the promised seed,
To lone Moriah's steep, and offer him
Upon its heights, a smoking sacrifice.
Yea, father, in Jehovah, God, trust now
As thou hast ever done: He doeth right.
JEPHTHAH.
I thank thee for those words. 'T is the one drop
That's pleasant in this cup of bitterness,
That hopeful thought of holy Abraham.
God did provide the lamb: He may again.
ADAH.
Nay, nay, I meant not that — only that he
Did not bewail or hesitate, when God
Commanded him to take his only son,
The promised seed, in whom all nations should
Be blessed, and bind him to ready pile.
I had forgot the rest.
JEPHTHAH
And so should I.
Daughter, I am rebuked. God did but try
His faith. I must be punished for my sin
For that desire of exaltation, so intense
That it forgot all else.
(Adah makes no reply, but stands with one hand over her eyes, her head bent down in a thoughtful attitude. Jephthah noticing it, and that it seems she makes no reply to what he has said, gloomily continues, as if to himself.)
I wonder not she has no word for me.
ADAH.
I have; I have. What askest thou? My mind
Was buried in its thoughts.
JEPHTHAH.
And I would ask
What were those thoughts?

ADAH.
Of death, of leaving thee,
My mother, all I love; to be no more.
Of the dark grave, and what a contrast in
My early youth to lay me down within
Its narrow walls, shut from the glorious light
Of heaven; and for companionship, instead
Of thee and her, the greedy, gloating worm.
    JEPHTHAH, (*weeping.*)
Go on.
    ADAH.
The shivering cold for warmth, darkness
For light, silence for pleasant sounds, these limbs,
Rigid and still, instead of airy life's
Quick, varied movements; and drear loneliness
For most beloved companionship. Yet think
Not that I shrink, appalling though it be —
Right must be done, whate'er the cost to me.
I have no fear; like Job, I, too, can say,
"Though worms devour this skin of mine, yet in
My flesh shall I see God." Father, thy vow
Must be fulfilled! Yet make I one request.
    JEPHTHAH.
Thou couldst ask nothing that I would not grant.
    ADAH.
Give me, I pray thee, two short months, in which
I may prepare me for my fate. Thou know'st
What was to be. I did look forward to
The time, my height of joy should be to make
Another happy, and I thought too much,
It may be, of the bliss that should be mine
When yet another should dwell in our home,
Alike beloved by *her* and *thee* and me,
And sons and daughters should be born to thee
In place of those Jehovah had denied
To thine own wedlock. No sweet, cherub lip,
Pressed close to mine, shall ever call me by
That dearest name that woman ever bore.
I'll not repine; my grief is not my own:
'T is *thine*, and *hers*, and his. O, God! for *him* —

Jephthah's Daughter

JEPHTHAH.
My daughter, Adah, wilt thou break my heart?
ADAH.
Nay, father, nay; but I do think of him, —
Eber, in all his young and joyous years
Doomed to be desolate; to bear a heart
Widowed, bereaved, just as he enters on
Life's opening threshhold; his bright morning sky
Beclouded ere life's sun had fairly risen.
Thou wilt console him; let him be to thee
E'en as he would have been, although no bride
His yearning heart find here. Thou 'lt promise this?
JEPHTHAH
I promise all. Say on. Ask what thou wilt.
ADAH.
My mother loves me, father. O! how can
She bear to be alone? Her child reft from
Her arms, and none to dwell with her: alone!
Oh! comfort her.
JEPHTHAH.
And who shall comfort me?
Thou think'st of all, of every one but me.
Hast thou no love for me? Shall *I* not, too,
Be left alone? Will not *my* home be dark? —
My heart be desolate? Hast thou no love
For *me,* my child?
ADAH.
Ah, yes, too much for all.
Forgive me if I thought of others first,
Each is so dear; it is so hard to feel
I can no longer have a place among
Ye all; can come no more with heart so full
Of gushing love, to cheer in sorrow, soothe
In suffering hours, and be a part of all,
In joy or grief.
JEPHTHAH.
Look, Adah; there she comes!
How shall I meet her? Oh! how break
To her this woe?

ADAH.
I will away, I can
Not meet her now. Thy blessing, once more,
Father, on thine Adah's head.
(*She kneels. He places his hand on her head. Telah comes in full view, as he does it, and the curtain drops.*)
END OF SCENE FOURTH

Scene Fifth

"And the daughters of Israel went out, four days in the year, to mourn and lament for her."

Scene — the mountain, with trees and rocks. A green mound, under which are the remains of Jephthah's daughter. To one side, and partially hidden, is Eber, the betrothed of Adah bowed under a covering of sackcloth. From the opposite side of the stage advance six maidens, clad in white robes, carrying baskets of flowers, and singing as they come.

MAIDENS.
SONG.
Here we come, a band of maidens,
    To these lonely rocks and glades;
Bright the blue sky bends above us,
    Cool and green, the leafy shades.
Come we here to mourn a lost one,
    Loved and lost one to bewail:
Fitting spot for lamentation
    O'er our lost one of the vale.
It was here she was lamenting,
    Till two moons had paled and gone,
Gaining strength, and faith, and courage,
    In these solitudes, alone.
On the mountain, where she perished,
    Where she spent those lonely days,
Every year we come to mourn her,
    Come, this noble maid to praise.
(*They discover Eber sitting on the far side of the mound. He slowly raises the sackcloth from his face, and they see who it is. A maiden speaks.*)

Jephthah's Daughter

MAIDEN.
Comest thou here to mourn and weep,
Eber? Worthy was she that's here
Beneath this lonely mound.
   EBER.
Ye come
But once a year, for she was naught
To you but a sweet friend. To me
My sun, my life — my every thing;
And I come — when, I scarcely know,
Nor, yet, how long I stay. There is
No joy remaining, now, save here
To bow by this green mound and feel
I shall be with her soon. How long!
How long! Oh, cruel vow! Was He,
The God of mercy, pleased with such
A sacrifice?
   MAIDEN.
Eber, thou griev'st
As one that hath no hope.
   EBER.
Grief is
No name for all the pangs I feel;
For, with such love as I have borne,
'T is the survivor dies. Long woe,
With ecstasy of torture, kills
At last — but O! how long. No death
The dying hath, like unto that
The living feels, to wander on
Alone; of all earth's joys bereft —
Its glorious sun extinct; life's light
To darkness turned, and all its flowers
To noxious weeds; the poor, numb soul,
Unknowing when 't is change of day,
Or night, or seasons, e'en. The crushed,
Torn heart-strings, rent away from all
About which twined their joy,
Lie trampled, bleeding, thrilled with pain,
And yet there's no desire to take

Them up, and soothe, and nurse them back
To ease, and strength, and life again.
The once glad, joyous heart, bounding
In youthful gladsomeness, crushed down,
A heavy lead-like thing within
The bosom's core, which ne'er again
Uplifts itself, but slowly wears
Its lingering tenement away,
Mourning a form that hath none, and
A voice it can not hear.
(*He slowly moves away.*)
(*Six voices chanting separately, as numbered.*)
    FIRST VOICE.
Joy beamed in her eye as she went forth to meet him.
    SECOND VOICE.
Skill born of her gladness brought mirth from the tabret.
    THIRD VOICE.
Fleet moved her light steps in the joy of his coming.
    FOURTH VOICE.
She met him; her eye beamed no longer in brightness.
    FIFTH VOICE.
Dropped quickly her fingers, forgetting their cunning.
    SIXTH VOICE.
And stayed were the steps that had bounded in gladness.
    FIRST VOICE.
But paled not the cheek of the maid as she listened.
    SECOND VOICE.
Her people were saved — she was ready to perish.
    THIRD VOICE.
Meek, bent the young head in its quiet submission.
    FOURTH VOICE.
O! daughter of Jephthah, most worthy of honor.
    FIFTH VOICE.
Nor daughter of Jephthah alone, but of Israel.
    SIXTH VOICE.
A nation laments while its maids are bewailing.
    ALL.
And the tribes of the earth, through all time, shall thee honor.

Jephthah's Daughter

SONG.
Daughter, in thy narrow bed,
Sister, from whom life hath fled,
Jewish maiden, o'er thy head,
Loving hands delight to fling
Sweetest blossoms of the spring
Nature's holy offering.
(*They scatter flowers upon the mound from their baskets, and continue to do it, from time to time, through the song.*)
Jewish maiden, virtues rare
Made thee e'en more good, than fair;
Pure as ever maidens are;
Meekly bent her drooping head,
Every thought of self had fled —
"Father, be't as thou hast said."

Other daughters have been good,
But, among them, she hath stood
Crown of virgin womanhood.
Round this mound sad hearts await,
Here to weep thine early fate,
And thy goodness emulate.

Jewish maiden! fair and young,
Ever shall thy praise be sung,
All the maids of earth among.
Purity beamed in thine eye —
All the virtues that could die
Wafted thy pure soul on high.
(*Six voices chanting, each, a separate sentiment.*)
    FIRST VOICE.
Whose heart was so strong as this beautiful maid's?
    SECOND VOICE.
Whose filial devotion so perfect and pure?
    THIRD VOICE.
No son of Judea was like unto her.
    FOURTH VOICE.
Who'll teach us our duty now she lieth low?

FIFTH VOICE.
The maidens of Israel are poor in her loss.
SIXTH VOICE.
The God of our fathers make us, even us,
ALL.
Like unto the maiden we come to bewail.
SONG.
Woe! for the vow that the warrior made,
The warrior and father, that Ammon be stayed,
And his country be freed from the grasp of the foe,
Who the altars of God in the valleys laid low.
Bereaved is a household — *one* heart is a wreck,
Which thought for the bridal, its treasure to deck;
Her life is aweary, uncheered, and alone,
There beameth no future when hope is unknown.
Sleep sweetly, pure maiden, disturbed by no fears,
We'll keep the turf green by our sorrowing tears,
And the blossoms we bring thee, renew when they fade,
Lamenting, bewailing thee, beautiful maid.
SONG.
(*With voices alternating.*)
ONE VOICE.
He that sleeps, shall wake no more.
ALL.
Yes, upon the morrow.
ONE VOICE.
Years, the dead can not restore.
ALL.
But they ease our sorrow.
ONE VOICE.
All must die, though live they would —
ALL.
Every life's a debtor.
ONE VOICE.
Weeping, mourning, do no good, —
ALL.
Sadness maketh better.
ONE VOICE.
It is sad to mourn and weep.

Jephthah's Daughter

ALL.
Sad, and yet a pleasure.
> ONE VOICE.
Let each sorrowing memory sleep.
> ALL.
Memory is a treasure.
Memories of the pure and good
Make our own hearts better.
This pure maiden, if we could,
We would not forget her.
> SONG.

They met, and proud Ammon was conquered at last,
And the tramp of his warriors went hurrying past;
His towns and his cities were swept from his hands,
And the conquered oppressor hath sought other lands.
There's a chieftain in Israel, once haughty and bold,
But the light, in his dark eye, is altered and cold;
There's a Judge, too, in Israel, loves justice and right,
But the honors, they pay him, can bring no delight.
He knoweth the price of proud Ammon's defeat,
For a face is upturning, so pleadingly sweet;
'T is the picture that's ever his vision before,
And 't will fade from his sight, nevermore, nevermore.
There's a memory, haunting, will never depart,
And the sweet light of hope is shut out of his heart.
He is ruler, he's judge, but he's childless and lone,
For *her* life was the price of the victories won.
> SONG.

(*With alternate voices, one alone, and all answering.*)
> ONE VOICE.
Sing of all that's good and fair,
> ALL.
She was better fairer:
> ONE VOICE.
Sing of all that's bright and rare,
> ALL.
She was brighter, rarer.
> ONE VOICE.
Liken her to earth's flower-queen,

ALL.
Lily of the valley.
ONE VOICE.
Breathing fragrance, though unseen
ALL.
When the light winds dally
ONE VOICE.
Liken her to brighter flowers,
ALL.
Sharon's precious roses,
ONE VOICE.
Making glad the passing hours
ALL.
As each cup uncloses.
ONE VOICE.
Liken her to stars of night;
ALL.
They're too far above us;
ONE VOICE.
They are pure, and they are bright,
ALL.
But they can not love us.
ONE VOICE.
Liken her to all pure things;
ALL.
Snow upon the mountain;
Dewdrops, snow, and flowers and springs;
 Water from the fountain.
Yet is naught so pure and bright,
 As this peerless daughter,
Turning meekly from the light
 To the dark doom brought her.
CLOSING SONG.
(*One Voice.*)
Her life bought our freedom,
 For the nation paid;
Israel can but honor
 This devoted maid.

Jephthah's Daughter

Prophet's hymning, tender,
    Ready writer's praise,
Ever shall commend her,
    Through all lapse of days.

And though Israel perish,
    Prophet, priest, and king,
Yet the world shall cherish
    Her of whom we sing.

Distant times and sages
    Shall her fame rehearse,
Ages upon ages
    Weave it into verse.

And no brighter luster
    Ever deed surround,
Never mem'ry juster,
    Through all time be found.

All the world shall claim her,
    Like the sun and showers,
Though we love to name her
    Israel's and ours.
END OF SCENE FIFTH.

Source: Adelia C. Graves, *Jephthah's Daughter: A Drama in Five Acts* (Memphis: South-Western Publishing House, 1867), 5–8, 23, 103–44.

ROSE TERRY COOKE

Cursed Above All Women

Rose Terry Cooke (1827–92), daughter of Anne Wright Hurlbut and Henry Wadsworth Terry, a landscape gardener who instilled in his daughter a love for nature, was born near Hartford, Connecticut.[26] Initially schooled by her mother, she entered the renowned Hartford Female Seminary at ten. She had a conversion experience as a teenager and belonged to a Congregationalist Church. She taught in private schools and worked as a governess to support herself from the age of sixteen, when she received a small inheritance, which allowed her to focus on her writing. She raised her sister's children as her own and at the age of forty-six entered into a financially disastrous marriage with thirty-year-old Rollin Cooke. Cooke supported her family by publishing hundreds of poems, short stories, and essays, as well as three novels and a play. While much of her writing has been dismissed as being overly sentimental, her work depicting life in nineteenth-century rural New England is still anthologized. Cooke often wrote about the hardships of women's lives; her female characters often suffered abuse from the men in their lives. At the same time, she wrote critically about the women's rights movement and women's suffrage.[27]

Cooke's sentimental poem "Jephtha's Daughter" reads against the grain of the biblical story in that it focuses entirely on the feelings and thoughts of Jephthah's daughter. Like Adelia Graves, Cooke appeals especially to the tender romantic feelings of the female reader as she describes babies' soft fingers and the sound of their footsteps. Like so many other authors in this chapter, Cooke immortalizes Jephthah's daughter in a way that her girlhood friends could not. Her poem is a commentary on the Woman Question. Like Caroline Gilman, she protests women's hard lot in life and at the same time encourages women to rise above their natural responses to suffering and duty. Although the poem holds out little hope, it does end with the daughter's prayer to Jesus, the "Pride of Judah's princes," to uphold her failing breath as she faces "a woman's mortal weakness," death.

26. "Rose Terry Cooke," in Judith Fetterley, *Provisions: A Reader from 19th-Century American Women* (Bloomington: Indiana University Press, 1985), 343–49.

27. See Cooke's essays that explore various issues regarding women's place, rights, and suffrage in *The North American Review*, vols. 148–50 (1889–91).

Jephthah's Daughter

Jeptha's Daughter

And she said unto her father, Let this thing be done for me; let me alone two months, that I may go up and down upon the mountains, and bewail my virginity.

Judges xi,37.

Alone, alone on the mountains, the mountains wild and high,
Far below in midnight the sleeping cities lie,
Strange and fearful silence! Is it life or after-death
That folds me in its shadow, and crushes out my breath?

Far above is heaven, far below is earth:
Heaven with stars of glory, the world with songs of mirth,
And I alone between them, a spirit cold and gray,
Lingering in the body, afraid to pass away.

"Mourn!" says the wind-swept ether. "Mourn!" the echoes cry.
"Weep for the hopes that perish; weep for the dreams that die!"
Along the light horizon a troop of visions pass
Frail as wandering shadows the clouds make on the grass.

Crowding wistful faces, their eyes as dark as mine,
Over their loosened tresses the crowns of Judah shine.
O my lost! my darlings! who never shall be born,
Fading into glory as stars fade into morn.

No soft baby fingers tinged like an ocean shell,
No light baby footsteps within my tent shall dwell;
The maidens of my kindred shall know a mother's heart,
But Death and I together in the bridal train depart.

Deeper in the vision I see a face divine,
Woman-born Redeemer! Hope of David's line.
Oh! cursed above all women! I daughter of dust and shame!
Forgotten among Israel! He shall not bear thy name.

The girls who loved my girlhood come from the sleeping plain,
I hear their mingled voices that wail my life in vain.

Lost in mountain caverns, to them the echoes sigh,
My soul shall fall in darkness that murmurs no reply.

I have said my sorrow, I have mourned my death:
Pride of Judah's princes, uphold my failing breath!
A woman's mortal weakness has had its mortal sway.
Calm as the dawn that breaketh my soul shall glide away.

Source: Rose Terry Cooke, *Poems* (New York: William S. Gottsberger, 1888), 176–77.

Cecil Frances Alexander

Saintly Sacrifice

Fanny Alexander (1818–95) was a renowned Irish Anglo-Catholic hymn-writer poet.[28] The collection of her poetry published a year after her death contains her poem on Jephthah's daughter.

Alexander's poem focuses particularly on the final days of Jephthah's daughter's life as she mourns her impending death. She calls all nature to listen to her cries, for "the lily that was sweetest, fairest, Shall not blossom next year in thy shades." For she is about to offer what Alexander calls the "first, and best, in strong devotion / To the altar of the King of kings." Alexander spiritualizes Jephthah's daughter's act of devotion to her father, construing her as a saint and type of virtue.[29] By imbuing Jephthah's daughter's life and death with meaning not present in the text, Alexander redeems the story and allows the daughter's voice to continue to speak into the lives of her readers.

---

28. For a fuller discussion of Alexander, see "From Scarlet Thread to Blood Drops" in the Rahab chapter.

29. Compare Christina G. Rossetti's discussion of virginal spirituality in her comments on the unmarried woman in 1 Corinthians 7:34-35 in *Letter and Spirit: Notes on the Commandments* (London: SPCK, 1883). Like Alexander, Rossetti views Jephthah's daughter as a model or type. "[The virgin's] spiritual eyes behold the King in His beauty; wherefore she forgets, by comparison, her own people and her father's house.... She contemplates Him, and abhors herself in dust and ashes. She contemplates Him, and forgets herself in Him. If she rejoices, it is on spiritual heights, with Blessed Mary magnifying the Lord; if she laments, it is still on spiritual mountain-tops, making with Jephthah's daughter a pure oblation of unflinching self-sacrifice"; *Letter and Spirit: Notes on the Commandments* (London: SPCK, 1883), 91–92.

Jephthah's Daughter

Her figural reading of the story is in line with her allegiance to the Oxford Movement, which encouraged typological readings.

Jephthah's Daughter

And she went with her companions and bewailed her virginity upon the mountains.

Judges xi,38.

Through the woods and pastures comes a crying,
A sweet voice that neither fears nor hopes,
Mid the ancient oaks of Bashan dying,
Dying on green Hermon's sunny slopes.

Not the mother, when her grief is sorest
For her nest and nestlings torn away,
Sends a sadder wailing through the forest,
Sitting lonely on her hawthorn-spray.

Not the wild deer, wounded by the fountain,
Gasping out his life with heavy moan,
Draws a wilder echo from the mountain,
Hath a stranger anguish in his tone.

For she waileth, waileth, in the hollows,
On the hill-tops rich with many a stripe
Of green pasture, where the wild goat follows
Shepherd's call, or note of pastoral pipe.

Hearken, Gilead! where, with foamy waters,
Arnon runneth down to Jordan's shore,
In her youth, the fairest of thy daughters
Passeth from thy plains for evermore.

Hearken, Bashan; where thine old oaks hoary
Guard the silver lilies at their feet,

When the sunlight crowns them with a glory,
Streaming inward where thy branches meet.

For the lily that was sweetest, fairest,
Shall not blossom next year in thy shades,
She, of all thy flowers that was the rarest,
Never more shall bloom along thy glades.

O wild forest! O ye upland meadows,
Like green oceans, tossing to and fro!
Ye can only see Heaven's lights and shadows,
Can but hear a natural voice of woe,

Knowing nothing of the heart's emotion,
Nothing of the earnest love that brings
All its first, and best, in strong devotion
To the altar of the King of kings.

But to us, she singeth, singeth faintly,
Going up and down that mountain sod,
"Nought is grievous to the spirit saintly,
Dearest things, and purest, are for GOD.

Therefore laid I, on the shrine of duty,
All sweet flowers that used to bind my brow;
So I went down in my youth, and beauty,
Went a victim to my father's vow."

Source: Mrs. C. F. Alexander, "Jephthah's Daughter," in *Poems on Subjects in the Old Testament*, 3rd edition (London: J. Masters & Co., 1888 [originally 1854]), 91.

Jephthah's Daughter

Leigh Norval

Like Father, Like Daughter

Leigh Norval (fl. 1889) is a forgotten author of a book on women of the Bible written for children in the Methodist Episcopal Church.[30] Her exposition of the story of Jephthah's daughter is found in her 1889 publication *Women of the Bible: Sketches of All the Prominent Female Characters in the Old and the New Testament*. In her retelling, Norval moves away from the exemplary hermeneutic used by most authors and evaluates the religious and cultural values assumed by Jephthah and his daughter, highlighting the inadequacies of both father and daughter. Norval admits that the sad story of the heroic fate of a young girl elicits "a tender concern for her," but she vilifies her theology: "The girl had her father's valiant spirit and patriotism, and shared his superstition."[31]

Jephthah's daughter . . . is briefly mentioned, but her youth and sad yet heroic fate arouse a tender concern for her. Her father mingled a pitiable superstition with a faith which brought victory over armies of foes. He vowed, as he went forth to fight, that he would offer as a sacrifice when he went home "whatsoever cometh forth of the doors of my house to meet me." The Lord punished him for the rashness of the vow. His darling and only child, a young daughter, came first to meet him with timbrels and dances. Jephthah was stricken with grief, but instead of repenting of his reckless vow he added the sin of performing it. The girl had her father's valiant spirit and patriotism, and shared his superstition. She professed herself willing to die, as the Lord had destroyed the enemies of Israel. The only request she made was that for two months she should go into the mountains with her girl friends and bewail her approaching death. "And it came to pass at the end of two months,

---

30. For a fuller discussion of Norval, see "Daring to Be Different" in the Rahab chapter.
31. Similarly, Jewish educators Constance and Annie de Rothschild judge that the vow itself was "impious" and unacceptable to God, the offer of his daughter being "detestable blasphemy." They attribute the errors of father and daughter to "the confusion of the lawless times in which such deeds could be publicly done and regarded as meritorious"; *The History and Literature of the Israelites according to the Old Testament and the Apocrypha*, vol. 1: *The Historical Books* (London: Longmans, Green & Co., 1870), 302.

that she returned unto her father, who did with her according to his vow." For four days every year the women of Israel lamented the high-spirited but misguided young maiden's death.

Source: Leigh Norval, *Women of the Bible: Sketches of All the Prominent Female Characters in the Old and the New Testament* (Nashville, Tenn.: Publishing House of the M. E. Church, South, Sunday-School Department, 1889), 87–88.

Elizabeth Cady Stanton

A Woman in the "No-Name Series"

Elizabeth Cady Stanton (1815–1902) worked tirelessly for women's rights in the United States throughout her life.[32] Stanton's comments on the story of Jephthah and his daughter are in the second volume of *The Woman's Bible*. Stanton uses the story as a platform for promoting her views on Scripture's authority and her values. She criticizes the ideologies ensconced in the story and censures what she regards as "the pitiful and painful view" advocated by most of the interpreters featured in this chapter, that Jephthah's daughter is a model of virtue and submission. To this end she rewrites the story, challenging its patriarchy and filial devotion and promoting her own political and religious agenda. Her daughter figure, for example, declares, "My first duty is to develop all the powers given to me and to make the most of myself and my own life. Self-development is a higher duty than self-sacrifice." The issues Stanton raises in her commentary — such as the daughter's lack of name, power, and voice; the authority of the father; the nature of vows; and traditional interpretations of the story — are not new, but they are radicalized.

A woman's vow, as we have already seen, could be disallowed at the pleasure of any male relative; but a man's was considered sacred even though it involved the violation of the sixth commandment, the violation of the

---

32. For a fuller discussion of Stanton, see "The Question of Motives" in the Rahab chapter.

individual rights of another human being. These loving fathers in the Old Testament, like Jephthah and Abraham, thought to make themselves specially pleasing to the Lord by sacrificing their children to Him as burnt offerings. If the ethics of their moral code had permitted suicide, they might with some show of justice have offered themselves, if they thought that the first-born kid would not do; but what right had they to offer up their sons and daughters in return for supposed favors from the Lord?

The submission of Isaac and Jephthah's daughter to this violation of their most sacred rights is truly pathetic. But, like all oppressed classes, they were ignorant of the fact that they had any natural, inalienable rights. We have such a type of womanhood even in our day. If any man had asked Jephthah's daughter if she would not like to have the Jewish law on vows so amended that she might disallow her father's vow, and thus secure to herself the right of life, she would no doubt have said, "No; I have all the rights I want," just as a class of New York women said in 1895, when it was proposed to amend the constitution of the State in their favor.

The only favor which Jephthah's daughter asks, is that she may have two months of solitude on the mountain tops to bewail the fact that she will die childless. Motherhood among the Jewish women was considered the highest honor and glory ever vouchsafed to mortals. So she was permitted for a brief period to enjoy her freedom, accompanied by young Jewish maidens who had hoped to dance at her wedding.

Commentators differ as to the probable fate of Jephthah's daughter. Some think that she was merely sequestered in some religious retreat, others that the Lord spoke to Jephthah as He did to Abraham forbidding the sacrifice. We might attribute this helpless condition of woman to the benighted state of those times if we did not see the trail of the serpent through our civil laws and church discipline.

This Jewish maiden is known in history only as Jephthah's daughter — she belongs to the no-name series. The father owns her absolutely, having her life even at his disposal. We often hear people laud the beautiful submission and the self-sacrifice of this nameless maiden. To me it is pitiful and painful. I would that this page of history were gilded with a dignified whole-souled rebellion. I would have had the daughter receive the father's confession with a stern rebuke, saying: "I will not consent to such a sacrifice. Your vow must be disallowed. You may sacrifice your own life as you please, but you have no right over mine. I am on the threshold of life, the joys of youth and of middle age are all before me. You are in the sunset; you have had your blessings and your triumphs; but mine are yet to come. Life is to me full of hope and of happiness. Better that you die than I, if the God whom you worship is pleased with the sacrifice of human life. I consider that God has made me the arbiter of my own fate and all my possibilities. My first duty is to develop all the powers given to me and to make the most of myself and my own life. Self-development is a higher duty than self-sacrifice. I demand the immediate abolition of the Jewish law on vows. Not with my consent can you fulfill yours." This would have been a position worthy of a brave woman. — E.C.S.

Source: Elizabeth Cady Stanton, "The Book of Judges, Chapter II," in *The Woman's Bible, Part II: Joshua to Revelation,* ed. Elizabeth Cady Stanton (Boston: Northeastern University Press, 1898), 24–26.

Louisa Southworth

Only a Girl

Louisa Stark (1831–90s) and her husband, William Palmer Southworth, were wealthy and prominent citizens in Cleveland, Ohio, where William owned the W. P. Southworth Company, a wholesale and retail grocery company and was president of Society National Bank. The home they built in 1879 still stands as a historic site. The Ohio census of 1880 lists four Southworth children and two servants. Louisa was active in the women's suffrage movement, writing articles on suffrage and heading up a local effort to get signatures in support of women's right to vote in 1893. She joined other prominent suffragists on the writing team of Elizabeth Cady Stanton's *The Woman's Bible.*

Like Stanton, Southworth criticizes the way "that the popular mind has become too benumbed to perceive its great injustice." She challenges traditional portraits of women as inferior and submissive, concluding: "The unalterable subserviency of woman in her natural condition can never be overcome and social development progress so long as there is a lack of distributive justice to every living soul without discrimination of sex." Like Stanton, she views the Bible itself as a barrier to progress.

Jephthah's Daughter

The ideal womanhood portrayed by ancient writers has had by far too much sway. The prevailing type which permeates all literature is that of inferiority and subjection. In early times Oriental poets often likened woman to some clear, flawless jewel, and made them serve simply as ornaments, while, on the other hand, they were made subordinate by the legislation of barbarous minds; and men, because of their selfish passion, have inflicted woe after woe upon them. Ancient literature is wholly against the equality of the sexes or the rights of women, and subordinates them in every relation of life.

The writings of the Bible, especially the Old Testament, are no exception to this rule. The reference, "The sons of God and daughters of men," while it admits of many interpolations, legendary or mythical as it may be, portrays the real animus of the Scriptures. To what extent the sentiment of the Hebrews favored sons rather than daughters, and the injustice of this distinction, is fully exemplified by the stories of Abraham and Isaac and of Jephthah and his daughter. Abraham was commanded by his God to sacrifice his son Isaac, after the manner of the Canaanites, who often slew their children and burnt them upon their altars in honor of their deities. But when all was made ready for the sacrifice an angel of Jehovah appeared, the hand of Abraham was stayed, and a ram was made a substitute for the son of promise.

The conditions were quite different in the case of Jephthah and his daughter. The Israelites had been brought very low in their contest with the Ammonites, and they chose the famous warrior, Jephthah, to lead them against their foe, who with warlike zeal summoned the hosts to battle. The risk was enormous, the enemy powerful, and the general, burning for victory, intent on securing the assistance of the Deity, made a solemn and fatal vow.

In the first case it was a direct command of God, but means were found to revoke this explicit command with regard to a son; in the second case it was only a hasty and unwise promise of a general going to war, and the prevailing sentiment of the age felt it unnecessary to evade its fulfillment — the victim was only a girl. The unhappy father must sacrifice his daughter!

What a masculine coloring is given to the rest of the narrative: "A maiden who did not mourn her death, but wandered up and down the mountain mourning her virginity." So much glamor has been thrown by poetry and by song over the sacrifice of this Jewish maiden that the popular mind has become too benumbed to perceive its great injustice. The Iphigenias[33] have been many and are still too numerous to awaken compassion. We must

---

33. In Greek mythology, Agamemnon was commanded to sacrifice his daughter, Iphigenia, so that his ships could sail to Troy.

destroy the root of this false and pernicious teaching, and plant in its place a just and righteous doctrine.

What women have to win for the race is a theory of conduct which shall be more equitable. The unalterable subserviency of woman in her natural condition can never be overcome and social development progress so long as there is a lack of distributive justice to every living soul without discrimination of sex. — L.S.

Source: Louisa Southworth, "The Book of Judges, Chapter II," in *The Woman's Bible, Part II: Joshua to Revelation*, ed. Elizabeth Cady Stanton (Boston: Northeastern University Press, 1898), 27–28.

STUDY QUESTIONS

1. What was the content of Jephthah's vow (Judges 11:30)? Why did he keep it? Discuss the interpretive crux of the story, namely, was Jephthah's daughter killed by her father or dedicated to a life a virginity? What is the support for each position? Which position is stronger?
2. Compare this story with that of the sacrifice of Isaac in Genesis 22:1–19 and the oath of Saul and deliverance of Jonathan in 1 Samuel 14:24–30, 43–45. Does gender play a role in the different outcomes of these narratives?
3. Where are the gaps in this story? How do different commentators fill these gaps? Respond to some of these imaginative readings. Which do you find most compelling?
4. The submission of Jephthah's daughter is evaluated in different ways by nineteenth-century commentators. Describe these views. What is your own? Which is supported by this text and by Scripture as a whole?
5. Jephthah's daughter is another "unnamed woman." Can you think of reasons why she was not named, even though she was memorialized? How do you respond to commentators who give her a name?
6. Try dramatizing parts of Adelia Graves's play, or reading the poems aloud. How does hearing these works read affect your perception of the story?

6

Manoah's Wife

The little-known narrative of the woman remembered as Manoah's wife and Samson's mother in Judges 13 is a self-contained gem that raised numerous issues for nineteenth-century women interpreters. The historical setting is the conflict between the Philistines and the Israelites for control of the land between the Jordan River and the Mediterranean Sea. According to the text, the tribes of Israel are loosely organized, and because of their faithlessness, no "judge" has arisen to deliver them from the Philistines. In this context, an angel appears to Manoah's barren wife announcing that she will bear a son, commanding her not to drink any alcohol or eat anything unclean during her pregnancy, for the boy will be a Nazirite (dedicated) to God. Manoah's wife reports her experience of meeting the angelic man of God to her husband. Manoah prays that the messenger return, and the "man of God" indeed reappears to his wife while she is on her own in a field. When Manoah finally meets the messenger, the instructions given to his wife are repeated. The husband invites the messenger to a meal, but the "man of God" will not eat their food. Instead they are directed to offer the kid as a burnt offering to the Lord. When Manoah asks him for his name, the request is refused with the reason that it "is too wonderful." The penultimate scene depicts the "angel of the LORD" ascending in the flames from the burnt offering. Realizing that the "man" was indeed an angel, Manoah laments that they will "surely die" for they have "seen God." His wife does not share his fear, reasoning that their offering would not have been accepted, nor would they have been promised a child, if God intended to kill them. The story closes by reporting that Manoah's wife bore a son named Samson and that the Lord blessed him and God's spirit began to stir in him — the beginning of the fulfillment of the "man of God's" proclamation that Samson would "deliver Israel from the hand of the Philistines."

Most interpreters expected the biblical stories to speak into their lives. They found many points of connection with the story of Samson's mother. Supporters of the temperance movement highlighted the explicit instructions to refrain from drink during pregnancy as well as the expectation that, due to his calling to be a Nazirite, Samson would perpetually abstain from alcohol. The angel's instructions about prenatal care elicited comments about Victorian concerns on the subject. Mary Beck, for example, read into the angel's instructions a specific commendation of a Victorian campaign to encourage pregnant mothers to care for themselves along with a general affirmation of God's desire that men and women alike become teetotalers.

Since the story featured a marriage in which the wife seemed to be superior to her husband, many interpreters commented about marital relations. Affirming a wife's dominant role chafed against the traditional nineteenth-century view that men should lead and even the more liberal opinion that women and men should be equal partners in marriage. A number of women mused on differences between men and women, triggered by the difference between Manoah's and his wife's responses to the angel's visit. The blessings of motherhood were also extolled, and Christian interpreters, such as Edith Dewhurst, connected the desire for a child with the yearning to birth the awaited Messiah, a view that Jewish interpreter Grace Aguilar contested. A few women observed that Manoah's wife is not identified by name, but apart from Elizabeth Cady Stanton they did not connect this silence to its patriarchal context.

Commentators on this story often raised the theological problem of the identification of the messenger. Many Christian interpreters followed the traditional identification of the man of God who rose in the fire from the altar as God incarnate, but this conflation was contested by Aguilar, who argued that the man was described as a messenger and as such did not suggest the second person of the Trinity. Clara Neyman, a Freethinker, also understood the identity of the angel differently, concluding that the description of the "man of God" was no more than a figure of speech.

Manoah's Wife

GRACE AGUILAR

Concealing Your Superiority

Grace Aguilar (1816–47), prolific English author, supported Judaism and religious tolerance at a time in Britain when Jews were under pressure to convert to Christianity.[1] She intended her popular book *The Women of Israel* to encourage Jewish women to be proud of their foremothers who were a "true and perfect mirror of themselves"[2] and to appreciate the benefits of their own faith traditions.

Aguilar's essay on Manoah's wife defends a Jewish reading of the story. Aguilar discusses barrenness, countering the idea that all Israelite women longed to bear the Messiah, instead claiming that children are a blessing from God. She also counters the Christian understanding of the necessity of Christ as mediator by noting that Manoah turns directly to God in prayer. She suggests that his prayer points to the importance of extemporaneous as opposed to formulaic prayer. Her lengthiest defense of Judaism over against Nazarene, that is, Christian, readings occurs in her discussion on Manoah's words, "We have seen God," traditionally understood by Christians to refer to the preexistent Christ. She also explains why Jewish men and women need to understand their own faith and the faith of their majority culture. Aguilar distinguishes interfaith dialogue and the conversations of missionaries intent on conversion, seeking to equip Jewish women to defend their own faith. She does not, however, encourage Jews to mimic Christians by trying to convert them. Rather, their attitude should be one of charity toward "those of other and less enlightened creeds."

Aguilar also explores the story's "bearings on our history as women." She sees this narrative as providing a model of a righteous husband and wife. She applauds the wife for her "ready wit and quickness of intelligence," noting that the messenger approached her first. Yet she cautions women from revealing their superiority. In language that could be deemed manipulative, Aguilar admonishes women to conceal their wisdom in an effort to fulfill their calling to influence, but not to control, their husbands, cautioning that a man will not be susceptible to influence if he feels inferior to his wife. Her writing reflects the complicated position of nineteenth-century women who were charged with the role of being "the angel of the home" while remaining dependent upon and subordinate to their husbands.

---

1. For a fuller biography, see "Achsah and the Age of Chivalry" in the Achsah chapter.
2. Grace Aguilar, *The Women of Israel* (New York: D. Appleton & Co., 1872), 2.

Wife of Manoah

Several years passed since the death of Deborah. Gideon, Tolo, Jair, Jepthah, Ibzan, Elon, and Abdan, had successively judged Israel, often with interregnums of rebellion, apostasy, and anarchy. After the death of the last-mentioned judge, "the children of Israel again did evil in the sight of the Lord, and He delivered them into the hands of the Philistines forty years." We now come to another incident in the history of the women of Israel demanding our attention. In the tribe of Dan was a certain man of the city of Zorah, named Manoah, whose wife had no children, always a source of grief in the families of Israel; not, as the Christians believe, from the idea of becoming the mother of the promised Messiah (who is scarcely mentioned till the time of the prophets, when the awfully threatened chastisement of the Eternal needed such consolatory promises), but because children were always considered proofs of the Lord's love, a privilege granted from Him as the recompense of faithful service; as we read in the words of David, "Lo, children are an heritage of the Lord: and the fruit of the womb is His REWARD," Psalm cxxvii. And, again, "Thy wife shall be as a fruitful vine by the sides of thine house: and thy children like olive plants around thy table. Behold, *thus shall* the man *be blessed* that feareth the Lord. Thou shalt see thy children's children, and peace on Israel," Psalm cxxviii. To go down childless to the grave, and so prevent the name from being "built up" in Israel, was deemed a heavy affliction, inferring, for some secret sin or public transgression, the anger of the Lord.

Sacred Writ is silent as to the reason of the Eternal's selection falling on the family of Manoah for a deliverer in part from the Philistines, but we are justified in inferring from the context, that they were one of the few faithful followers of Israel, by whom the Law was in all points obeyed. Be that, however, as it may, this is certain, that it was to the WOMAN, not to the man, the Most High deigned to send His angelic messenger, with not only the blessed revelation that He would grant her a son; but deigning to instruct her as to the food and drink she was to refrain from taking herself, and to the devoting her babe as a Nazarite to the Lord, even from his infancy; thus making the direct commands of the Immutable agree in all points with the Law which His wisdom and mercy had already given.

Naturally astonished, for such revelations were not even then common in

Israel, we find "the woman" following the impulse of her confiding nature, hastening on the instant to her husband, and informing him that a man of God had come unto her, and his countenance was very terrible (signifying, not actually terrible, but grand and imposing), like the countenance of an angel of the Lord; but "I asked him not whence he was, neither told he me his name." From this description of the heavenly messenger, it appears that the woman did not consider him in reality an angel, supposing him a man of God or prophet, bearing a message from the Most High, as was usual in Israel, yet still struck by the imposing beauty of his countenance, and feeling it possessed something beyond mortality.

Equally astonished, but *believing*, Manoah lost no time in idle speculation, but betook himself instantly to prayer; thus confirming our idea of his faithfulness and piety, and proving one grand and important national truth, that the Israelites needed no *mediator* whatever, be he man or angel, to bring up their prayers before God, and obtain His gracious reply. Here was Manoah, living on his own estates, in his own tribe, far removed from the priests of the Lord and the tabernacle, through the first of whom alone it is declared, by our opponents, that the prayers of Israel could be acceptably offered up. No priest near, of whom he could either ask or obtain counsel; no wise man or judge, of whom he might demand advice or explanation. Yet the law was then in force all over Israel, and if it had been illegal and derogatory to the dignity of the Lord to address Him in prayer from any place, or at any time, we should have found Manoah hastening without a moment's delay to the appointed spot, and offering sacrifices to obtain the mediation of the anointed priest, knowing that through him only he could obtain reply.

Instead of which, we find him, without even pause or hesitation, believing the words of his wife so implicitly, as to offer up a prayer of such simple construction that it clearly proves how little the Most High regards mere formula in prayer, when springing, as did Manoah's, from humility and faith. "Then Manoah entreated the Lord, and said, O my Lord, let the man of God which Thou didst send come again to us, and teach us what we shall do unto the child that shall be born." Here is no doubt expressed as to the reality of the blessing proffered: "The child that shall be born," reveals how fully he believed in the promise; but, as was natural to humanity, he entreated a confirmation of the instructions vouchsafed, not knowing how far the imagination and the fears of his wife might have tinctured her relation.

"And God hearkened to the voice of Manoah." Did we need any further incentive to "entreat the Lord" in all things, surely we have it here. Manoah had simply spoken the thoughts of his heart in words, which would be their natural vehicle of expression. He had prayed through the merits of neither dead nor living, man nor angel, but in lowly trusting faith, and God hearkened and answered. [Aguilar quotes the rest of the story.]

We have quoted this chapter almost at length, because it contains so much which it is almost imperative for us to consider in a national point of view, before we can come to regard it in its bearings on our history as women. Any elucidation or defence of our national belief will not, we trust, be deemed out of place in a Jewish work, however little it may be pronounced to have to do with the main point of its subject. In an age when so much of controversy is going on, when even the intimate association, and often friendships, between Hebrew and Gentile may bring forward peculiar points of belief, to inquire their differences or varying modes of interpretation — it becomes imperatively necessary for the young Hebrew of either sex to be provided with such defence as will, at least, satisfy his own heart and conscience, and render him invulnerable to the peculiar expositions proffered to his attention, however little such defence may weigh with the hereditary prejudices of his opponents. There is a wide difference between an argument seeking the conversion of another, and that merely defending our own belief in the same sacred authority as gives a supposed foundation for the belief of an opponent. As long as the Christian confines his arguments and quotations to the New Testament, the Israelite feels perfectly secure, from his entire rejection of such authority as Divine. But when the words of the Old Testament are so explained as to bear almost startlingly upon the creed of our adversaries, then it is we need careful, though perfectly simple, training, to provide us both with reply and defence....

The chapter under consideration is one of those much regarded by the Nazarene, and always brought forward in controversial discussion. From Manoah's simple words, "We have seen God," they believe, that wherever the "angel of the Lord" is mentioned, it signifies the second person of the Godhead; and that as He took visible form to our ancestors of old, so we might equally believe in His taking the form of Jesus to save the world.

To a mere superficial thinker this argument might prove dangerous; and we are therefore anxious to explain this chapter according to the Israelite's belief. In the first place, we refuse to see in this messenger anything more than the Word of God declares, "an angel of the Lord," simply because the Eternal said unto Moses, in answer to his earnest entreaty, "Show me Thy glory," "THOU CANST NOT SEE MY FACE: FOR THERE SHALL NO MAN SEE ME, AND LIVE."[3] And we therefore know, that no man has or ever can see His

---

3. [Exodus 33:18, 20.]

face, and live; for God is a God of truth, and knows not the very shadow of a change. That which He has once said is immutable, unwavering, changeless as Himself. That there may be, even in the books of Moses, one or two verses seeming to contradict this assertion, as in Exodus xxiv., verses 10 and 11, and in verse 11 of chapter xxxiii., is of no importance, being either a wrong translation, or the mere manner of writing, to bring down the solemn appearance of the glory of God to the comprehension of the mixed multitude, and impossible to be weighed a single moment with the words of the Most High Himself. Would He declare the solemn truth in one part of His Holy Word, confirming it by every prophet, and in another part command His people, as a condition of their salvation, to believe on His appearing on earth, and conversing face to face with man, first as an angel, and then in human form? The very words of Manoah confirm this belief, and prove it was entertained as strongly by the ancient as the modern Jews. The Nazarenes take only the last member of this sentence, forgetting the important fact, "*We shall surely die, if, indeed,* we have seen God," for such is the real meaning of his words, and that he did not die; and the simple truth of his wife's suggestion convinced him, no doubt, as it convinces us, that it was not God whom he had seen, but one of those angelic messengers whom it some-times pleased the Lord to employ to deliver His missions unto man. The nature of such beings it needs not now to inquire; but the belief in the existence of angels is so twined with the belief in the Bible, that if we disbelieve the one, we must disbelieve the other. The very word מַלְאָךְ, derived from the Arabic לְאַךְ, *to send, or employ,* signifies merely a messenger, a legate, used indiscriminately for one employed by a king as ambassador, or by the Lord as an angel, prophet, or priest; and sometimes also applied to whatever is sent by the Eternal to execute His will, even as winds and plagues....

A layman, and a lowly individual of his father's tribe, it was not unnatural that Manoah should even be more awe-struck, than rejoiced, at the revelation so graciously vouchsafed; and while the mistaken idea engrossed him, if, indeed, it ever did, that he had conversed with God, he could not do otherwise than fear instant death, for, like all his brethren, he knew the God of Israel was a God of truth; and therefore, if he had seen Him, he must cease to live. The ready answer of his wife removed these groundless fears; and while it told him, that if it had pleased the Lord to kill them, He would not have accepted offerings at their hands, or so revealed His will, it must equally have convinced him, as a believer in the revelation of the Lord through Moses, that it was *not God,* but His messenger whom he had seen.

Such is the simple rendering of this very simple chapter; while the second commandment, and the words already quoted, "No man can see Me, and live," with the firm belief that God is TRUTH, are all sufficient wherewith satisfactorily to explain, both to our own hearts and to those of our children, every verse that may seem to read slightly contradictory, and supply us with an impenetrable shield, against which the reasonings of our opponents must fall blunted and harmless to the ground.

Regarding this narrative in its bearings on our history as Women of Israel, it is confirmation strong of our always attested declaration, that neither Written nor Oral Law interfered with the perfect equality of man and wife. The chapter before us displays a simple and natural picture of conjugal confidence and equality, and of the respective peculiarities of man and woman. It is impossible to read this chapter, without perceiving that Manoah's wife was a perfectly free agent, only bound by the links of love and confidence which the marriage law enjoins. As the mother of the child selected to deliver Israel in part from the Philistines, she was even of more importance in the sight of God than her husband, a fact inferred from the angel appearing both times to *her*, and only addressing Manoah when addressed by him. We find, too, Manoah including her alike in all he said and did. "Let *us* detain thee, until *we* have prepared a kid," etc. In the religious observance of the burnt-offering, and in the lowly prostration acknowledging the divine power, Manoah and his *wife* are separately named, proving her perfect equality in all religious observances, and her *right* to partake of them. That the angel never again appeared either to Manoah or his *wife*, is the proof to them that he was a messenger from the Lord. The words, "we shall surely die," included her in the penalty supposed to have been incurred, and mark the female as equally a responsible agent as the male. Still more clearly demonstrative that the Hebrew wife really occupied the free and equal position which the laws of God Himself assigned her, is the fact that it was her ready wit, and quickness of intellect, which reassured her husband. She had been awe-struck like himself, but yet, perfectly in accordance with woman's nature, was the first to comprehend the real intention of the revelation. Man's more solid nature and deeper thought, require time for mature judgment — woman's quicker fancy, and often more easily excited feeling, give her the advantage in the rapidity of comprehension, and, very often, in the correctness of judgment, which man's greater solidity strengthens and matures.

But that Manoah's wife could thus comprehend, and thus correctly judge, implies a domestic and social position which not only permitted, but exercised these peculiar faculties. In an enslaved and degraded position, their possession was practically and theoretically impossible.

Manoah's Wife

We find, then, much even in this brief chapter to interest and instruct us, alike as Hebrew women, and as women taken generally. In the latter, we shall do well to reflect on the simple trusting confidence of Manoah's wife, seeming the more tender and deferential from the greater correctness of judgment manifested afterward. And so it should always be. However woman may be naturally endowed with superior attainments, with, perhaps, even a greater share of strength and firmness, and a quicker aptitude for intellectual acquirements, still it is her bounden duty so to guide and use these gifts, that they shall never in any way jar upon the feelings of the one chosen as her husband; and check mutual confidence and love by that assumption of superiority, even granted it exist, of all things most irritating to man's nature. It is woman's province to *influence,* never to *dictate;* to conceal, rather than assume superiority. She may find many and many an opportunity to use it for the good of her husband and children, as was the case with the wife of Manoah; but never let her display it — never let her permit her husband to feel his inferiority — never let her withhold confidence, from the mistaken notion that as her judgment is as good, if not better than his, she cannot need his advice or interference — for if she does, she may rest assured that from that instant her influence is at an end forever.

Source: Grace Aguilar, *The Women of Israel* (London: Groombridge & Sons, 1845), 211–19.

MARY ELIZABETH BECK

Drink Milk Not Beer

Mary Elizabeth Beck (fl. 1872–1908), a prominent member of England's Society of Friends, was a teacher, preacher, and a prolific writer of poetry, journal articles, and books on the Bible, church history, and theology. She published under her initials M.E.B. and also as Mary E. Beck. Beck was a woman of means and documented her travels to the Holy Land and America in her popular 1872 publication *East and West*. Other noteworthy publications include *Heavenly Relationships* (1885), *Fresh Diggings in an Old Mine* (1885), *Collateral Testimonies to Quaker Principles* (1887), and *Turning Points in the Lives of Eminent Christians* (1888).

Beck's *Bible Readings on Bible Women* (1892) began as addresses or sermons given to women in London. The book consists of a series of seventeen short chapters, fourteen of which tell the story of a woman or group of women from the Bible. The first three chapters provide introductory material on the Bible, focusing on sin and redemption. Beck intended her addresses to be read aloud or preached at mothers' meetings or women's Bible study groups.

The primary lesson Beck draws from the story of Manoah's wife is total abstinence: "Mothers, heed the story well, for the text is plain; / For your own and children's sake, From strong drink abstain." The messenger's requirement that Samson's mother take no drink during her pregnancy becomes an occasion to speak to the problems that result from women drinking during pregnancy, including the claim that their children will be born with the tendency to drink. Beck also discusses infant nutrition, citing the support of doctors for her nutritional advice and providing recipes for oatmeal porridge with milk. She provides not only a glimpse of nineteenth-century ideas about pregnancy and nursing, but a picture of how the temperance movement persuaded Christians to become teetotalers. Her story of the husband and wife who both took "the pledge" shows that Beck believed a woman is responsible to influence her husband for good. By her example and prayers, the wife can persuade the husband to give up drinking.

Like Grace Aguilar, Beck reinforces the traditional role for women as mothers responsible for shaping their children's lives. She calls for educational reform, especially education for women. She quotes the French philosopher Mirabeau (1749–91), a politician who governed France in the early stages of the French Revolution, to support the notion that women need to be educated so that they in turn can educate their sons.

The Story of Samson's Mother:
A Lesson on Total Abstinence

Mothers, heed the story well, For the text is plain;
For your own and children's sake, From strong drink abstain.

Read aloud, Judges xiii.1–24.

We must call her Manoah's wife, or Samson's mother, for no other name has come down to us. And yet she was one of those favoured women who, having almost given up the hope of the highest crown of woman, motherhood, received the promise of a son through an angel visitant. Sarah, the mother of Isaac; Hannah, the mother of Samuel; and Elizabeth, the mother of John the Baptist, were similar cases, and all of these had remarkable sons. If an angel were suddenly to appear to any of us, how attentively we should listen to every word he said, especially if he were to give us any directions for our future conduct.

The Lord, in His pity toward the children of Israel, who had been forty years oppressed by the Philistines on account of their sins, was about to send them a deliverer; but the right preparation of the child for so important a commission was to begin even before he was born! A celebrated French philosopher, named Mirabeau, being asked how soon the education of a boy should begin, is reported to have said, "Twenty years before his birth, by educating his mother."

The angel's instructions were short, but emphatic: — the woman could not forget them. She was not told what to do, but *what she was not to do*. "Drink no wine nor strong drink." Her boy was to be a Nazarite to God, devoted to Him from his birth, and he was not to inherit from his mother a taste for that which all Nazarites were strictly forbidden. The mother was to be in a healthy state of body, in order that her child might be born under favourable conditions.

Manoah was naturally very much impressed by the wonderful circumstance of which his wife told him, and, without any misgiving of its truth, he besought the Lord to send His messenger again, with directions as to how the promised boy was to be brought up.

It is rather remarkable that all we hear during the second visit respecting the command of the angel is the repetition of his first message; but it must have made it doubly impressive.

This time there were miraculous signs attending, so that there could be no doubt in their minds that they had received a direct ambassador from Heaven. The woman, wiser than her husband, stilled his fears, and in time her faith was rewarded, and her highest wishes fulfilled. And now, what sort of a boy was this Samson, the child of a total-abstaining mother? Of course his extraordinary strength was not natural, or from natural causes; it was distinctly a Divine gift, to answer a grand purpose. But still there is deep teaching in it. It shows us that God would have us take our part in helping on His work. If strong drink would have increased his supernatural strength, would he have been forbidden all use of it? If strong drink would have made his mother stronger in body, would she have been twice told by the angel to beware of touching it?

What, then, is the lesson to the mothers of the present day? Prepare for the duties and responsibilities of your motherhood. Do not let one drop of intoxicating drink flow through your system.

It is a solemn fact that many innocent babies are born with a tendency to like drink, which they have inherited from their mothers.

If mothers would only substitute milk or oatmeal porridge for beer or porter, it would be much better for their own health, and far safer for their little ones.

Mrs. Reaney tells a story of a young mother who wished to bring up her baby on total abstinence principles, and begged that she might not have stout given her at lunch. The nurse, however, insisted that she must take it, and the mother reluctantly yielded. One day, being rather in haste, she took her stout at one draught, and nursed her baby directly afterwards, returning it to its nurse. The next morning the lunch was sent up without the stout. The mother noticed it, but said nothing. The day following, and the day after that, it was the same. Then the lady said, "Nurse, are you going to let me do without my stout?" The nurse saw it was now time for an explanation, and confessed that she had noticed the stiffened limbs of the child, and the strange look in its eyes, when the mother had finished nursing it, and she thought, "If that is the effect on the *body* of the infant, what effect may be produced on its *soul*?" She ended by saying that what she had just seen had made her a teetotaller.

"But hard-working nursing mothers must have something to keep up their strength." Quite true, and let us hear what Dr. Edmunds, who has had large experience in the Temperance Hospital in London, has to say on this subject. "Oatmeal porridge with milk is a most digestible and sustaining food. For nursing mothers it is *the* food which makes the very best food, with the least strain upon the mother's system." But, then, it should be carefully made — clean boiling water, a clean saucepan, and good meal. Mix three tablespoonfuls of oatmeal very smoothly with a quarter of a pint of milk and three-quarters of a pint of boiling water. Boil gently for two hours, and flavour as you please.

Oatmeal drink made in this way is recommended by Dr. Richardson, and it cannot possibly have any injurious effect on the young life entrusted to your care.

Before we conclude our lesson on this subject, may I ask you who are wives and mothers to consider how great is your influence with regard to strong drink over your husbands and children? If you take your "little drop" at lunch or supper, how can you expect your husband, whose temptations are so great, to give it up altogether? If you wish to have a sober husband and happy home, make it as easy as possible for him to abstain. Be willing to set the example yourself, and provide him with some substitute for beer if he has to work all day without coming home. Nothing is better than oatmeal drink for this purpose. It has been fairly tried by working men on extensive railway works, and in the hay and harvest fields, with complete success; the men worked with better tempers, and got through more work in less time than the beer-drinkers. I will finish this chapter by a true account taken from a little tract called "The Wife's Story."[4] It was related by the wife herself to a gentleman whom I know. She said, "I gave my heart to the Lord many years ago.... It was, however, only some eighteen months before Tom signed the pledge that I myself saw through the sin and danger of the drinking system, and became a teetotaller. When I had put away my own beer, I began steadily praying that the drunkard's cup might be taken from my husband's hands; and many an hour have I spent upon my knees, with my finger upon some of the promises of God which are written in His blessed Book. The day that Tom signed I was working my sewing machine in the evening. When he came home, he flung a bit of paper in the work-basket. 'Look at that,' said he. 'I will in a moment,' I answered. Again he said a second and a third time, rather sharply, 'Look at that paper.' So I stopped work and read it. Oh! what a glorious surprise! So long praying, so long hoping against hope as I had been — and now the answer had come, just as I had wanted it, but all in a moment, and so unexpectedly. For some time I could hardly believe my eyes. I was like the Hebrews when they were liberated from Babylon, as you may read in the 120th Psalm.... There are tens of thousands of wives praying for husbands ... and parents praying over their wandering boys and erring daughters. Let them pray on, and never get disheartened. The dear Lord hears them, and sends His Holy Spirit into their hearts to convince them of sin. Let them be patient and kind, and themselves give up the drink which has been such a terrible snare to their loved ones. Prayer and precept and example must all go together if the Lord is to do 'great things' for us and make us glad." This story was told by the happy wife six years after her husband had become an abstainer, and "had stuck to it well," she said, "through thick and thin"; and "our house," she added, "is like a little Paradise to what it used to be."

But, though reformation is a good thing, it is better after all to *begin* right, and to have a Christian and teetotal home from the first. Solomon says, "Train up a child in the way he should go, and when he is old he will not

---

4. One of the Leominster series of Gospel Temperance Tracts by F. Sessions.

depart from it."[5] Let the noble resolution of Joshua be yours: "As for me and my house, we will serve the Lord."[6]

Source: Mary E. Beck, *Bible Readings on Bible Women: Illustrated by Incidents in Daily Life* (London: S. W. Partridge & Co., 1892), 25–32.

Edith M. Dewhurst

Nameless But Known

Little is known about English Anglican educator and author Edith Dewhurst (fl. 1888–1903). She published a series of outlines for mothers' meetings and Bible classes on women in the Old Testament and in the Gospels, believing that "they being dead, yet speak."[7] In addition to her teaching and writing ministry to women, Dewhurst taught and published for children of various ages. Her book *Pleasant Fruits: Thoughts after Confirmation* (1892) shows her ability to reflect practically and theologically for a teenaged audience. Several of her writings are tied into the liturgical calendar, notably the series of readings she prepared on *The King and His Servants* (1899) and her lessons for infant classes from Christmas to Easter (1903).[8] The preface to *The Women of the Old Testament: Outlines for Mothers' Meetings*, written by Reverend C. J. Atherton, a missioner with the Church of England, suggests that Dewhurst's ministry and writing were highly valued in the church. She begins her thirteen addresses on the Old Testament with Eve and ends with Ruth.

Dewhurst outlines a classic three-point sermon on Manoah's wife. The first point explores the namelessness of Manoah's wife and the divine messenger. She, like Mary Beck, calls attention to Manoah's wife's namelessness,

---

5. [Proverbs 22:6.]
6. [Joshua 24:15.]
7. Edith M. Dewhurst, *"They Being Dead, Yet Speak": Outlines for Mothers' Meetings and Women's Bible Classes,* second series of "Women of the Old Testament" (London: Marshall Bros., 1890).
8. Edith M. Dewhurst, *The King and His Servants: Advent to Trinity, Trinity to Advent* (London: Elliot Stock, 1899); idem, *Sunday Afternoons with the Little Ones: Lessons from Christmas to Easter* (London: Marshall Bros., 1903).

an issue that bothered later feminists such as Elizabeth Cady Stanton.[9] Dewhurst assuages the problem with her suggestion that the Lord knew her and includes her in the "records of heaven." She then explores the question of the identity of the messenger, providing an example of the type of Christian interpretation to which Grace Aguilar was responding. Dewhurst equates the man of God with the "Lord of Hosts Himself" and goes on to claim that he was "the Son of God in angelic form." She weaves together Old and New Testament texts to defend her reading. For example, she connects the angel's ascending in the flame of the altar with the ascension of Jesus in Acts 1:9.

Dewhurst's second point focuses on the promise and command given to Manoah's wife. She explains the claim that every Jewish woman longed to be the mother of the long-awaited Messiah, and it was for this reason that Manoah's wife was overjoyed to receive the news of the angel. She also suggests that the story calls listeners to be separate from the world, as Samson and his mother were called to be separate. Unlike Mary Beck, she does not make the practical application of abstaining from drinking, nor does she give any other examples of what it means to be separate.

Dewhurst's third point again focuses on Manoah's wife's exemplary spirituality. Just as her assurance arose out of her faith and obedience, so the assurance of Christians is based on Jesus's "full, perfect and sufficient sacrifice" on the cross.

Manoah's Wife

Text: — Ps. xxv.14.
Passage of Scripture to be Read or Referred to: — Judges xiii.

We know the names of the husband and son of the woman whom we are about to consider, but her own name we know not. "The *Lord* knoweth them that are His,"[10] and from what we read of Manoah's wife, we are sure that her name is written in the records of heaven,[11] though it may be written in no other record.

---

9. See "Mrs. Manoah Doe" below and Adele Reinhartz, *"Why Ask My Name?" Anonymity and Identity in Biblical Narrative* (New York: Oxford University Press, 1998).
10. [2 Timothy 2:19.]
11. [Luke 10:20.]

To this woman was it granted to meet with the Lord of Hosts Himself in the person of "a man of God, whose countenance was like the countenance of an angel of God, very terrible."

Evidently it was the Son of God Himself in angelic form, who came to this woman with a promise, and a command from God. "His *countenance* was very terrible" (ver. 6). Long afterwards, before that same countenance, unbelieving men "did shake for fear, and became as dead" (St. Matt. xxviii.3, 4).

And again, when He appeared to His beloved disciple with "His countenance as the sun shining in his strength," that disciple "fell at His feet as dead," so great was his awe and reverence (Rev. i.16, 17).

His *name* was "secret," or "wonderful" (ver. 18).

"His name shall be called wonderful," was the prophecy concerning the Son of God, who was the "mighty God" Himself (Isa. ix.6).

"The angel *did wondrously,* and Manoah and his wife looked on" (ver. 19).

Long afterwards, none of the disciples durst ask the risen Christ, "Who art Thou? knowing that it was the Lord," because of His wondrous acts (St. John xxi.12).

The angel of the Lord "*ascended* in the flame of the altar" (ver. 20).

"While they beheld, He was taken up; and a cloud received Him out of their sight," is spoken of the risen Saviour (Acts i.9).

II. The Lord gave Manoah's wife a promise, and a command (ver. 7, 14).

She was to have a son. That was the great desire of every Jewish woman, who hoped that to her might be granted the great honour of being an ancestor of the promised Messiah. But there was a command connected with the promise. The child was to be *separated unto God* from the womb, therefore he was to be kept separate from all that might defile him. He was to drink no wine or strong drink. For the Lord's work, he must have no artificial strength, he must be filled only with the Spirit of the Lord.

In order that he might be separate, his mother must be separate (ver. 7).

She was to be a sharer in his great work of beginning to deliver Israel out of the hands of the Philistines (ver. 5).

III. The woman's assurance arising from faith and obedience (ver. 23).

She feared, and worshipped, and yet she trusted; rather, it was because she did fear and worship, that she learnt to trust (ver. 20, 23).

God had accepted her offering, therefore He could not reject *her*; God had revealed to her His will, therefore He would enable her to fulfill it (ver. 23).

"The Word was made flesh, and *dwelt among* us (and we beheld His glory, the glory as of the only begotten of the Father) full of grace and truth" (St. John i.14).

Manoah's Wife

We have a clearer vision of God than Manoah's wife knew anything of. He has given us a promise and a command. "Come out from among them, and be ye separate, saith the Lord, and touch not the unclean thing; and I will receive you, and will be a Father unto you, and ye shall be My sons and daughters, saith the Lord Almighty" (2 Cor. vi.17, 18).

God wants to separate us and our children unto Himself. He wants to have us altogether belonging to Him, without any opposing influence, that He may save us, that He may use us, that He may satisfy us.

There will come a day when Christians will be separated from the world; the one will be on Christ's right hand, the other on His left.

Who does not desire for herself and children to be found on the right hand then? Then let us see to it, that in simple obedience to God's command we separate ourselves here from all that would prevent us yielding our hearts to Him, and determine to serve Him, and Him only.

Manoah's wife had confidence because God had accepted her offering. May we assure our hearts before Him, because we believe He has accepted the "full, perfect, and sufficient sacrifice"[12] which Christ made for us on the Cross.

Manoah's wife was not afraid of God's will, for she knew He would give her strength to fulfill it.

"What man is he that feareth the Lord? him shall He teach in the way that He shall choose. His soul shall dwell at ease, and his seed shall inherit the earth. The secret of the Lord is with them that fear Him, and He will show them His covenant" (Ps. xxv.12–14).

Source: Edith M. Dewhurst, *The Women of the Old Testament: Outlines for Mothers' Meetings*, first series (London: Marshall Bros., 1889), 125–31.

M.G.

Saintly Mothers

M.G. published her book *Women Like Ourselves: Short Addresses for Mothers' Meetings, Bible Classes, etc.* (1893) as a resource for inexperienced teachers. In

---

12. [Quotation from the service of Holy Communion in the Book of Common Prayer.]

her addresses on the stories of women in Scripture, M.G. looked for points of connection with her audience, assuming that biblical characters acted "exactly as we ourselves would be likely to act under the same circumstances."[13] Not surprisingly M.G.'s address focuses on Samson's God-fearing mother, the unnamed heroine of Judges 13, as a role model for the Christian mother. She notices that Samson's mother gave up all thoughts of self and considered only the "welfare of the unborn babe." She reminds mothers of their great responsibilities for both the physical and spiritual well-being of a child. She not only refers to the Bible to convince women of their high calling as mothers, but also quotes Napoleon Bonaparte to claim that good French soldiers are the result of good mothers. Unlike the other women excerpted in this chapter, M.G. reflects on the difficult truth that, although Samson's mother was a paragon of virtue, her son was not, and she supposes that Samson's "ungodly marriage" must "have cost his mother many a bitter heartache." However, because Samson, in the end, died having been restored to God's favour, she encourages mothers to persevere in their prayers for their wayward children. The story of Monica's prayers for Augustine, a wild youth who eventually became the Bishop of Hippo, is cited as another example of a son who eventually returned to the church.

M.G.'s philosophy of Christian motherhood is summed up in the mandate, "nurse your child for God." Her practical suggestions for mothers include prenatal care, catechizing children at home, and advocating for religious education and prayer in Board Schools. In her applications of the Bible to daily life we see her blurring the traditional separation of private and public life; she calls for women to see that their role as mothers extends outside the home.

M.G.'s interpretation of Judges 13 also includes a figural reading. Like Edith Dewhurst, Anglo-Catholic M.G. understands the messenger as the preexistent Christ, but she goes on to reveal her theology of the Eucharist, suggesting that that same Christ "comes down to be with us upon His Altar under the outward symbols of Bread and Wine." M.G. similarly provides a figural reading of the story of Moses's rescue in this address; the Egyptian princess is a type of Christ and of the church.

M.G. concludes her sermon with a summary of the story of the mother of the seven sons found in 2 Maccabees, an apocryphal book with deuterocanonical status in the Anglican Church. She ends with a prayer that the

---

13. M.G., *Women Like Ourselves: Short Addresses for Mothers' Meetings, Bible Classes, etc.* (London: Society for the Promotion of Christian Knowledge, 1893), iv.

mothers in the meeting would live up to their high calling so that at the last judgment they may stand with confidence before their God, a God of retributive justice.

The Mothers of Samson and of Moses

The influence of a mother upon her children is, for the most part, such a quiet, hidden thing, that we need not be surprised that we do not find in the Old Testament any continuous story giving a striking illustration of a mother's life. Here and there we have a touching picture: Rebekah by her deceit losing her favourite son; the Shunammite owning through her tears that all was well with her dead child; Rizpah watching day and night over the bodies of her sons (2 Sam. xxi.8–12).

But for the most part the work of the mother is unseen, and only known by the results. When you see a green spot upon the moor, you say, "There is a spring of water there." And so we feel sure, in many cases, that a God-fearing mother has trained some noble character.

I think that the mother of Samson, in Judges xiii., gives us the most beautiful picture we can find of the spirit in which a mother should undertake her great trust. I want to point out to you the care which she was bidden to observe from the moment that she first knew she would be blessed with a child. She was no longer to please herself and to indulge in even lawful pleasures; her one thought and prayer was to be, "How shall we order the child? and what shall we do unto him?" (ver. 12). You mothers know well how much your actions influence the bodily health and welfare of the unborn babe. Do not forget that you are also responsible in a great measure for its spiritual well-being; any strong passions, any self-indulgence, will probably be reproduced in the mind of your offspring. Try then, during those months of anticipation, to be what you would have your child to be; and pray daily, like Manoah and his wife (ver. 8), "O, my Lord, teach us what we shall do unto the child that shall be born." For it is a great responsibility to be the means of bringing a man into the world, for that soul which takes its life from you will never die, that little body which you bear will rise again, either to everlasting glory or everlasting torment. That child of yours is sent to do a special work for God upon earth. What that work may be you cannot foresee, but you may feel certain that God *has* a purpose for him or her, in one way or another, to fight the battle of the Lord against sin and Satan, of whom the Philistines were the type (see ver. 5).

See, then, that you do your part to prepare your child for the work. When Napoleon Bounaparte [*sic*] was asked what was needed to make Frenchmen brave soldiers, he answered at once, "They want good mothers." Do you then pray and resolve that as far as your power can effect it, your sons and daughters may be consecrated to God's service from the womb to the day of their death (ver. 7). They may break away from that service in after years, and cause you much disappointment and grief of heart. Samson's life was far from being as pure and true as it should have been, and must have cost his mother many a bitter heartache. In vain she and his father tried to dissuade him from making an ungodly marriage (chap. xiv.3, 4), not knowing that God would bring good even out of that act of folly and disobedience to God's law. But still, in the end, the fervent prayers of that godly couple were answered, for we may believe that the return of Samson's strength was a mark of the restoration of God's favour after his bitter humiliation.

Many years ago, a saintly woman named Monica had a son, whom she had dedicated to God before he was born, and whom she endeavoured to train to His service. But to her unspeakable grief he grew up wild and sinful, and utterly despised his mother's counsels. At last she poured out all her trouble on his account to the holy Bishop of that city, and was greatly comforted by his assuring her — "Fear not; for it is impossible that the child of so many prayers should perish." So Monica prayed on in faith, in spite of many disappointments, until at length the good news reached her of her son's conversion; and that wild youth became one of the greatest and holiest Bishops the world has ever seen, known throughout the Church as Saint Augustine of Hippo.

This fervent, unflagging prayer, then, should be the foundation of the mother's work. The little ones whom God gives you, are but lent to you to train for Him; so that in every particular that concerns either their souls or bodies, your hearts should look up to Him to know how He would have you treat them. "How shall we order the child? and what shall we do unto him?" Especially should you come to Him with this prayer for help and guidance at the time when He, Who appeared to Manoah and his wife in the form of an angel, comes down to be with us upon His Altar, under the outward symbols of Bread and Wine. Then, indeed, He does "wondrously" (ver. 19), for then He makes Himself known to us in breaking of Bread; and well may we, recognizing His Presence, fall on our faces with trembling awe (ver. 20). There, while the pure flame of our devotion ascends to heaven, may we seek from Him in sweet communion all the wisdom and all the grace we need, for "how shall we not prevail with God," says an old writer (S. Chrysostom),[14] "when that great Sacrifice is displayed?"

And now let us turn to the time when the infant Moses was given into the arms of his mother, Jochebed, by the king's daughter. "Take this child," she said, "and nurse it for me, and I will give thee thy wages" (Exod. ii.9). Is not this what Christ says to each mother when a dear little baby is born? — "This little one is lent to you to nurse and train *for Me*, that when I send for him he may be fit to dwell in My palace." He says the same by the mouth of the Church (of whom the king's daughter is a type) to parents and godparents when their little charge is given back to them fresh from the waters of Holy Baptism: "It is your parts and duties to provide that this child may be virtuously brought up to lead a godly and a Christian life."[15]

Here, in these brief words to Jochebed, we see the outward duties of mothers towards their children, as in the stories of Manoah's wife and of Monica we saw that they must be preceded and accompanied by heartfelt devotion and prayer. Christ has taken the little ones especially under His protection, and promises that everything done to one of them shall be reckoned as done to Him. "For ME!" Bear these words in mind when you are tempted to be impatient with the little children, or to weary of telling them what their little minds so quickly forget. Bear them in mind when you feel tempted to "let things go," when it is a question whether you have time to teach them their hymns, or to hear them lisp their infant prayers. They are not your own, to do what you like with, to care for or to neglect. You are nursing them for Jesus Christ, therefore you *must* correct each little fault as you see it; you *must* talk to them about Him, and teach them to love Him and to pray to Him; you *must* treat their little bodies carefully and reverently as belonging to Him.

It grieves me very much to find how few of my little Sunday scholars are taught at home to say any morning prayers. "Mother hasn't time to hear us," they say; and if I go to their mothers to talk to them about it, they candidly answer, "Well, ma'am, you see I'm so busy in a morning." Surely, surely, nothing else that you may have to do can be sufficiently important to prevent your bringing the little ones for their morning greeting to their heavenly Father, and teaching them to seek His guidance and protection at the beginning of the day. And remember that in this, as in all else, your own example will go further with your children than any mere teaching could do.

---

14. A reference to St. John Chrysostom (ca. 347–407), Archbishop of Constantinople and renowned preacher.

15. See the Baptismal Service in the Book of Common Prayer.

Once again, if it is for God that you have to train your child, and not merely for his own worldly advantage or yours, will you not take care, when the time comes to send him to school, that you will have him (or her) go to a school where a sound *religious* education may be had? There are some Board Schools, you know, where they have grand buildings and clever teachers, but where the Bible is never explained, the Catechism never taught, and if any religious teaching is given at all, it is watered down to suit Jews and Roman Catholics and Unitarians just as well as children of the Church; while in some Board Schools even the Creed, and the Lord's Prayer, and the Ten Commandments are forbidden. That is scarcely the sort of school where you would like to send the child that you are nursing for the Lord Jesus, is it? You want to send it where it will be taught God's will and to know more about Him. You want it to be taught a reason for the faith that is in it,[16] better than you can teach. You want God's Child to be where God is loved and reverenced even when it is learning secular lessons. Try, then, and send it to a Voluntary School — a Church School, if you can — rather than to a Board School. There are some people who, for their own purposes, are making a great noise in the country, and trying to get all religious teaching done away with in weekday schools. They want to set up Board Schools everywhere, and have nothing but secular instruction given; but the working-men and women of England, whose children are chiefly concerned in the matter, have spoken out well against it, and have signed, thousands of them, that Petition which we were all asked to sign not long ago, asking that instead of doing them away, Government would do more to help those schools, which generous Church-people have built on purpose that the children of the poor should have not only a good worldly education, but a good religious education as well, such as befits children who are to dwell hereafter in the Palace of the King of kings, that they may know as much as it is possible for them to learn about Him.

For the same reason, you will not leave the child to please him or herself as to what Sunday School it goes to, nor will you just send it off to the one where they give most prizes and best treats, nor take it away in a temper because it is reproved. You are nursing your child for God, and therefore it should be trained as a faithful member of that Church into which it was baptized, and sent to the Sunday School, which has been called "the nursery of the Church."

Let me tell you a story in conclusion out of the Apocrypha, which is

---

16. [1 Peter 3:15.]

bound up with some of our Bibles. At the time when Jerusalem was conquered by the heathen, many of those Jews who would not renounce their religion were tortured to death. Among others, a mother was brought before the tyrant with her seven sons, and commanded to eat pork, contrary to the Jewish law. On their refusal, one after another was tortured before their mother's eyes in the most horrible manner, till but one, the youngest, was left alive. The king then told his mother to reason with him and persuade him to save his life. "Yes," she said, "I will counsel him"; and, turning to him, she besought him, "O, my son, have pity upon me that bare thee nine months . . . and nourished thee and brought thee up. . . . Fear not this tormentor, but being worthy of thy brethren take thy death, that I may receive thee again in mercy with thy brethren."[17] She had brought them up for God, and she was faithful to her trust to the last; and now she has received her "wages," even "a glorious kingdom and a beautiful crown from the LORD's hand,"[18] the crown of martyrdom; and surrounded once more by her seven brave sons, she and they stand among the noble army of martyrs in glory everlasting. The same reward, differing only in degree, is waiting for every faithful mother now. God grant that each one of us may so fulfil her trust here, that we may stand before Him at the day of reward in confidence, knowing that He "is not unrighteous to forget your work and labour of love."[19]

Source: M.G., *Women Like Ourselves: Short Addresses for Mothers' Meetings, Bible Classes, etc.* (London: Society for the Promotion of Christian Knowledge, 1893), 66–73.

CLARA B. NEYMAN

Demythologizing the Angel

Very little is known about Clara Neyman (fl. 1890s) apart from her involvement with the movement for women's suffrage in the United States and her association with Freethinkers.[20] Unlike the other women excerpted in this

---

17. [2 Maccabees 7:1–29.]
18. [Wisdom of Solomon 5:15.]
19. [Hebrews 6:10.]
20. For more information on Neyman, see "Genius Knows No Sex" in the Deborah chapter.

chapter, Neyman demythologized the story, concluding that the angel was likely Manoah's wife's "own inner sense" and that the angel's appearance to Manoah and his wife "a figure of speech" rather than an "actual occurrence." Neyman also held to the notion, common in the nineteenth century, that in the history of humanity there had been an initial matriarchy that had degenerated into a patriarchy and, consequently, that the battle for woman's suffrage was a battle of regaining what women had lost.[21] This view of history underlies her claims that knowledge about how prenatal care affects the life of the unborn child was lost when a woman was no longer permitted to be the "arbiter of her own destiny."

Neyman had a very high view of the importance of mothers in the formation of children and, like M.G., wondered how Samson's mother might have failed him. She reasons that instructions given to Samson's mother concerned only Samson's physical well-being and neglected his moral or "psychical" health. This omission explains why Samson displayed physical prowess but lacked moral strength. She observes that, for this reason, Samson, a Nazirite, was no more virtuous than his enemies, the Philistines, because both practiced "vengeance, cruelty, deceit." Neyman looks forward to a time when children will be raised to be virtuous by "an intelligent, pure fatherhood, and a wise, loving motherhood," descriptions that, though lofty, repeat the stereotypes of men being rational and women being emotional.

We come now to a very interesting incident, giving proof of the remarkable knowledge which the writers had of some intrinsic laws and the power of transmission which, even today, are known and adhered to only by a very small minority of wise, thoughtful mothers. However, the wife of Manoah, the future mother of Samson, is visited by an angel, giving her instructions as to her way of living during pregnancy. It appears that the writer was acquainted with some pre-natal influences and their effect upon the unborn.

We are just now beginning to investigate the important problem of child culture. Many good thoughts have been given on this subject by earnest

---

21. This view was held by Stanton also, and is most clearly articulated in the speech she gave in 1891 entitled, "The Matriarchate, or Mother State," included in the anthology *Elizabeth Cady Stanton: Feminist as Thinker*, ed. Ellen Carol Du Bois and Richard Candida Smith (New York: New York University Press, 2007), 264–75.

thinkers. A knowledge of these important laws of life will do away with the most harassing evils and sins which human flesh is heir to. Intelligent, free mothers will be enabled to forecast not only the physical, but also the psychical, traits of their offspring. How and why this once recognized knowledge was lost we know not. We may, however, rightly infer that so long as woman was not the arbiter of her own destiny she had no power to make use of this knowledge. Only the thoughtful, independent wife can administer the laws and the rules necessary for her own well-being and that of her offspring. Freedom is the first prerequisite to a noble life.

Observe how simple and trustful the relation is between this husband and wife. Manoah is thoughtful and ready to unite with his wife in all that the angel had commanded. There is no trace of disunion or of disobedience to the higher law which his wife had been instructed to follow. To her the law was revealed, and he sustained her in its observance. Mark, however, one difference from our interpretation of today, and how the omission of it worked out the destruction of the child. All the injunctions received were of a physical nature; strength of body and faith in God were to be the attributes through which Samson was to serve his people. The absence of moral traits is very evident in Samson; and this is the reason why he fell an easy prey to the wiles of designing women. It was not moral, but physical heroism which distinguished Samson from his combatants. Vengeance, cruelty, deceit, cunning devices were practised not only by the Philistines, but likewise by the Nazarite.

The angel who appeared to Manoah's wife was probably her own inner sense, and the appearance is to be understood rather as a figure of speech than as an actual occurrence, although there may have been, as there are today, people who were so credulous as to believe that such things actually occurred. The angel who whispers into our ears is knowledge, foresight, high motive, ideality, unselfish love. A conscious attitude towards the ideal still unattained, a lofty standard of virtue for the coming offspring, an intelligent, pure fatherhood, and a wise, loving motherhood must take the place of a mysterious, instinctive trust — the blind faith of the past. C.B.N.

Source: Clara B. Neyman, "The Book of Judges, Chapter III," in *The Woman's Bible, Part II: Joshua to Revelation,* ed. Elizabeth Cady Stanton (Boston: Northeastern University Press, 1898), 28–29.

WOMEN OF WAR, WOMEN OF WOE

Elizabeth Cady Stanton

Mrs. Manoah Doe

Elizabeth Cady Stanton (1815–1902) was a well-educated American social activist, abolitionist, and champion of women's rights. Her brief commentary on the story of Manoah's wife was published when Stanton was eighty-three.[22] Stanton makes only two points. First she draws attention to Manoah's wife's namelessness and draws a trajectory from this biblical practice to her experience in the nineteenth century when women were still defined in terms of their husband. She chides women who divorce and keep their ex-husband's surname (even after they remarry), claiming that they ignore their own family name, "the father from whom she may have derived all of her talent." Interestingly, in her comments Stanton ignores her own mother as a source of her own talent. In encouraging women to carry on their father's name, she seems unaware that she is still perpetuating patriarchy by identifying women only in relation to their fathers. Continuing this line of thought, Stanton also reflects on the only named woman in the Samson story being Delilah, a woman known for her ill repute and deviousness.

Stanton's second point picks up on an issue discussed by most women excerpted in this chapter, namely, the "absolute power for weal or for woe over the immortal being" that a mother has when the child is in utero. She ends her commentary with a brief survey of ideas about the degree to which a child is malleable, a significant concern in a century that considered eugenics and the possibility of restricting the right to bear children. In addition to quoting the well-known philosophers John Locke (1632–1704) and René Descartes (1596–1650), she includes the Latin proverb *"Nascitur, non fit"*[23] and notes that Elihu Burritt (1810-1979), an American philanthropist and social activist, reversed the motto.

One would suppose that this woman, so honored of God, worthy to converse with angels on the most delicate of her domestic relations, might have had a name to designate her personality instead of being mentioned merely as

---

22. For a fuller biography of Stanton, see "The Question of Motives" in the Rahab chapter.
23. Born, not made.

the wife of Manoah or the mother of Samson. I suppose that it is from these Biblical examples that the wives of this Republic are known as Mrs. John Doe or Mrs. Richard Roe, to whatever Roe or Doe she may belong. If she chance to marry two or three times, the woman's identity is wholly lost. To make this custom more ludicrous, women sometimes keep the names of two husbands, clinging only to the maiden name, as Dolly Doe Roe, ignoring her family name, the father from whom she may have derived all of her talent. Samson's wife had no name, nor had the second woman on whom he bestowed his attentions; to the third one is vouchsafed the name of Delilah, but no family name is mentioned. All three represented one type of character and betrayed the "consecrated Nazarite," "the canonized Judge of Israel."

It would be a great blessing to the race, if parents would take heed to the important lesson taught in the above texts. The nine months of ante-natal life is the period when the mother can make the deepest impression in forming future character, when she has absolute power for weal or for woe over the immortal being. Locke, the philosopher, said, "Every child is born into the world with a mind like a piece of blank paper, and we may write thereon whatever we will"; but Descartes said, "Nay, nay; the child is born with all its possibilities. You can develop all you find there, but you cannot add genius or power." "*Nascitur, non fit,*" although our learned blacksmith, Elihu Burritt, always reversed this motto. E.C.S.

Source: Elizabeth Cady Stanton, "The Book of Judges, Chapter III," in *The Woman's Bible, Part II: Joshua to Revelation*, ed. Elizabeth Cady Stanton (Boston: Northeastern University Press, 1898), 30.

STUDY QUESTIONS

1. In this chapter the "man of God" and Samson's mother are not named. Why would their names be omitted?
2. Manoah's wife seemed to possess superior spiritual discernment. How did commentators respond to what they viewed as an unusual reversal of roles?
3. What do these commentaries on the story of Manoah's wife reveal about nineteenth-century views of motherhood, antenatal care, and temperance? Provide some examples of how ideological and theological presuppositions influence interpretation.

4. Discuss the theological problem inherent in the identification of the man of God in this story. Are there "appearances" of God today? How are they explained?

7

Delilah

The notorious figure of Delilah appears in the final episode of the story of Samson found in Judges 13–16. After taking a fancy to a prostitute in Gaza — an encounter that nearly costs him his life — Samson falls in love with Delilah (Judges 16:4-22). She is identified only in terms of her home in the valley of Sorek (Philistine territory), and while Delilah is not explicitly called a prostitute, neither is she described as Samson's wife. After this relationship begins, the Philistine leaders bribe Delilah into using her powers to help them defeat Samson. Three times Delilah questions Samson about the origin of his strength, and three times he fabricates a false answer. Delilah, believing him each time, attempts to use the information against him so that the Philistines can capture Samson, but he easily defeats them again and again. Finally, on her fourth try, Delilah's nagging and begging are successful, and she learns the true source of his great strength: his hair, which has never been cut because of his dedication as a Nazirite while still in his mother's womb. Samson falls asleep on her lap, Delilah arranges for his hair to be cut, and when the Philistines attack, Samson cannot defeat them; they gouge out his eyes, take him prisoner, bind him with shackles, and force him to grind grain at the mill.

This racy narrative drew relatively little comment from nineteenth-century women interpreters, who typically avoided interpreting texts involving sexuality. With the possible exception of Harriet Beecher Stowe, who raises the issue of literary genre, interpreters assumed it was reliable history. Sarah Hale even dates the events to 1120 B.C., following Bishop James Ussher's seventeenth-century chronology. Mary Cornwallis draws upon what is known about Eastern customs to explain Samson's position of repose upon Delilah's lap. Stowe draws considerable attention to Delilah's status as a foreigner. Her Delilah belongs to a class of idolatrous heathen "bad" women who use their "arts and devices" for evil. An American, Ella Wilcox reveals her geographical origins when she describes Delilah as a "Southern beauty"; the jewel-toned chromolithograph of Delilah that illustrates Stowe's essay highlights a beautiful woman in a low-cut dress.

While commentators approached the historicity of the text in similar fashion, they came to very different conclusions about Samson and Delilah's actions and respective culpability. Samson is portrayed as lewd and Delilah as a villain by Cornwallis, Stowe views Delilah as an evil, manipulative destroyer, but Hale blames Samson more than Delilah because he does not marry her. Wilcox's poem depicts Samson as victim of his passion and written from his point of view, it vividly portrays the strength of Samson's lust and his inability to resist Delilah's lure. Wilcox's poem is a testimony to the power of women's beauty and sensuality. All the interpreters bring their assumptions about the nature of male and female to their reading. Even Ella Wilcox and Clara Neyman, writing in the 1880s and late 1890s respectively, stress differences between women and men's nature. The infamous seductress of Proverbs 7 is an important intertext for Cornwallis and Stowe, while Neyman likens Delilah to Vivian from the Tales of King Arthur.

Mary Cornwallis

A Cautionary Tale

Mary Cornwallis (1758–1836), wife of the rector of an Anglican parish in Wittersham, Kent, published a remarkable four-volume commentary on the entire Bible in 1817.[1] Her comments on Delilah are part of her exposition of the book of Judges.

Cornwallis, who writes her comments with young men, such as her grandson, in mind, sees the narrative as a cautionary tale and condemns both Samson and Delilah. Samson is lewd, but Delilah is manipulative, mercenary, and treacherous, and Cornwallis concludes that human nature has not changed in the intervening millennia. She reads intertextually and connects Delilah with Dame Folly in Proverbs 7. She also sets the story in its

---

1. For more information on Cornwallis, see "Using the Only Means in Her Power" in the Jael chapter.

Delilah

ancient context, drawing on the works of scholars and travelers to explain Samson's sleeping posture. Cornwallis explores the significance of Samson's hair, claiming that it was not the hair itself that was the source of Samson's strength; rather it was symbolic of his Nazirite vow. This interpretation would make sense given her Anglican background; Samson's strength came from God, who had bestowed the special power upon him in order to fulfill a holy purpose, and not from "magic" derived from uncut hair. Logically, then, Cornwallis interpreted Samson's capture and defeat as just punishment for his life of debauchery. Accordingly, she infers that the return of Samson's strength showed that he had sincerely repented and subsequently received God's forgiveness.

When it is considered that Samson was not only a Nazirite, but a Judge of Israel, his flagitious conduct appears doubly criminal; and, though he was permitted by his invincible strength to effect his deliverance from Gaza, and twice from the hands of Delilah, yet we see that in the end he suffered the just consequences of his profligacy, and continued resistance of the Divine grace. The artful blandishments, the mercenary disposition, and the treachery of a prostitute, are admirably portrayed in the person of Delilah; and the infatuation of a man given up to lewdness is equally so in that of Samson. Human nature has been the same in all ages; and young men may derive very important instruction from this chapter, if they peruse it with the seriousness and attention it deserves. The character of such a woman as Delilah is finely drawn, Prov vii. We are not to suppose that any strength was derived to Samson through his hair; but that it was permitted by Providence that the breach of his vow as a Nazarite, of which his hair was a token, should be published by the loss of that strength, which was a Divine gift, only bestowed on him for particular ends. From the attitude of Samson, as described in ver. 19, we may suppose that Delilah was seated, after the eastern fashion, upon the cushion of her divan. Braithwaite, in his journey to Morocco, describes a favourite court lady, in whose lap the emperor constantly slept, when intoxicated. The frequency, therefore, of this situation, in an intercourse of depraved gallantry, might prevent any suspicion from arising in the mind of Samson, when thus invited to repose himself. Sins and imprudences usually bring their punishment sooner or later; this Samson experienced, when he was betrayed into the power of the Philistines: nor is it possible to conceive a person on whom slavery and contempt would sit heavier. It is to be hoped, and indeed it may be inferred from the return of his strength, that the deprivation of his sight, and imprisonment, produced a sincere repentance; and, although his last prayer carries the aspect of revenge, it may be supposed that the desperate act which closed his life was dictated by a divine impulse.

Source: Mary Cornwallis, *Observations, Critical, Explanatory, and Practical, on the Canonical Scriptures*, 2nd edition (London: Baldwin, Cradock & Joy, 1820 [originally 1817]), 2.357–58.

Sarah Hale

Samson the Traitor

Sarah Hale (1788–1879) was a very successful American editor and prolific author.[2] Hale's firm belief that women are morally and spiritually superior to men is featured in her massive tome *Woman's Record; or, Sketches of All Distinguished Women from the Beginning till A.D. 1850*.[3] In her entry on Delilah, Hale's favorable bias toward women's natures is evident. Indeed she claims that Samson's history is "the history of the triumphs of woman's's [sic] spiritual nature over the physical strength and mental powers of man." According to Hale, Delilah conquered Samson because she was more subtle due to her spiritual nature. Because she was his "paramour, perhaps his victim," Hale judges Delilah less culpable than Samson, who was a champion gifted by God and therefore must be held to a higher standard.

It is important to Hale to separate the biblical text from how the story of Samson and Delilah is told by John Milton, which indicates how familiar her contemporaries would have been with his dramatic poem *Samson Agonistes* (1671). Hale implicitly criticizes Milton's presentation of Delilah as Samson's wife when she implores her audience to read the story in the Bible only. Milton's version, of course, makes Samson a victim and Delilah the villain,

---

2. For more information on Hale, see "Redeeming Rahab" in the Rahab chapter.
3. This work went through several editions. The edition excerpted here has the year 1854 in the title.

Delilah

which runs contrary to Hale's argument that Delilah owed Samson neither obedience nor faith because they were not married. Hale draws her line boldly: Delilah was in no way traitorous, as it was Samson who was clearly disloyal to the God who gave him his strength.

Delilah

Of Sorek, a Philistine woman, who enticed Samson to reveal to her the secret of his supernatural strength, which was in his hair. This she caused to be cut off, and thus delivered him, helpless, into the hands of his enemies.

The history of Samson is the history of the triumphs of womans's [sic] spiritual nature over the physical strength and mental powers of man. Samson's birth, character and mission were first revealed to his mother; the angel appearing twice to her before her husband was permitted to see the heavenly messenger. All the preparatory regimen to ensure this wonderful son was appointed as the mother's duty; and when the angel of the Lord was revealed, the man's earthly nature was overwhelmed with fear; the woman's spiritual nature held its heavenly trust unshaken. The arguments of the wife, to comfort and sustain her husband, are as well-reasoned as any to be found in man's philosophy.[4]

Next, the "woman in Timnath," the wife of Samson, persuaded him to tell her his riddle or enigma, then considered a remarkable proof of genius to make. His wisdom was weakness weighed with her attractions. But his great physical strength remained a secret still. It was the especial gift of God, confided to him that he might become the deliverer of his nation. Yet this endowment was rendered of little real avail, because he devoted it to unworthy purposes, either to gratify his sensual passions or to escape the snares into which these had led him. The last trial of his strength, mental and bodily, against the subtlety of the woman's spirit, proved her superior power. Delilah conquered Samson, and in the means she employed she was far less culpable than he; because she was his paramour, perhaps his victim, and he the heaven-gifted champion of Israel. Read the history as recorded in the Bible, not in Milton's "Samson Agonistes," where the whole is set in a false light. Delilah was not the wife of Samson. She owed him no obedience,

---

4. [Judges 3:2–25.]

no faith. But his strength was consecrated to God — he was the traitor, when he disclosed the secret. See Judges, from chapters xiii. to xvii. These events occurred B.C. 1120.

Source: Sarah Hale, *Woman's Record; or, Sketches of All Distinguished Women, from the Creation to A.D. 1854* (New York: Harper & Bros., 1855), 36.

Harriet Beecher Stowe

Delilah the Destroyer or the Bad Power of a Bad Woman

Distinguished American author Harriet Beecher Stowe (1811–96) drew on her husband's knowledge and the resources in his considerable library and her own experiences in her writing of *Woman in Sacred History* (1873).[5] Referring to her essay on Delilah in a letter to her son, Stowe revealed that she was indebted to "Mr Manricis lectures on the O[ld] T[estament] which he gave to The Working Men's College in London."[6]

Stowe introduces her discussion of Delilah with a discussion of the story's setting in the idolatrous times of the Judges and argues that "the arts and devices of heathen women" are largely to blame for the introduction of idolatry into "the Jewish race." Stowe moves from discussing the historical setting of the story to consider the issue of literary genre, likening it to allegory and legend. The story's moral, Stowe suggests, is "the power of the evil woman," a phenomenon that "has repeated itself from age to age" and is "repeating itself today." Like Mary Cornwallis, Stowe regards Delilah as a type of the foreign seductress of Proverbs 7. She embellishes the portrait of Delilah found in Judges, explaining Delilah's wants: money and power and male "slaves to do her pleasure." Not surprisingly, the jewel-toned chromolithograph of Delilah that is included in Stowe's book highlights a beautiful woman in a gown with a plunging neckline.

---

5. For a fuller discussion of Stowe as a biblical interpreter, see "An Inspired Poet" in the Deborah chapter.

6. See Joan D. Hedrick, *Harriet Beecher Stowe: A Life* (New York: Oxford University Press, 1994), 388.

Delilah

Delilah the Destroyer

The pictures of womanhood in the Bible are not confined to subjects of the better class.

There is always a shadow to light; and shadows are deep, intense, in proportion as light is vivid. There is in bad women a terrible energy of evil which lies over against the angelic and prophetic power given to them, as Hell against Heaven.

In the long struggles of the Divine Lawgiver with the idolatrous tendencies of man, the evil as well as the good influence of woman is recognized. There are a few representations of loathsome vice and impurity left in the sacred records, to show how utterly and hopelessly corrupt the nations had become whom the Jews were commanded to exterminate. Incurable licentiousness and unnatural vice had destroyed the family state, transformed religious services into orgies of lust, and made woman a corrupter, instead of a saviour. The idolatrous temples and groves and high places against which the prophets continually thunder were scenes of abominable vice and demoralization.

No danger of the Jewish race is more insisted on in sacred history and literature than the bad power of bad women, and the weakness of men in their hands. Whenever idolatry is introduced among them it is always largely owing to the arts and devices of heathen women.

The story of Samson seems to have been specially arranged as a warning in this regard. It is a picture drawn in such exaggerated colors and proportions that it might strike of the lowest mind and be understood by the dullest. As we have spoken of the period of the Judges as corresponding to the Dark Ages of Christianity; so the story of Samson corresponds in some points with the medieval history of St. Christopher. In both is presented the idea of a rugged animal nature, the impersonation of physical strength, without much moral element, but seized on and used by a divine impulse for a beneficent purpose. Samson had strength, and he used it to keep alive this sacerdotal nation, this race from whom were to spring the future apostles and prophets and teachers of Christianity. . . .

With the history of this inspired giant is entwined that of a woman whose name has come to stand as a generic term for a class — Delilah! It is astonishing with what wonderful dramatic vigor a few verses create before us this woman so vividly and so perfectly that she has been recognized from age to age.

Delilah! Not the frail sinner falling through too much love; not the weak, downtrodden woman, the prey of man's superior force; but the terrible creature, artful and powerful, who triumphs over man, and uses man's passions for her own ends, without an answering throb of passion. As the strength of Samson lies in his hair, so the strength of Delilah lies in her hardness of heart. If she could love, her power would depart from her. Love brings weakness and tears that make the hand tremble and the eye dim. But she who cannot love is guarded at all points; *her* hand never trembles, and no soft, fond weakness dims her eye so that she cannot see the exact spot where to strike. Delilah has her wants, — she wants money, she wants power, — and men are her instruments; she will make them her slaves to do her pleasure.

Samson, like the great class of men in whom physical strength predominates, appears to have been constitutionally good-natured and persuadable, with a heart particularly soft towards woman. He first falls in love with a Philistine woman whom he sees, surrendering almost without parley. His love is animal passion, with good-natured softness of temper; it is inconsiderate, insisting on immediate gratification. Though a Nazarite, vowed to the service of the Lord, yet happening to see this women, he says forthwith: "I have seen a woman in Timnath. . . . Get her for me; for she pleaseth me well."

She is got; and then we find the strong man, through his passion for her, becoming the victim of the Philistines. He puts out a riddle for them to guess. "And they said to Samson's wife, entice thy husband that he may declare unto us the riddle. And Samson's wife wept before him . . . seven days, and on the seventh day he told her." A picture this of what has been done in kings' palaces and poor men's hovels ever since, — man's strength was overcome and made the tool of woman's weakness.

We now have a record of the way this wife was taken from him, and of the war he declared against the Philistines, and of exploits which caused him to be regarded as the champion of his nation by the Hebrews, and as a terror by his enemies. He holds them in check, and defends his people, through a course of years; and could he have ruled his own passions, he might have died victorious. The charms of a Philistine woman were stronger over the strong man than all the spears or swords of his enemies.

The rest of the story reads like an allegory, so exactly does it describe that unworthy subservience of man to his own passions, wherein bad women in all ages have fastened poisonous roots of power. The man is deceived and betrayed, with his eyes open, by a woman whom he does not respect, and

Delilah

who he can see is betraying him. The story is for all time. The temptress says, "How canst thou say, I love thee, when thy heart is not with me? Thou hast mocked me these three times, and hast not told me wherein thy great strength lieth. And it came to pass when she pressed him daily with her words, and urged him so that his soul was vexed to death, that he told her all his heart.... And she made him sleep upon her knees; and called for a man, and bade him shave off his seven locks, and his strength went from him.... the Philistines took him, and put on him fetters of brass, and he did grind in their prison house."

Thus ignobly ends the career of a deliverer whose birth was promised to his parents by an angel, who was vowed to God, and had the gift of strength to redeem a nation. Under the wiles of an evil woman he lost all, and sunk lower than any slave into irredeemable servitude.

The legends of ancient history have their parallels. Hercules, the deliverer, made the scoff and slave of Omphale, and Anthony, become the tool and scorn of Cleopatra, are but repetitions of the same story. Samson victorious, all-powerful, carrying the gates of Gaza on his back, and the hope of his countrymen and the terror of his enemies; and Samson shorn, degraded, bound, eyeless, grinding in the prison-house of those he might have subdued, — such was the lesson given to the Jews of the power of the evil woman. And the story which has repeated itself from age to age, is repeated in itself to-day. There are women on whose knees men sleep, to awaken shorn of manliness, to be seized, bound, blinded, and made to grind in unmanly servitude forever.

"She hath cast down many wounded,
Yea, many strong men hath she slain;
Her house is the way to Hell,
Going down to the chambers of Death."[7]

Source: Harriet Beecher Stowe, *Woman in Sacred History* (New York: J. B. Ford & Co., 1873), 91-99.

---

7. [Proverbs 7:26–27.]

Ella Wheeler Wilcox

The Road to Sweet Hell

The famous lines "Laugh, and the world laughs with you; Weep, and you weep alone," were written by Ella Wheeler (1850–1919), who was born on a farm in Johnstown, Wisconsin, and grew up north of Madison. She began writing poetry as a child and gained local recognition by the time she had graduated from high school. Her most famous poem, "Solitude," is included in Wilcox's collection *Poems of Passion*, which also contains her poem "Delilah." Soon after Wheeler married Robert Wilcox in 1884 she became interested in theosophy, New Thought, and spiritualism. Together they owned properties in Branford, Connecticut, and these became gathering places for literary and artistic friends. She continued to pursue literary and religious interests her whole life, and, after her husband's death in 1916, she became involved in Rosicrucian philosophy. She published her autobiography a year before her death. Wilcox is still revered as an American poet; the Ella Wheeler Wilcox Society continues to promote her religious views and practices.

Wilcox's "Delilah" is written from Samson's point of view, graphically portraying his passion for Delilah, whom she describes as a southern beauty. All Samson's resolve dissolves in her presence, and his joy in their lovemaking causes him to put away God, the world, and all hope for eternity. The poem suggests no hint of regret, even though it closes with the image of Samson descending into hell, taking Delilah with him. Like Mary Cornwallis's interpretation, this dark descent resonates with Proverbs 7:27, where Dame Folly draws men down to the grave. The poem is a testament to the power of women's beauty and illicit love, and Samson's apparent weakness to resist, or even want to resist temptation. The poem implies that the straight and narrow path is filled with less joy and passion than the alternative. While heaven is to be desired, Wilcox seems to say, the road that leads to it is dreary.

Delilah

In the midnight of darkness and terror,
When I would grope nearer to God,
With my back to a record of error

Delilah

And the highway of sin I have trod,
There come to me shapes I would banish —
The shapes of the deeds I have done;
And I pray and I plead till they vanish —
All vanish and leave me, save one.

That one, with a smile like the splendor
Of the sun in the middle-day skies —
That one, with a spell that is tender —
That one with a dream in her eyes —
Cometh close, in her rare Southern beauty,
Her languor, her indolent grace;
And my soul turns its back on its duty,
To live in the light of her face.

She touches my cheek, and I quiver —
I tremble with exquisite pains;
She sighs — like an overcharged river
My blood rushes on through my veins;
She smiles — and in mad-tiger fashion,
As a she-tiger fondles her own,
I clasp her with fierceness and passion,
And kiss her with shudder and groan.

Once more, in our love's sweet beginning,
I put away God and the World;
Once more, in the joys of our sinning,
Are the hopes of eternity hurled.
There is nothing my soul lacks or misses
As I clasp the dream-shape to my breast;
In the passion and pain of her kisses
Life blooms to its richest and best.

O ghost of dead sin unrelenting,
Go back to the dust and the sod!
Too dear and too sweet for repenting,
Ye stand between me and my God.
If I, by the Throne, should behold you,
Smiling up with those eyes loved so well,

Close, close in my arms I would fold you,
And drop with you down to sweet Hell!

Source: Ella Wheeler Wilcox, *Poems of Passion* (Chicago: W. B. Conkey Co., 1883), 46–48.

Clara B. Neyman

The Double Standard

Clara Neyman (fl. 1890s) was a member of the writing team for the second volume of Elizabeth Cady Stanton's *The Woman's Bible* (1895).[8] Neyman's entry on Delilah may be very brief but it offers important insight. Delilah is held responsible for her behavior; Neyman castigates her for using the gifts of "beauty and personal attractiveness" for a "sinister purpose." Neyman cautions women against following her example, arguing that women should be pure and attract men through their spiritual nature. At the same time Neyman explores the context that contributed to Delilah's behavior. Neyman is the only author excerpted in this chapter to recognize that men are responsible for the institution of prostitution, stating that if man overcame "the lust of his eyes," prostitution would end. Closing her commentary by warning that women's chastity is at risk because a double standard exists, Neyman recognizes that women are judged more harshly for any deviance in their sexual behavior. She argues that as long as men can be sexually promiscuous with little or no negative repercussions, women will be in danger and the relationship between the genders will be that of predator and prey.

The writer of the Book of Judges would fail in his endeavor to present a complete picture of his time, did he omit the important characteristic of a woman and her influence upon man therein portrayed.

In Delilah, the treacherous, the sinister, the sensuous side of woman is

---

8. For more information on Neyman, see "Genius Knows No Sex" in the Deborah chapter.

Delilah

depicted. Like Vivian, in the Idyls of King Arthur, Delilah uses — nay, abuses — the power which she had gained over Samson by virtue of her beauty and her personal attractions. She uses these personal gifts for a sinister purpose. They serve her as a snare to beguile the man whose lust she had aroused.

What a lesson this story teaches to men as well as to women! Let man overcome the lust of his eyes and prostitution will die a natural death. Let woman beware that her influence is of the purest and highest; let her spiritual nature be so attractive that man will be drawn toward it. Forever "the eternal womanly draweth man"[9] onward and upward. Soul unity will become the rule when the same chastity and purity are demanded of the sexes alike. Woman's chastity is never secure as long as there are two standards of morality. C.B.N.

Source: Clara B. Neyman, "The Book of Judges, Chapter III," in *The Woman's Bible, Part II: Joshua to Revelation*, ed. Elizabeth Cady Stanton (Boston: Northeastern University Press, 1898), 34.

STUDY QUESTIONS

1. Few nineteenth-century women commented on the story of Samson and Delilah. Why do you think they avoided the story? Does the story make you uncomfortable?
2. The commentators draw different conclusions about the morality of Samson and Delilah's actions. Describe the differences between their views. What evidence do commentators rely upon to make their case? For example, does it matter whether Samson and Delilah were married?
3. What nineteenth-century assumptions about the nature of male and female affect their interpretations of the story?
4. Sarah Hale describes Delilah as Samson's "paramour, perhaps his victim," and judges Samson more harshly than Delilah. Is it fair to have a higher moral standard for God's people than for foreigners?

---

9. Neyman is paraphrasing Goethe's *Faust*, "das Ewig-Weibliche zieht uns hinan": "The eternal feminine spirit draws us ever upward."

8

The Levite's Concubine

The gruesome story of the Levite's concubine and its violent consequences concludes the book of Judges by presenting the depravity of God's people. The story begins with a Levite from the hill country of Ephraim taking a concubine from Bethlehem and then notes that she was unfaithful or that she was angry and subsequently returned to her father's house.[1] After four months, the Levite and his servant travel to the woman's father's house to persuade her to return, and the Levite is welcomed lavishly for several days. One night during the journey home, the couple finds themselves without shelter until an old man from the hill country of Ephraim living in Gibeah finds them in the town square and offers them hospitality. He warns them of the dangers of spending the night in the open, but these dangers follow them back to the old man's house as the men of the city surround it and demand sex with the Levite. The men of the city refuse the old man's offer of his virgin daughter and the Levite's concubine. The Levite pushes his concubine outside anyway, where she is raped and abused throughout the night. At daybreak, the concubine falls at the door, where she lies until the Levite opens it, demanding that she get up. When she gives no answer, he places her on his donkey, returns home, dismembers her, and sends her twelve body parts to the various tribes, demanding that action be taken against those who caused her death.

When the tribes learn of what happened they are disgusted, and under the direction of the Levite mount an attack against Gibeah. The Benjamites,

---

1. The Hebrew phrase "she fornicated against him" was translated in the King James Version as "his concubine played the whore against him." The Revised Standard Version and New Revised Standard Version translate the verb in Judges 19:2 as "became angry" following the Septuagint and Old Latin translations.

refusing to attack their fellow Israelites living in Gibeah, respond by defending Gibeah, and a bloody battle ensues, killing thousands of Benjamites and destroying their towns. Four hundred virgins from Jabesh Gilead are spared to become wives for Benjamites who survive the slaughter, while six hundred men who still need wives abduct girls from Shiloh as they dance at an annual festival.

It is not surprising that very few nineteenth-century women commented on the story of the Levite's concubine as they generally avoided discussing scriptural texts addressing issues relating to rape and violence. In her commentary on the Bible published in 1805, for example, Anglican educator Sarah Trimmer summarized Judges 19–21 in one succinct paragraph, giving no mention of the rape, which occasioned the subsequent violence:

> These chapters give an account of some shocking and dreadful things that happened in Israel in the days of Phineas, the son of Eleazer, the grandson of Aaron, when the Israelites had in great measure forsaken the Lord, particularly the tribe of Benjamin, and committed all kinds of abominable deeds, which at last occasioned a civil war, and almost all the tribes of Benjamin were cut off. Observe, that the tribes were now made instruments of punishment to one another.[2]

In her more comprehensive 1817 commentary, Mary Cornwallis focuses on the chronology and ancient setting of the story. She notes its thematic links to the story of Sodom in Genesis 19 and comments "to what a romantic height the laws of hospitality were carried for many centuries." Unlike Trimmer, Cornwallis voices her disapproval, suggesting it would have been better for the men inside the house "to have defended life and honour to the last, than to have made such a horrid compromise with monsters in wickedness." Free-thought writer Annie Besant (1847–1933) simply acknowledges the sordid nature of the story, describing it as "the horribly disgusting tale of the Levite and his concubine."[3]

---

2. Sarah Trimmer, *A Help to the Unlearned in the Study of the Holy Scripture: Being an Attempt to Explain the Bible in a Familiar Way, Adapted to the Common Apprehensions, and according to the Opinions of Approved Commentators* (London: Rivington, 1805), 174. For a brief biography and analysis of her work, see *Handbook of Women Biblical Interpreters: A Historical and Biographical Guide*, ed. Marion A. Taylor and Agnes Choi (Grand Rapids: Baker, 2012), 505–9.

3. Annie Besant, *Woman's Position according to the Bible* (London: Freethought Publishing, 1885), 3.

Unlike Victorian interpreters who avoided or commented only tersely on the story, Anglican social activist Josephine Butler engages the story of the Levite's concubine fully. In lectures and in print, she dares to rehearse the story's darkest scenes, finding in them God's message for her world. Butler interprets the story in its canonical context, focusing particularly on the plight of the concubine and her treatment by the men in her life. She then fuses the horizons of the original story and the present, reading it as a story about women who are trafficked and those who either victimize or ignore them.

Mary Cornwallis

Abused to Death

An Anglican rector's wife, Mary Cornwallis (1758–1836) published her four-volume commentary *Observations, Critical, Explanatory, and Practical on the Canonical Scriptures* in 1817, with a second edition appearing in 1820. Her work follows the format of a standard commentary. Cornwallis is interested in questions of history and raises the problem of chronology in the book of Judges. She suggests that the story of the Levite's concubine happened "about the same time" as the story of Micah's idolatry in Judges 18. She compares it to Genesis 19, commenting on the ancient customs of hospitality. Unlike Sarah Trimmer, Cornwallis engages the horror of the concubine's rape and voices her strong disapproval of the actions of the men in the story. Her commentary on the sequel to the "atrocious act" in Judges 20–21 again highlights the evil times. Cornwallis does not draw specific moral lessons from Judges, but in her final comments at the end of the book of Judges she focuses on the recurrent problem of human sin, tracing a grim picture of salvation history beginning with Adam and continuing to the present. She concludes: "But every effort of Infinite mercy, to secure the happiness of mankind, has been in turn abused or rejected, and nothing remains, within the limits of Divine justice, but a separation of the righteous from the wicked at the last awful day of general judgment."

Chapter XIX

1. A Levite of mount Ephraim goeth to Bethlehem to fetch home his concubine. 16. An old man entertaineth him. 22. The men of the city beset the house: to prevent which the man yieldeth up his concubine, who is abused by them to death. 29. He divideth her into twelve parts, which he sendeth to the twelve tribes of Israel.

It is very uncertain at what period of time the dreadful transaction here recorded took place; some suppose it to have happened between the death of Joshua and the government of Othniel; but it is not likely that the people could have fallen into such a state of apostasy, so soon after the death of that excellent man, and the worthy elders who succeeded him; indeed we are told that, by their example and good advice, they preserved the people in obedience to the Divine commands. It is more probable that the idolatry of Micah, and this atrocious act, happened about the same time, when there was no regular government. The manner in which this murderous act was made known to the different tribes, was according to the usage of ancient nations, as well pagans, as worshippers of the true God. "Saul, "we are told, "took a yoke of oxen and hewed them in pieces, and sent them throughout all the coasts of Israel by the hand of messengers; saying, Whosoever cometh not forth after Saul, and after Samuel, so shall it be done unto his oxen; and the fear of the Lord fell on the people, and they came out with one consent."[4] By this we see that the bloody mandate was understood, and that a confederacy was immediately formed to avenge an injury, or to support a war. A human victim must have excited peculiar horror, and the text well expresses the general consternation: "And all that saw it said there was no such deed done, nor seen, from the day that the children of Israel came up out of the land of Egypt, unto this day: consider of it, take advice, and speak your minds." The history of Lot in Sodom, and that contained in the present chapter, show to what a romantic height the laws of hospitality were carried for many centuries. Under such distressing circumstances it would have been more agreeable to reason and religions to have kept the door fast as long as possible, to have committed the innocent inhabitants to the Divine protection, and to have defended life and honour to the last, than to have made such a horrid compromise with monsters in wickedness. . . .

---

4. 1 Samuel 11:7.

Chapter XXI

This chapter confirms what was before surmised, that the tribes assembled to chastise their brother Benjamin were highly deserving of punishment themselves. Every act here recorded was base and abominable, the result of human wisdom, not the counsel of God; who appears to have given no answer to the application of the people, when they appeared before him. "Every man did that which was right in his own eyes." "For want of a supreme authority," observes Archbishop Ussher, "every tribe, every city, nay every private man, committed many horrid things which were not publicly punished. This was the case of Micah's idolatry; of the Benjamites' filthiness; and now of these enormous things done by all the Israelites, in killing all the Benjamites without distinction, when the law required that the children should not suffer for the parent's offences; in binding themselves by such a rash oath to give them none of their daughters to be their wives; in killing all the women of Jabesh-Gilead, who were not virgins; and now in permitting, nay ordering this rape, rather than break a rash oath, which should teach men to be thankful for the authority which is set over them, to preserve them from such enormities."

Source: Mary Cornwallis, *Observations, Critical, Explanatory, and Practical, on the Canonical Scriptures,* 2nd edition (London: Baldwin, Cradock & Joy, 1820 [originally 1817]), 2.361–65.

JOSEPHINE BUTLER

The Weak and Prostrate Figure Lying at Our Door

Josephine Butler (1828–1906) led the Ladies' Association against the Contagious Diseases Acts[5] and campaigned for women's rights in education, law,

---

5. Contagious Diseases Acts were enacted by the English Parliament in 1864 and amended and extended by acts of 1866 and 1869. This legislation and its subsequent amendments allowed magistrates to conduct a physical examination of a prostitute for venereal disease. Women found with a sexually transmitted disease were hospitalized until cured; women who refused examination were imprisoned. The Contagious Disease Acts intended to protect men from

and employment throughout her life.[6] She was a renowned lecturer and writer. Though not formally trained to interpret Scripture, she believed that she had a prophetic call to listen to and to proclaim God's whispers in her public addresses and writings. Her peers recognized the fresh and prophetic quality of her exegesis.

As part of her address before four hundred women whom she was trying to recruit to support the campaign against the Contagious Diseases Acts in 1870, Butler rehearsed the story of the Levite's concubine. The address, initially published as "The Duty of Women," became part of a much longer essay on prostitution in the *Contemporary Review*. Butler's retelling of Judges 19 focuses on the "ghastly details" of the story — "the clamouring of the sons of Belial round the door, the suspense, the parley, till, in the cowardice of self-defense, the man brings out that helpless woman, and casts her among the hellish horrors of that awful night." Butler discloses her hermeneutical approach when she describes this story as one of the "many tragical histories recorded in the Old Testament — that true mirror of the faith and the righteousness, but also of the depravity of man." She calls attention to the poignant parallels between the abuse of the concubine and the situation of contemporary prostitutes, declaring, "There is a weak and prostrate figure lying at our door; to this door she turns for help." She also reads the story within its larger canonical context, using such intertexts as Luke's story of Jesus being anointed by the immoral woman of the city who perfumed and kissed his feet and then experienced Jesus's forgiveness (Luke 7:36–50), Revelation 3:20 ("Behold, I stand at the door, and knock"), and the story of the woman with the issue of blood touching the hem of Jesus's garment (Luke 8:40–48) to bring Jesus into the story of the rape of the Levite's concubine. To the poignant theological question, "Where is God in the midst of this horrific story?," Butler answers that Jesus is there at the door with the concubine. Not surprisingly, Butler concludes her address/sermon with a call to women to extend their love to fallen women, outcasts, and sinners, as they too are made in God's image.

---

infected women. Butler and others felt that the laws discriminated against women, as the legislation contained no similar sanctions against men.

6. For more information on Butler, see "The Saving Shelter of the Home" in the Rahab chapter.

There are many tragical histories recorded in the Old Testament — that true mirror of the faith and the righteousness, but also of the depravity of man: few are more tragical than that story in the Book of Judges of the wayfaring Levite who halted at Gibeah of Benjamin, and lodged there with the woman, his companion. We read with a shudder the ghastly details — the clamoring of the sons of Belial round the door, the suspense, the parley, till in the cowardice of self-defense the man brings out that helpless woman, and casts her among the hellish horrors of that awful night. "All night until the morning," she endured, "until the day began to spring. Then came the woman in the dawning of the day, and fell down at the door of the man's house where her lord was, till it was light. And her lord rose up in the morning, and opened the doors of the house, and went out to go his way; and, behold, the woman was fallen down at the door of the house, and her hands were upon the threshold. And he said unto her, Up, and let us be going. But none answered." She was dead.

Christian people! there is a weak and prostrate figure lying at our door; to this door she turns for help, though it be but in her dying fall; her hands are upon the threshold — dead hands flung forward in mute and terrible appeal to the God above, who, looking down from heaven, sees not the prostrate form alone, but on the one side the powers of hell, on the other, in their safe dwelling-place, the selfish sleepers to whom the pale cold hands appeal in vain. The night is far spent. Throughout the world's long night the fate of the Levite's concubine has been outcast woman's fate, cast forth in answer to the clamorous cries of insatiable human lusts, and then left to perish in the outer darkness; while "her lord," ordained her protector by nature and by the law of God,[7] slumbers unheeding. Her voice is too weak to be heard, the door is too heavily barred for her to open, that she might cross the threshold again; her only appeal is her heavy corpse-like fall beside the door, her silence when invoked, and her cold dead hands stretched forth. It might well make our morning slumbers uneasy, and cause us to murmur in our dreams of coming judgment, to know that there lies a corpse at our door, an outraged corpse, crushed with the heaped and pitiless weight of the sins of others and her own.

But the day is at hand. We have slept long and soundly, while that woman bore the hell without. Shall we sleep still? What if the Judge should come and find us scarcely risen from our torpor, our door scarcely opened, our morning salutation scarcely uttered to the victim whose voice is stilled in

---

7. [1 Peter 3:6.]

The Levite's Concubine

death — should come and should require of us an account of our protectorship, and show to us such mercy as we have shown to her?[8]

There are, thank God, signs at last, and in certain parts of the earth, of a movement among the sleepers, a haunting consciousness of somewhat [sic] leaning heavily on our door, a gradual awakening to a sense of pain and fear and duty unfulfilled — nay, of partnership in guilt, with the present immunity from its penalties, which presses heavier than all else upon a conscience lit with the fires of coming wrath, or on a heart capable of a generous sorrow. Some, thank God, have started from their beds and gone forth in the morning twilight to find the prostrate body, wherein yet perchance is life, and have uttered, not ineffectually, the words, "Up, let us be going"; and have gathered in their arms, and have sustained and comforted, and when healing was not too late, have healed.

Yet those who, waking late, are working now, work ever with the sad and humbling memory of past centuries of injury and neglect in this matter. They who have themselves been guiltless of actual wrong towards the fallen, feel the most acutely in the tenderness of their souls the wrong done by their forefathers, who, since the foundation of the world till now, have dedicated by millions these weaker vessels to profanest service — sacrificing them with impious rites to a so-called necessity — a Moloch to whom all the kingdoms of the earth have caused armies of their daughters to pass through the fire,[9] generation after generation. These vessels, once defiled, were, as our fathers judged, incapable of cleansing, never again to be restored to sweet and honourable household use, too vile for hand of just man or pure woman to touch; albeit One, the ever blessed, the only pure, had not disdained to raise such a vessel to His sacred lips, and with richest draughts from thence to allay the thirst of His Divine soul for his creature's love. Nay, He complains of the strong uninjured vessels that they give not as the broken give: to the honoured of men, firmly holding his position in society, "Thou gavest me no kiss," He said; "but *this woman* hath not ceased to kiss my feet."[10]

We cannot know how many of "this woman's" character and kin may not have kissed secretly those blessed feet, even in the darkness outside the door; more perhaps than we, who pity, dare to hope — more certainly than Simon thinks, while he sits eating and drinking there, and shuddering at the

---

8. [Matthew 25:5; Romans 13:12.]
9. [Leviticus 18:21.]
10. [Luke 7:45.]

thought that any guest of his should suffer the approach of so vile a thing; for He who gives his feet to be kissed,[11] have we not His voice to the end of the Dispensation — "Behold, I stand at the door and knock"?[12] His head is filled with the dew and His locks with the drops of the night,[13] and it may be that at the same closed door these two, the slain woman and the Saviour, have met many a time while we slept and knew it not; it may be that those cold faint hands, falling upon the threshold, groping hopelessly, have stolen in the darkness some virtue from His garment's hem;[14] and though the fount of weeping, which despair has dried, may have given no more tears to "distil like amber on the royal feet of the Anointed,"[15] yet may they have been pressed instead with the cold death-dews of a forehead branded with shame and hiding itself in the dust.

Every act of our Lord's, emphatically recorded by the Evangelists, has a deep and an everlasting significance. A single act of his towards a single individual was designed to be the type, for all ages, of the acts required of every Christian in every similar case — a seed intended to bring forth fruit a thousandfold;[16] on each is plainly written the command, "Go thou and do likewise."[17] The Lord manifested a peculiar compassion for lepers, and from that time forth the Gentile Christians ceased to treat the leper as he had been treated among the Jews, and the saints of the early Church vied with each other in acts of charity towards the victims of this loathsome disease, that thus in the persons of his afflicted members they might do honour of their Lord. Jesus Christ blessed little children,[18] and this has been recognized by Christendom as significant of the part to be acted by and towards the Christian child. The Lord especially honoured the poor;[19] so likewise has the Church ever considered the poor her especial charge, and the care of the poor one of the first of social obligations. But how has

---

11. [Luke 7:40–50.]
12. [Revelation 3:20.]
13. [Song of Songs 5:2.]
14. [Luke 8:44–45.]
15. In her unpublished doctoral thesis, Amanda Russell Jones suggests that Butler may have had William Holman Hunt's paintings, *The Light of the World* and *The Awakening Conscience* (1853-1855), in mind when she describes Jesus and the Levite's concubine meeting at the door. See "The Voice of the Outcast: Josephine Butler's Biblical Interpretation & Public Theology," submitted to the University of Birmingham, December 2014.
16. [Matthew 13:23.]
17. [Luke 10:37.]
18. [Mark 10:13–15.]
19. [Matthew 5:3.]

it been the matter of our Lord's treatment of fallen women? Was ever act of His more marked, or more prominent, or more designedly typical, than His conduct towards these? As if to enforce the duty of society towards them with a special recommendation, He is seen, not once, but again and again, by His marked reception of these women, to give as it were to the world a key-note upon which to tune its voice to the Magdalene to the end of time.... [Butler continues by tracing a history of prostitution and the church's response to it.]

Source: Josephine Butler, "The Lovers of the Lost," *Contemporary Review* 13 (1870): 16–19.

Josephine Butler

Cold Dead Hands upon Our Threshold

Josephine Butler often revisited the "terrible and pathetic story" of the Levite's concubine, viewing it as the best example of a representative story in the Old Testament. In her 1898 reflection on the story, Butler focuses more on the Levite's hard-hearted response and extends her exposition to include Judges 20–21, arguing for a connection "between the passions and lusts which curse our domestic and social life, and those which break out, ever and anon, in hatred between nations, and which give full play to the instinct of destruction." She testifies to her own spiritual experience of having had her heart "pierced" by God for these outcasts; blending the image of the "cold outstretched hands" of the concubine with images of apocalyptic hope from the prophets and the apocalypse, she avers that her sorrows will be comforted only when the sorrows of victims are assuaged. She pleads passionately that her readers will hear that voice of the outcast: "O! hear it, I beseech you!" Butler's words of benediction are both hopeful and ominous; her hope is based on God's sovereignty and signs of the coming kingdom, which brings judgment and the end of suffering.

A Typical Tragedy: Dead Hands upon the Threshold

There are certain brief and tragical incidents recorded in the Old Testament Scriptures which are strikingly typical. They represent, in miniature, portions of the history of mankind as a whole; none more so than the story related in the last chapters of the book of Judges.

It is a terrible and pathetic story; too terrible to quote at length in our bald, strong Saxon translation of the Bible. I have never heard it commented upon by any preacher or writer in any public manner; and never indeed in any way do I remember to have seen its terrible typical significance suggested.

Here it is. A Levite was travelling with a "damsel," his wife, or concubine. They arrived at Gibeah of Bethlehem, and lodged in the house of a man of that city. Certain "sons of Belial" besieged the house at night, calling upon the old man its master to bring forth the young Levite.

In order to *save himself* from the degradation which he foresaw from the treatment of these Satyrs, the Levite took his companion, the woman, and thrust her forth to become, in his place, the victim of their diabolical passions. And he! he returned to his rest till the morning. Mark the tragic pathos of what follows: "Then came the woman in the dawning of the day," (after a long night of horror and slow death,) "and fell down at the door of the man's house where her lord was, till it was light. And her lord rose up in the morning, and opened the doors of the house, and went out to go his way; and behold the woman was fallen down at the doors of the house, and her hands were upon the threshold."

"And he said unto her, 'Up, and let us be going.' But none answered," she was dead.

At this close of the year 1898, let me, once more, O! Christian people, implore you to look back over the history of the world, and to realize this tragedy has been repeated all through the centuries; that the story I have cited is the story of the egotism of man and the sacrifice of womanhood to that egotism, invoking a curse which is to this day hanging like a dark and threatening cloud over the nations of the earth.

To what end was this machinery of the State regulation of vice invented and enforced, except in order to save the man at the expense of the woman whom God formed to be his companion and help-mate?[20] What is the motive of all these immoral Army arrangements except to save the health of

---

20. [Genesis 2:18.]

troops of men, by the casting out for destruction of the womanhood of whatever neighbourhood, colony, or country they may be in?

These men of Belial were entreated "not to do so vile a thing" as to harm the man, the Levite. (Judges xix.24.) But the Levite and his host alike accepted it as natural and not so vile a thing, that the woman (the weaker and more delicately fashioned) should be made a forced minister to demoniacal lust.

And it has been so through the long, long night of the world's history. "They abused her all the night until the morning." "Then came the woman at the dawning of the day, and fell down at the door of the man's house, where her lord was" who had deliberately sacrificed her in his strong instinct of self-preservation.

"The dawning of the day," — may it be this day, the present day in which light is breaking at last through the thick cloud which has so long shrouded the selfishness and the agony! In the dim twilight she lay prostrate "till it was light," and the light brought to the consciousness of her selfish lord the horrible truth that he had devoted her to death.

Careless of, or stupidly denying to himself the inevitably tragic end of his companion, he opens the doors to "go his way," and as usual he gives her his orders which she has ever too abjectly obeyed. "Up, and let us be going," he said. Note the callousness, the ignorance or wilful denial of the nature of woman, its delicacy of structure and essence, its liability to swift and complete destruction. "Up," he says, "why do you lie sleeping there? It is time to go on our journey." Yes, you, man, Levite, having saved yourself by decreeing the outcast, can go on your journey. But she, nevermore!

But his lordship over her is at an end. He cannot wake the dead. He may feel some pangs of self-reproach, but his evil deed can never be undone.

"Her hands were upon the threshold." *They are there still.* That corpse lies at our doors, prone. Its cold dead hands are upon our threshold, stretched out in dumb dread appeal to all the families and homes of the earth. We are none of us guiltless, men or women. Our silent acquiescence in the crime of this murder has contributed, is contributing, to the woe which follows and is following.

For, mark the end: a fire was kindled through this one act of guilty cowardice in yielding to the claims of fiendish lust, a war was proclaimed which resulted in the *destruction of a whole tribe.* The tribe of Benjamin, among whom the sons of Belial were found, was cut off. The children of Israel "wept before the Lord" for the destruction of Benjamin and said, "there is one tribe cut off from Israel this day." Though the Benjamites were mighty men skilled in war; "twenty-six thousand men who drew sword," among whom were troops of "chosen men left-handed, everyone of whom could sling stones at a hairsbreadth and not miss." (Judges 20:16.) (What could the right hand not do?) Yet they were "slain with a mighty slaughter."

There is significance in the French saying: *"Cherchez la femme,"* — "Seek the woman," — who is supposed to be found, in one way or another, at the base of every social tragedy; and she is generally, if not always, there; and in a larger sense her degradation heralds national collapse. Lucretia and Virginia in the old Roman times are themselves symbolic of the larger desolation.[21]

Womanhood prostrate, breathing her last, is most surely found on the stage of a drama of the people's decay or a nation's overthrow. There, under the trampling feet of men and armies, she lies, unmarked save by the recording angel; but her dead hands are stretched forth over the earth in dreadful appeal, prophetic of judgment.

Dervishes who for centuries have strewn the desert with the bones of outraged wives and maidens; Turks who have tortured tens of thousands of the women whom they pronounce to be soulless with a cruelty exceeding the imagination of man; — What is their end? What will it be? Degradation of their manhood, ever deeper and deeper, the fiendish nature ever more intensified, until, fierce and unyielding soldiers as they are, meeting death like lions, they will, nevertheless, by a law of their own nature, be cleared off the face of the earth.

And what of our civilized European races, with their refinements of scientific torture, applied in the interests of debauchery? Theirs is not the coarse outrage of the Turkish soldiery; it goes deeper; it slays not less surely; it acts more slowly and with greater anguish for the finer and more emotional part of womanhood.

Whenever a portion of womankind is devoted by the State of infamy, respect for woman becomes weaker and dies. Her voice is scarcely heard when, with pure lips and burning heart she pleads for the release from shameful bondage of her sisters. Every year which passes in cities where the State has made woman its slave for the fancied protection of man increases the diffi-

---

21. [Lucretia, a legendary figure in Roman history, was raped by the king's son and committed suicide, an act that incited the revolution that led to the establishment of the Roman Republic. Virginia, another figure from a story of old Rome, was the beautiful betrothed daughter of the centurion Lucius Verginius who rejected the advances of another and was eventually killed by her father, an incident that provoked further violence and the eventual reestablishment of the Roman Republic.]

culty of her emancipation, because of the familiarizing of men's minds with the horror of this enslavement. Their hearts become harder year by year; their consciences "seared as with a hot iron."[22]

For thirty years past I have pleaded as well as I could the cause of the outcast. The time may not be long in which I shall be permitted to continue to plead it in this world. Pardon me then, Christian people, — and all just men and just women, Christian or not, — for uttering this cry from the depths of my soul, at this close of the year, and approaching close of the century. The happiest of women, myself, in all the relations of life, — God has done me the great favour of allowing me, in a manner, to be, for these thirty years, the representative of the outcast — of "the woman of the city who was a sinner."[23] It is *her* voice which I utter. O! hear it, I beseech you! It is by right of the great sorrow with which God pierced my heart long ago for his outcasts, that I speak; — a sorrow which will never be wholly comforted till the day when I shall see millions of those cold dead hands now stretched upon the threshold of our social and national life, lifted to the throne of God in adoring and wondering praise for his final deliverance. "Thy dead men shall live,"[24] all who have been done to death in sorrow and anguish; and "God shall wipe the tears from all faces."[25]

And even for the present, for the near future there is hope, abundant hope, for Jehovah reigns, and the day of sifting has dawned.

Source: Josephine Butler, "A Typical Tragedy: Dead Hands upon the Threshold," *The Storm Bell* 10 (1898): 111–14.

STUDY QUESTIONS

1. Some of the commentators discussed chose to avoid addressing the violence in the story of the Levite's concubine. Why did they avoid it? Is it still avoided? What are we missing if we silence this narrative?
2. How does Josephine Butler answer the question: "Where is God in this

---

22. [1 Timothy 4:2.]
23. [Luke 7:37.]
24. [Isaiah 26:19.]
25. [Isaiah 25:8.]

horrific story?" What about the other commentators? Where would you say God is found here?
3. Does any figure in this story resonate with you? Do you think that readers' experience of violence affects how they read this story?
4. Mary Cornwallis connects this text with the story of Lot in Genesis 19, while Josephine Butler relates it to Luke 7:36–50; Luke 8:40–48; Revelation 3:20; and other intertexts. What are the significant connections among these texts? What other Old Testament and New Testament passages relate to the themes in this passage?

Bibliography

Primary Sources

Aguilar, Grace. *The Women of Israel*. London: Groombridge & Sons, 1845.

Alexander, Cecil Frances. "Jephthah's Daughter." In *Poems on Subjects in the Old Testament*. 3rd ed. London: J. Masters & Co., 1888.

———. *Poems,* edited with a preface by William Alexander, Archbishop of Armagh and Primate of All Ireland. London: Macmillan, 1896.

A.L.O.E. [Charlotte Maria Tucker]. "Achsah." In *Glimpses of the Unseen: Poems*. Edinburgh: Gall & Inglis, 1854.

———. *House Beautiful*. London: T. Nelson & Sons, 1868.

Balfour, Clara Lucas. *The Women of Scripture*. London: Houlston & Stoneman, 1847.

Baxter, Mrs. M. [Elizabeth]. *The Women in the Word*. 2nd ed. London: Christian Herald, 1897.

Beck, Mary E. *Bible Readings on Bible Women: Illustrated by Incidents in Daily Life*. London: S. W. Partridge & Co., 1892.

Butler, Josephine. *The Lady of Shunem*. London: H. Marshall, 1894.

———. "The Lovers of the Lost." *Contemporary Review* 13 (1870): 16–19.

———. "A Typical Tragedy: Dead Hands upon the Threshold." *The Storm Bell* 10 (1898): 111–14.

A Clergyman's Daughter [Eliza Smith]. *The Battles of the Bible*. Edinburgh: Paton & Ritchie, 1852.

Cooke, Rose Terry. *Poems*. New York: William S. Gottsberger, 1888.

Cornwallis, Mary. *Observations, Critical, Explanatory, and Practical, on the Canonical Scriptures*. 2nd ed. London: Baldwin, Cradock & Joy, 1820.

Dewhurst, Edith M. *The Women of the Old Testament: Outlines for Mothers' Meetings*, 1st ser. London: Marshall Bros., 1889.

Farningham, Marianne. *Women and Their Work*. London: J. Clark, 1906.

G., M. *Women Like Ourselves: Short Addresses for Mothers' Meetings, Bible Classes, etc.* London: SPCK, 1893.

Gilman, Caroline Howard. *Verses of a Lifetime*. Boston: James Munroe & Co., 1848.

Graves, Adelia C. *Jephthah's Daughter: A Drama in Five Acts*. Memphis: South-Western Publishing House, 1867.

Hale, Sarah. *Woman's Record; or, Sketches of All Distinguished Women, from the Creation to A.D. 1854*. New York: Harper & Bros., 1855.

Hall, Sarah Ewing (A Lady of Philadelphia). *Conversations on the Bible*. 4th ed. Philadelphia: Harrison Hall, 1827.

Kellison, Barbara. *Rights of Women in the Church*. Dayton: Herald & Banner Office, 1862.

Lydia. "Female Biography of the Scriptures: Achsah." *The Christian Lady's Magazine* 10 (July–December 1838): 156–63.

Mercier, Anne. *The Story of Salvation: Thoughts on the Historic Study of Scripture*. London: Rivingtons, 1887.

Neyman, Clara B. "The Book of Judges, Chapter II." In *The Woman's Bible. Part 2: Joshua to Revelation*, edited by Elizabeth Cady Stanton. Boston: Northeastern University Press, 1898.

———. "The Book of Judges, Chapter III." In Stanton, *The Woman's Bible, Part 2*.

Norval, Leigh. *Women of the Bible: Sketches of All the Prominent Female Characters in the Old and the New Testament*. Nashville: Publishing House of the M. E. Church, South, Sunday-School Department, 1889.

Owen, Mrs. Octavius Friere. *The Heroines of History*. London: George Routledge & Co., 1854.

Rothschild, Constance de, and Annie Henrietta de Rothschild. *The History and Literature of the Israelites, according to the Old Testament and the Apocrypha. Vol. 1: The Historical Books*. 2nd ed. London: Longmans, Green & Co., 1871.

Rowson, Susanna. *Biblical Dialogues between a Father and His Family Comprising Sacred History from the Creation to the Death of Our Saviour Christ*. Boston: Richardson & Lord, 1822.

Schimmelpenninck, Mary Anne. *Biblical Fragments*. London: Ogle, Duncan & Co., 1821.

Southworth, Louisa. "The Book of Judges, Chapter II." In Stanton, *The Woman's Bible, Part 2*.

Stanton, Elizabeth Cady. "The Book of Joshua." In *The Woman's Bible. Part 2: Joshua to Revelation*. Boston: Northeastern University Press, 1898.
———. "The Book of Judges, Chapter II." In *The Woman's Bible, Part 2*.
———. "The Book of Judges, Chapter III." In *The Woman's Bible, Part 2*.
Steele, Eliza. *Heroines of Sacred History*. New York: John S. Taylor & M. W. Dodd, 1841.
Steele, Eliza R. Stansbury. *Heroines of Sacred History*. 4th ed. New York: John S. Taylor & M. W. Dodd, 1851.
Stowe, Harriet Beecher. *Woman in Sacred History*. New York: J. B. Ford & Co., 1873.
Whately, Elizabeth Jane. "Objections to the Old Testament." In *How to Answer Objections to Revealed Religion*. London: Religious Tract Society, 1875.
Wilcox, Ella Wheeler. *Poems of Passion*. Chicago: W. B. Conkey Co., 1883.
Woosnam, Etty. *The Women of the Bible: Old Testament*. 4th ed. London: S. W. Partridge & Co., 1881.
Wright, Julia McNair. *Saints and Sinners of the Bible*. Philadelphia: Ziegler & McCurdy, 1872.

General Bibliography

Adams, John Quincy. *Speech . . . Upon the Right of People, Men and Women, to Petition; on the Freedom of Speech and Debate in the House of Representatives*. Washington: Gales & Seaton, 1838.
Anonymous. "Ought Women to Learn the Alphabet?" *Atlantic Monthly* 3 (February 1859): 137–50.
Beal, Lissa M. Wray. "Schimmelpenninck, Mary Anne (1778–1856)." In *Handbook of Women Biblical Interpreters: A Historical and Biographical Guide*, edited by Marion Ann Taylor and Agnes Choi, 436–40.
Benckhuysen, Amanda. "Butler, Josephine Elizabeth Grey (1828–1906)," In Taylor and Choi, *Handbook of Women Biblical Interpreters*, 104–5. Grand Rapids: Baker, 2012.
Besant, Annie. *Woman's Position According to the Bible*. London: Freethought Publishing, 1885.
Bray, Gerald. *Biblical Interpretation: Past and Present*. Downers Grove: InterVarsity, 1996.
Brown, Callum G. *The Death of Christian Britain: Understanding Secularization, 1800–2000*. London: Routledge, 2001.

Burnett, J. J. *Sketches of Tennessee's Pioneer Baptist Preachers.* Nashville: Marshall & Bruce Co., 1919.

Calmet, Augustin, Charles Taylor, and Edward Robinson. *Calmet's Dictionary of the Holy Bible as Published by the Late Mr. Charles Taylor with the Fragments Incorporated,* revised by Edward Robinson. Boston: Crocker and Brewster, 1832.

Calvert-Koyzis, Nancy, and Heather E. Weir, eds. *Strangely Familiar: Protofeminist Interpretations of Patriarchal Biblical Texts.* Atlanta: Society of Biblical Literature, 2009.

Carruthers, Jo. "'Neither Maide, Wife or Widow': Ester Sowernam and the Book of Esther." *Prose Studies* 26.3 (December 2003): 321–43.

Carter, Jimmy. *A Call to Action: Women, Religion, Violence, and Power.* New York: Simon & Schuster, 2014.

Carus-Wilson, Mary L. G. *Unseal the Book: Practical Words for Plain Readers of Holy Scripture.* London: Religious Tract Society, 1899.

Childs, Brevard S. *Biblical Theology of the Old and New Testaments: Theological Reflection on the Christian Bible.* Minneapolis: Fortress, 1992.

Choi, Agnes. "Boddington, Gracilla (1801–87)." In Taylor and Choi, *Handbook of Women Biblical Interpreters,* 82–85.

Day, Linda, and Carolyn Pressler, eds. *Engaging the Bible in a Gendered World: An Introduction to Modern Feminist Biblical Interpretation.* Louisville: Westminster John Knox, 2006.

Dewhurst, Edith M. *The King and His Servants: Advent to Trinity, Trinity to Advent.* London: Elliot Stock, 1899.

———. *Sunday Afternoons with the Little Ones: Lessons from Christmas to Easter.* London: Marshall Bros., 1903.

———. *"They Being Dead, Yet Speak": Outlines for Mothers' Meetings and Women's Bible Classes.* Women of the Old Testament. Ser. 2. London: Marshall Bros., 1890.

Dibdin, Emily. *Lessons on Women of the Bible.* London: Church of England Sunday School Institute, 1893.

Doern, Kirstin G. "Balfour, Clara Lucas." In *The Oxford Dictionary of National Biography,* edited by H. C. G. Matthew and Brian Harrison, 3:514–15. Oxford: Oxford University Press, 2004.

Ellis, Sarah Stickney. *The Women of England: Their Social Duties and Domestic Habits.* London: Fisher, Son & Co, 1839. Reprint, Cambridge: Cambridge University Press, 2010.

Farningham, Marianne. *A Working Woman's Life: An Autobiography.* London: J. Clarke, 1907.

Fay, Elizabeth. "Grace Aguilar: Rewriting Scott Rewriting History." In *British Romanticism and the Jews: History, Culture, Literature,* edited by Sheila A Spector. New York: Palgrave Macmillan, 2002.

Fetterley, Judith. "Rose Terry Cooke." In *Provisions: A Reader from 19th-Century American Women,* edited by Judith Fetterley, 343–49. Bloomington: Indiana University Press, 1985.

Fitzmaurice, James, Josephine Roberts, Carol L. Barash, Eugene R. Cunnar, and Nancy A. Gutierrez, eds. *Major Women Writers of Seventeenth-Century England.* Ann Arbor: University of Michigan Press, 1997.

Glover, W. B. *Evangelical Nonconformists and Higher Criticism in the Nineteenth Century.* London: Independent Press, 1954.

Goldingay, John. *Theological Diversity and the Authority of the Old Testament.* Grand Rapids: Eerdmans, 1987.

Gould, Hannah Flagg. *Poems.* Boston: Hilliard, Gray & Co., 1839.

Groot, Christiana de. "Contextualizing *The Woman's Bible.*" *Studies in Religion* 41.4 (2012): 564–77.

———. "Florence Nightingale: A Mother to Many." In de Groot and Taylor, *Recovering Nineteenth-Century Women Interpreters of the Bible,* 117–33.

Groot, Christiana de, and Marion Ann Taylor, eds. *Recovering Nineteenth-Century Women Interpreters of the Bible.* Atlanta: Society of Biblical Literature, 2007.

Gunn, David. *Judges.* Oxford: Blackwell, 2005.

Hedrick, Joan D. *Harriet Beecher Stowe: A Life.* New York: Oxford University Press, 1994.

Herder, J. G. *The Spirit of Hebrew Poetry,* translated by James Marsh. 1782–83. Reprint, Burlington: Edward Smith, 1833.

Idestrom, Rebecca G. S. "Wordsworth, Elizabeth (1840–1932)." In Taylor and Choi, *Handbook of Women Biblical Interpreters,* 540–42.

Isichei, Elizabeth. *Victorian Quakers.* Oxford: Oxford University Press, 1970.

Jessopp, C. S. *Two Dreams: I. Jael, II. Bathsheba.* Norwich: A. H. Goose & Co., 1882.

Jones, Amanda Russell. "The Voice of the Outcast: Josephine Butler's Biblical Interpretation & Public Theology." PhD diss., University of Birmingham, 2014.

Jowett, Benjamin. "On the Interpretation of Scripture." In *Essays and Review,* edited by Frederick Temple. London: Parker & Sons, 1860.

Kellison, Barbara. *Rights of Women in the Church.* Dayton: Herald & Banner Office, 1862.

Kerfoot, Donna. "Etty Woosnam: A Woman of Wisdom and Conviction." In de Groot and Taylor, *Recovering Nineteenth-Century Women Interpreters of the Bible*, 217–31.

Lange, Johann Peter. *A Commentary on the Holy Scriptures: Critical, Doctrinal, and Homiletical, with Special Reference to Ministers and Students*, translated by Philip Schaff. New York: Charles Scribner's Sons, 1871.

Larsen, Timothy. *A People of One Book: The Bible and the Victorians*. Oxford: Oxford University Press, 2011.

Lee, Bernon. "Conversations on the Bible with a Lady of Philadelphia." In de Groot and Taylor, *Recovering Nineteenth-Century Women Interpreters of the Bible*, 45–62.

———. "Hall, Sarah (Ewing) (1761–1830)." In Taylor and Choi, *Handbook of Women Biblical Interpreters*, 240–42.

Litvack, Leon. "Alexander, Cecil Frances." In *The Oxford Dictionary of National Biography*, edited by H. C. G. Matthew and Brian Harrison, 1: 661–62. Oxford: Oxford University Press, 2004.

Macumber, Heather. "Hale, Sarah (1788–1879)." In Taylor and Choi, *Handbook of Women Biblical Interpreters*, 238–40.

McDonald, Lynn, ed. *Florence Nightingale's Spiritual Journey: Biblical Annotations, Sermons, and Journal Notes*. Vol. 2 of *Collected Works of Florence Nightingale*. Waterloo: Wilfred Laurier University Press, 2001.

———. *Florence Nightingale's Theology: Essays, Letters and Journal Notes*. Vol. 3 of *Collected Works of Florence Nightingale*. Waterloo: Wilfred Laurier University Press, 2002.

McKim, Donald K., ed. *Historical Handbook of Major Biblical Interpreters*. Downers Grove: InterVarsity, 1998.

Miller, Nancy K. *Subject to Change: Reading Feminist Writing*. New York: Columbia University Press, 1988.

Morgan, Lady Sydney. *Woman and Her Master*. Philadelphia: Carey & Hart, 1840.

Newsom, Carol A., Sharon H. Ringe, and Jacqueline E. Lapsley, eds. *Women's Bible Commentary: Twentieth-Anniversary Edition*. Louisville: Westminster John Knox, 2012.

Pilarski, Ahida E. "The Past and Future of Feminist Biblical Hermeneutics." *Biblical Theology Bulletin* 41 (2011): 16–23.

Pope-Levison, Priscilla. "Stanton, Elizabeth Cady (1815–1902)." In Taylor and Choi, *Handbook of Women Biblical Interpreters*, 469–73.

Reinhartz, Adele. *"Why Ask My Name?" Anonymity and Identity in Biblical Narrative*. New York: Oxford University Press, 1998.

Robertson, Darrel M. "The Feminization of American Religion: An Examination of Recent Interpretations of Women and Religion in Victorian America." *Christian Scholar's Review* 8.3 (1978): 238–46.

Robinson, Thomas. *Scripture Characters; or, A Practical Improvement of the Principal Histories in the Old and New Testament.* London: T. Bensley, 1793.

Rogerson, John. *Old Testament Criticism in the Nineteenth Century.* London: SPCK, 1984.

Rossetti, Christina G. *Letter and Spirit: Notes on the Commandments.* London: SPCK, 1883.

Scheinberg, Cynthia. "Aguilar, Grace (1816–47)." In Taylor and Choi, *Handbook of Women Biblical Interpreters*, 31–37.

Schroeder, Joy A. *Deborah's Daughters: Gender, Politics, and Biblical Interpretation.* New York: Oxford University Press, 2014.

———. *Dinah's Lament: The Biblical Legacy of Sexual Violence in Christian Interpretation.* Minneapolis: Fortress, 2007.

Schwartz, Laura. "The Bible and the Cause: Freethinking Feminists vs. Christianity, England 1870–1900." *Women: A Cultural Review* 21.3 (2010): 266–78.

Silsby, Susie. "Jephtha's Vow." In *Green Mountain Poets: A Collection of Poems from the Best Talent in the Green Mountain State (Vermont)*, edited by Albert J. Sanborn. Claremont: Claremont Manufacturing Co., 1872.

Slenker, Elmina Drake. *Studying the Bible; or, Brief Criticism of Some of the Principle Scriptural Texts.* Boston: Josiah P. Mendum, 1870.

Speer, William S. *Sketches of Prominent Tennesseans.* Nashville: Albert B. Travel, 1888.

Stanton, Elizabeth Cady. "The Matriarchate, or Mother State." In *Elizabeth Cady Stanton: Feminist as Thinker*, edited by Ellen Carol Du Bois and Richard Candida Smith, 264–75. New York: New York University Press, 2007.

———. "Preface to Part II." In *The Woman's Bible. Part 2: Joshua to Revelation*, edited by Elizabeth Cady Stanton. Boston: Northeastern University Press, 1898.

Stanton, Elizabeth Cady, Susan B. Anthony, and Mathilda Gage, eds. *History of Woman's Suffrage.* Rochester: Charles Mann, 1887.

Steele, Eliza R. *Sovereigns of the Bible.* New York: Dodd & Mead, 1851.

———. *A Summer Journey in the West.* New York: J. S. Taylor & Co., 1841.

Stiles, Cindy Ann. "Windows into Antebellum Charleston: Caroline Gilman and the *Southern Rose* Magazine." PhD diss., University of South Carolina, 1994.

Styler, Rebecca. "A Scripture of Their Own: Nineteenth-Century Bible Biography and Feminist Bible Criticism." *Christianity and Literature* 57.1 (2007): 65–85.

Sypherd, Wilbur Owen. *Jephthah and His Daughter: A Study in Comparative Literature.* University of Delaware, 1948.

Taylor, Marion Ann. "Cornwallis, Mary (1758–1836)." In Taylor and Choi, *Handbook of Women Biblical Interpreters,* 142–45.

―――. "Harriet Beecher Stowe and the Mingling of Two Worlds: The Kitchen and the Study." In de Groot and Taylor, *Recovering Nineteenth-Century Women Interpreters of the Bible,* 99–115.

―――. "The Psalms outside the Pulpit: Applications of the Psalms by Women of the Nineteenth Century." In *Interpreting the Psalms for Teaching and Preaching,* edited by Herbert W. Bateman IV and D. Brent Sandy, 219–32 and 284–86. St. Louis: Chalice, 2010.

―――. "The Resurrection of Jephta's Daughter: Reading Judges 11 with Nineteenth-Century Women." In *Strangely Familiar: Protofeminist Interpretations of Patriarchal Biblical Text,* edited by Nancy Calvert-Koyzis and Heather E. Weir, 57–73. Atlanta: Society of Biblical Literature, 2009.

―――. "Stowe, Harriet Beecher (1811–96)." In Taylor and Choi, *Handbook of Women Biblical Interpreters,* 482–87.

―――. "Women and Biblical Criticism in Nineteenth-Century England." In vol. 8.2 of *The Bible and Women: An Encyclopaedia of Exegesis and Cultural History,* edited by Ruth Albrecht and Michaela Sohn-Kronthaler. Atlanta: Society of Biblical Literature, forthcoming.

―――. "Words of a Mother: Mary Cornwallis, Nineteenth-Century Biblical Interpreter." In de Groot and Taylor, *Recovering Nineteenth-Century Women Interpreters of the Bible,* 39–44.

Taylor, Marion Ann, and Agnes Choi, eds. *Handbook of Women Biblical Interpreters: Historical and Biographical Guide.* Grand Rapids: Baker, 2012.

Taylor, Marion Ann, and Heather E. Weir. *Let Her Speak for Herself: Nineteenth-Century Women Writing on Women in Genesis.* Waco: Baylor University Press, 2006.

Thompson, John. *Reading the Bible with the Dead: What You Can Learn from the History of Exegesis That You Can't Learn from Exegesis Alone.* Grand Rapids: Eerdmans, 2007.

―――. *Writing the Wrongs: Women of the Old Testament among Bible Commentators from Philo through the Reformation.* Oxford: Oxford University Press, 2001.

Trible, Phyllis. *Texts of Terror.* Philadelphia: Fortress, 1984.

Bibliography

Trimmer, Sarah. *A Help to the Unlearned in the Study of the Holy Scripture: Being an Attempt to Explain the Bible in a Familiar Way, Adapted to the Common Apprehensions, and according to the Opinions of Approved Commentators.* London: Rivington, 1805.

Vining, James W., and Ben A. Smith. "Susanna Rowson: Early American Geography Educator." *Social Studies* 98 (1998): 263–70.

Walkowitz, Judith R. "Butler, Josephine Elizabeth." In *The Oxford Dictionary of National Biography,* edited by H. C. G. Matthew and Brian Harrison, 9:180–86. Oxford: Oxford University Press, 2004.

Weir, Heather. "Tonna, Charlotte Elizabeth (1790–1846)." In Taylor and Choi, *Handbook of Women Biblical Interpreters,* 500–502.

———. "Tucker, Charlotte, Maria (A.L.O.E.) (1821–93)." In Taylor and Choi, *Handbook of Women Biblical Interpreters,* 511–14.

Welter, Barbara. "The Cult of True Womanhood: 1820–1860." *American Quarterly* 18 (1966): 151–74.

———. *Dimity Convictions: The American Woman in the Nineteenth Century.* Columbus: Ohio State University Press, 1976.

———. "The Feminization of American Religion: 1800–1860." In *Clio's Consciousness Raised: New Perspectives on the History of Women,* edited by Mary S. Hartman and Lois Banner. New York: Harper & Row, 1974.

Whately, Elizabeth. "Objections to the Old Testament." In *How to Answer Objections to Revealed Religions.* London: Religious Tract Society, 1875.

White, Andrew Dickson. *A History of the Warfare of Science with Theology in Christendom,* vol. 2. New York: D. Appleton & Co., 1896.

Wijk-Bos, Johanna W. H. van. *Reformed and Feminist: A Challenge to the Church.* Louisville: Westminster John Knox, 1991.

Wilson, Linda. *Marianne Farningham: A Plain Woman Worker.* Colorado Springs: Paternoster, 2007.

Wiseman, Nathaniel. *Elizabeth Baxter: Saint, Evangelist, Preacher, Teacher, and Expositor.* London: Christian Herald, 1928.

Wolosky, Shira. "Women's Bibles: Biblical Interpretation in Nineteenth-Century American Women's Poetry." *Feminist Studies* 28.1 (2002): 191–211.

Yonge, I. (Juliana). *Practical and Explanatory Commentary on the Holy Bible: Taking the Whole in One Point of View from the Creation to the End of the World.* London: R. Faulder, 1787.

Index of Names and Subjects

Abraham, 40, 83, 175, 181, 199, 201
Abuse, 192, 243, 244, 246–47, 249, 255. See also Violence
Achsah, Caleb's daughter, 55- 74; dowry, 56, 60, 64, 71, 72; property rights, 14, 16, 56; virtue, 65
Adams, John Quincy, 99
Aguilar, Grace, Jewish author, 8, 10, 13, 16, 62–63, 77, 102, 205, 217; on Achsah, 56, 63–66, 68, 73; on Deborah, 76–84, 111; on Manoah's wife, 205–11, 217
Alcohol, 203–4, 211, 214, 215; beer 211, 214–15; wine, 61, 145, 213, 218, 220, 222. See Temperance movement
Alexander, Cecil Frances (Fanny), Irish hymn writer and poet, 15, 19, 33–34, 194–95; on Rahab, 34–36, 37; on Jephthah's daughter, 156, 195–96
Allegory. See Hermeneutics
A.L.O.E (A Lady of England). See Tucker, Charlotte Maria, 205–7
American Civil War, 5, 156, 175
Angel, angelic, archangel, vii, 7, 34, 36, 40, 48, 90, 161, 180, 201–13, 217–18, 222, 225–28, 237, 239, 256
Anglican, 7, 9, 16, 19–20, 33, 37, 47–48, 67, 85, 87, 105, 119, 132, 136, 141, 143, 148, 151, 216, 220, 232–33, 245, 246
Anglo-Catholic, 13, 15, 33, 149, 156, 194, 220
Anthony, 239. See also Cleopatra
Apocrypha, 121, 133, 220, 224

Arab(s), 116, 120. See also Eastern/Oriental: customs
Ark (of the Covenant), 24, 39, 46
Atonement, 34, 36, 42
Audience, 4, 9, 16, 21, 38, 85, 144, 149, 156, 220, 234; children, 12, 25, 37, 45, 67, 116–17, 129, 162, 166, 197; teenagers/youth, 116, 216; female, 30, 174, 192, 211; mothers, 212, 216
Augustine (of Hippo), Saint, 220, 222

Baal, 78, 95, 123–27, 129, 169
Balfour, Clara, Baptist temperance advocate, lecturer and author, 9–10, 17, 76–77, 85; on Deborah, 76–77, 85–91
Baptist, 70, 85, 174
Barak, 75–77, 80, 83, 87–88, 90, 92–93, 96–97, 100, 107–12, 114, 117–18, 126, 128, 136–37, 145, 148, 153
Barrenness, 203, 205
Baxter, Elizabeth, Anglican preacher, evangelist and writer, 10, 13, 16–17, 105; on Deborah, 76, 106–10
Beck, Mary Elizabeth, Quaker teacher, preacher and writer, 211–12; on Manoah's wife, 204, 212–16
Becker, Lydia, Anglican suffragist, 7
Belial, 249–50, 254–55
Besant, Annie, socialist, theosophist, writer, 245
Bible: authority of, 18, 141, 198, 208; as divinely inspired 21, 53, 58, 62, 115; impartiality of, 90; as infallible, 42;

Index of Names and Subjects

as revelation, 115, 148; as Sacred/Holy Writ, 58, 206; as the Word of God, 18, 93, 208

Boaz, 20, 27, 39, 43, 51

Boddington, Gracilla, Anglican commentator, 9

Bunyan, John; 37, 48. See *Pilgrim's Progress*

Buonaparte, Napoleon, 105, 220, 222

Burritt, Elihu, 228-29

Butler, Josephine Elizabeth, social justice advocate, 4-5, 14, 17, 47-48, 248-49: on Rahab, 19-20, 48-51; on the Levite's concubine, 6, 14, 246, 249-58

Caleb, 14, 55-73

Catholic, anti-Catholic, 16, 69, 93, 98, 141, 164, 223, 224

Children's rights, 162-64

Christian(s), 16-17, 34, 40-41, 48-49, 57, 59, 63, 70-71, 86, 91, 101-2, 105, 108, 117, 136, 144-47, 164, 204, 212, 217, 219-20, 223, 252, 257. See Nazarene

Christianity, 5, 7, 42, 63, 69, 76-77, 102-3, 111-12, 205-6, 208, 237

Church, 7, 15, 19, 40, 60, 92, 103, 108, 112, 138, 144-45, 152, 222-4, 252

Church of England, 87, 164. See Anglican

Chrysostom, John, 223

Class, 4, 7, 17, 63, 81, 104, 108, 139, 199, 231, 237, 238

Cleopatra, 239. See also Anthony

Commentator(s), 9-10, 19-20, 32, 55, 76, 77, 102, 106, 114-16, 118, 133, 142, 155, 163, 199, 204, 232

Common humanity, 1, 13-14, 58, 111

Concubine, 5-6, 8, 14-16, 102, 244-57. See also Levite's concubine

Congregationalist, 192

Conquest, 2, 5-6, 11, 13, 19, 23, 27, 29, 37, 51, 55, 59-60, 78, 80, 108, 144, 149

Conversion, 20, 31-32, 41-44, 52, 58, 63, 77, 205, 208, 222. See also Rahab: conversion

Cooke, Rose Terry, Congregationalist educator, writer, 191-92: on Jephthah's daughter, 14, 155, 193-94

Copley, Esther Hewlett, Baptist author, 9

Corday, Charlotte, French revolutionary hero, 148

Cornwallis, Mary, Anglican commentator, 9, 17, 119-20: on Jael, 120-21, 136; on Delilah, 231, 232-34

Creed, 83, 148, 205, 208, 224

Cult of domesticity/True womanhood, 6, 7, 10, 13, 63, 70, 83-84, 94, 95, 99, 106, 110, See Woman's traits

Culture: enlightened 13, 115; primitive 13, 115; progressive, 71, 120; static, 120. See also Eastern/Oriental: customs

Darwin, Erasmus, 164

Daughters of Zelophehad, 68-69

David, 22, 24, 27, 40, 43, 81, 83, 97, 193, 206

Deborah, 75-113; authority of, 87, 91-93, 107; chief magistrate, 103; conjugal duties, 79, 83-84; deliverer, 86, 103; domestic duties, 83; duties of prophetic office, 101; feminine character, 87-88, 90; head, 91-93; helpmeet, 91-93; high position, 95, 97; household duties, 13, 76, 79, 83, 106; inspired, 79, 102-4; judge, 14, 75-79, 81, 83, 86, 89, 92-95, 97, 106-8, 112, 117, 144, 149; leader, 76, 78, 85-86, 88-89, 91-92, 104, 106, 113-14; masculine mind, 125; model, 77, 86, 87 n. 11, 111; mother (in Israel), 75-76, 80-81, 86, 89, 92, 94, 96-97, 106, 108-10, 113, 124; office, 77-79, 81, 83, 85, 87, 92, 95, 97; palm tree of, 75, 79, 82-83, 87-88, 94-95, 104, 125, 128; poet, 76-78, 80-81, 85-86, 102, 104, 112, 115; poetic inspiration, 86, 104; priestess, 112; private sphere, 14; prophet (prophetess), 75-76, 78-81, 86, 89, 91-92, 95-97, 99, 101-2, 104-8, 112, 117, 119-20, 125, 139, 144, 149; public duties, 83; public sphere, 8, 13, 76, 85, 106; singer, 75-76, 78; song of, 77, 85, 102, 104, 109, 114, 139, 153; warrior, 14, 95

Deborah, character and qualities of, 6, 8, 11, 13-16, 30 n. 9, 59, 75-113; courage, 95-96; discretion, 97; devotion, 90; faith, 86, 95-96. 107; genius, 85-76,

88, 90; godliness, 95; heroic, 14, 112; holiness, 82; humility, 82, 95, 106; intellectual superiority, 87; meekness, 82; patriotism, 95–97, 102, 104; piety, 88, 90, 97, 125, 128; prideful, 106; role model 6, 8, 87, 111; self-sacrifice, 95–96; wisdom, 82, 88, 90, 97, 112, 119; woman of prayer, 94–95

Delilah, 231–43; and Dame Folly (Proverbs 7), 232, 236, 240; prostitute, 231, 233; temptress, 239; woman in Timnath, 235, 238; woman's power, 8

Descartes, René, 228–29

Dewhurst, Edith M., Anglican educator, 1, 204, 216–17; on Manoah's wife, 217–20

Double standard, 8, 15, 68, 242–43

Dunois, comte de, 100. See Joan of Arc

Eastern/Oriental: customs, 11–12, 22–23, 32, 72, 115, 120, 132, 148, 201, 231, 233. See Arab

Egalitarianism/Equality, 8, 52, 66, 69, 76–77, 78, 83, 94, 100–103, 111–12, 119, 201, 204, 210. See Woman's equality with men; Women's sphere: distinct from men

Ellis, Sarah Stickney, 63

Esther, 4, 121

Ethics: code of morality, 199; dilemmas, 6; of killing, 133; of lying 20, 29; moral code, 199; moral standards, 5; norms of society, 1; personal morality, 6; situational, 115, 136; of treachery, 134; two stands of morality, 243; of war, 31. See chapters on Rahab and Delilah

Eve, 2, 30, 57, 67, 107, 216

Evolutionary: biology, 13; model of human development, 77. See Stowe, Hariet Beecher; Progressive revelation; Human development

Exemplar/Example of imitation, in general, 58, 63–64; Achsah, 56, 63, 69, 71; Deborah, 77, 82; Jael, 120, 129, 146; Jephthah's daughter, 162; Rahab, 20, 27, 42. See also Hermeneutics: exemplary

Falsehood/Lying, 25–26, 29, 41, 120, 131

Farningham, Marianne, English author, 70; on Achsah, 56, 70–72.

Female education, 8, 77, 94, 98–99, 119

Feminist: agenda 8; consciousness, 14; hermeneutics, 6, 155; ideals, 8

Forgiveness, 42, 150–51, 170, 183, 233

Fry, Elizabeth, 5, 108

G., M.: pseudonymous Mothers' Meeting teacher/preacher, 13, 15, 149, 219–20: on Jael, 115–16, 149–52; on Manoah's wife, 220–26

Gender, 4, 7, 10, 14, 56, 73, 76, 92, 202, 242 . See Sex, sexuality

Gentiles, 40, 48–49, 51, 65, 208, 252

Gilman, Caroline Howard, Unitarian author, 157–58: on Jephthah's daughter, 14, 156, 158–61, 192

God's attributes: benevolent, 22, changeless, 69, 209; divine government, 50, 98; eternal, 43; immutable, 69, 209; justice of 19–20, 22, 24, 37, 221, 246; omnipotence of, 23; providence of, 90, 143; sovereignty of, 41, 253; is truth, 43, 49, 209, 210, 218

God's names: Almighty, 86, 87, 91, 219; Almighty Ruler 29; Deity, 201, 89; the Eternal, 65, 79, 80–82, 206, 208, 209; Father 44, 61, 68, 103; Father in Heaven, 60; Father of light, 159; Father of Spirits, 57, 61; the Giver 59, 83–84, 65, 79, 80–82, 206, 208–9; God of Families, 48; the God of Israel, 22–23, 26, 31, 33, 49, 80, 92, etc.; the God of the Hebrews, 32; the Great Proprietor, 61; the Immutable, 206; Jehovah, 59, 123, 126–29, 140, 165, 180–82, 201, 257; the King of kings, 194, 196, 234; the Lord God of Israel, 80, 92, 96, 109; the Maker, 29, 89; the Mighty Lord of Hosts, 35; the Most High 29, 206–7, 209; one Lord, 149; Our Sire, 56, 67–68; Parent, 57, 58, 61; Providence 87, 233; the Unseen, 109

Graves, Adelia C., Baptist educator and author: 11, 17, 174–75: on Jephthah's daughter, 11, 13, 15, 156, 175–92, 202

Greek language, 12, 17, 21, 98

Index of Names and Subjects

Hale, Sarah, American editor and writer, 10, 30–31, 234: on Rahab, 19, 31–33; on Delilah, 231, 234–36, 243

Hall, Sarah Ewing: American essayist and children's author, 21–22, 116–17, 129, 162; on Jael, 117–19, 136; on Jephthah's daughter, 162–64, 166; on Rahab, 20, 22–24, 37

Harlot. See Prostitute

Hearn, Mary Ann. See Farningham, Marianne

Hebrew: language of, 12, 17, 27, 31–32; poetry, 77, 80, 86, 104; religion, 24; scriptural text, 116, 142, 162, 166. See also Jewish: interpretations

Herder, Johann Gottfried, 77, 102, 104

Hermeneutics: allegory, 15, 236, 238; canonical setting, 115; Christian interpretation, 217; common relational connections, 14; exemplary, 13, 197, 217; female lens 4, 14, 156; feminist, 5, 8, 10, 14, 18, 57, 157; figural reading, 18, 130, 144, 149, 195, 220; historical setting, 203, 235–36; of informed trust, 18; issues 6; legend, 201; literal/historical sense, 11, 56, 61, 144; literary genre, 4, 16, 116, 156, 231, 236; methods of interpretation, 11; Protestant hermeneutic, 132; spiritual sense, 5, 15, 18, 34, 37, 56–57, 59, 144 (see Lydia, "Achsah Spiritually Considered"); of suspicion, 18; of sympathy, 18; typology, 15, 18, 37, 40, 42, 57–58, 115, 130–31, 144–45, 149–50, 156, 158, 194, 199, 201, 217, 220, 222–23, 226, 229, 236, 252

Hero (-ism), 14, 34, 51, 56, 63, 96, 112, 118, 122, 132–35, 137, 148, 152–53, 156, 158, 168, 172, 175–76, 197, 220, 227

Heynau (Austrian tyrant), 139

Historical sense. See Hermeneutics

Historicity, 11–12, 17–18, 20, 31, 56, 115–16, 120, 132, 136, 149, 232

History of interpretation, 2–4, 53, 76

History of the women of Israel, 206, 234, 235

Holy Spirit: being filled with, 147; comforter, 61; conviction of sin, 215; enlightening 43; purifier, 146; sanctifier 62; Spirit of the Lord, 155, 218

Hospitality, 12, 38, 115, 131, 134, 137, 148, 150–51, 153, 244–47

Huldah, 59, 91, 99, 104

Human development: evolutionary model, 11, 13, 68, 77, 102, 112, 120, 136, 200, 202

Human sacrifice, 5, 127, 156–57, 162–71, 199–201

Humility, 50, 76, 82, 95, 106, 176, 207. See Cult of domesticity

Idolatry/ Idolaters, 75, 81, 109, 122–23, 125, 136–37, 169, 236–37, 246–48

Imagination, 94, 113, 168. See also Hermeneutics

Interpretation. See Hermeneutics

Iphigenia, 201

Jabin, king of Canaan, 15, 75, 88–89, 92, 95–97, 108–9, 114, 117, 120, 127–28, 137, 144–45

Jael, 114–54; Deborah's praise of, 115, 128; deceitful, 114, 130, 135, 137, 149–50, 152; dishonourable, 149–50; heroine, 132–33, 135, 137, 148, 153; hospitality, 131, 134, 148, 153; malice, 134; masculine resolve, 116–19; most blessed of women, 5, 14, 114, 128, 131, 133, 135, 140; mother of Zillah (fictional daughter), 124–27; murderer, 5, 13, 114, 148; non-Israelite, 116, 120, 131, 136, 137, 150; treachery 118, 120, 131, 134–35, 139, 142; unwomanly/ unsexed, 143, 145, 149–50; violence of, 115, 117, 134, 147; wife of Heber the Kenite, 114, 116, 118, 130–31, 137; womanly nature of, 115, 133

Jephthah: book of Hebrews, 156; Cain-like, 180; conqueror, 159, 167, 169, 170, 189; hero, 156, 170; judge of Israel, 172, 189; patriotism, 156, 197; pride, 176, 180; sacrifice of his daughter, 155–58, 162–202; vow, 155–56, 159, 167; warrior, 155, 159, 169, 188–89, 201

Jephthah's daughter, 155–202; Christlike, 175; dedication of, 164–65; devotion, 161; dutiful, 167, 178, 187, 196, 200; feminine excellence, 176; fortitude, 161, 172; hero, 175, 176; model for women, 13, 162, 175; obedience, 175–176; patriotism, 162, 175, 176, 197; redemptive act, 157, 164, 167, 171; sacrifice of, 155–58, 162–202; self-sacrifice, 158, 175–76, 194, 198–200; single life, 162, 164–65; submission, 162, 198, 199; victim, 163, 170, 196, 201; virgin, 157, 167, 169, 171, 178, 187, 193–95, 201; virtues of, 160, 175–76, 187, 198

Jesus Christ: ascension of, 217–18; blessing children, 252; Captain of salvation, 147; cross of, 36, 42, 149, 151–52, 217, 219; and the Eucharist, 220; God incarnate, 204; lineage of Rahab, 43; mediator, 205, 207; messiah, 51, 134, 168, 173, 204–6, 217–28; Mighty God, 218; paschal lamb, 42; pre-existent Christ, 205, 220; Pride of Judah's princes, 192, 194; Prince of peace, 147; Redeemer, 172; Savior 39, 42, 172–73, 218, 252; second person of the Trinity, 204; Son of God, 217–18; type of Christ, 15, 220

Jewish: church, 103, 138; education, 63, 77, 224; interpretations, 204, 205–6, 209; interpreters, 62–63, 77, 132, 135, 197, 204, 205; laws, 13, 120, 139, 199–200, 225; race, 236–237; social organization, 59, 79, 83, 103, 112; women, 13, 16, 32, 48, 63, 103–4, 139, 199, 217–18, 237

Joan of Arc, 100, 106, 109, 145

Josephus, 92

Judaism, 32, 63, 69, 76, 83, 102, 111–12, 205

Justice: distributive, 202; retributive, 19, 221. See also God's attributes: justice of

Justification, 27, 41–42

Kellison, Barbara, preacher, author of Rights of Women in the Church, 91; on Deborah, 91–93

Kenites, 116, 118, 130, 136

King, Frances Elizabeth, Scripture biographer, 10

Language about God: inclusive, 57

Latin, language of, 12, 21, 30, 98, 100, 228, 244

Levite's concubine, 5–6, 8, 14–16, 244–57; and Benjamites, 244–45, 248, 255; Gibeah, 14, 244–45, 252, 254; hospitality, 244–47; Micah's idolatry, 246, 248; murder of 247, 255; rape of, 244–46, 248–49; rights of prostitutes, 8; sexual double standard, 8; victim, 14, 250, 253–54; violence, 245, 257

Locke, John, 228, 229

Lucretia, 256

Lydia, pseudonymous author, 16, 57; on Achsah, 58–62

Lying. See Falsehood

Male and female relationship: equality, 8, 52, 66, 69, 76–77, 78, 83, 94, 100–103, 111–12, 119, 201, 204, 210; harmony, 77

Man's inferiority, 205, 211. See also Woman's superiority

Man's nature, 106, 210–11, 235

Manoah, 203–5, 206–11, 213, 227

Manoah's wife, 203–30; barren, 1; exemplary spirituality, 217; faith of, 217–18, 222; heroine, 220; ideal mother, 14; intelligence, 205; namelessness, 216, 220, 228; obedience, 217–19; paragon of virtue, 220; role model for Christian mothers, 220; Samson's mother, 203–4, 221, 220, 226, 229; wit, 210

Marital relations: concealment of wife's wisdom, 210; equal partners in marriage, 204, 209; wife's dependence on husband, 204; wife's dominant role, 204; wife's influence on husband, 205; wife's subordination, 205; wife's superiority, 205

Mary, mother of Jesus, 2, 67, 102, 104,105, 114, 194

Masculine (masculinity): attributes 76, 87, 88, 116–18, 125; interpretation, 201; language for God, 57; traits 64, 76, 99, 117. See Hall, Sarah Ewing: on Jael; Woman's differences with man; Women's sphere

Mercier, Anne: Anglican author, 147–48: on Jael, 115, 148–49

Index of Names and Subjects

Methodist, 48, 63, 106,
Methodist Episcopal, 44–45, 197
Milton, John, 234–35. See also Samson Agonistes
Mirabeau (French philosopher), 212
Moravian, 164
Mothers' meetings, 149, 212, 216, 219,

Namelessness, 15, 199, 216, 228. See Manoah's wife
Nazarene(s) (or Christian), 205, 209
Nazarite, 206, 213, 227, 229; vow, 233, 238
New Thought, 45. See also Wilcox, Ella Wheeler; Neyman, Clara B.
Newman, Francis, 48
Neyman, Clara B., suffrage advocate and author, 16, 111, 225: on Deborah, 112–13; on Delilah, 242–43; on Manoah's wife, 204, 226–27
Nightingale, Florence, 6, 12, 13
Norval, Leigh, Methodist Episcopalian children's educator, 44, 197: on Rahab, 45–47; on Deborah, 106, 111; on Jephthah's daughter, 197–98
Nursing/lactation, 212, 214, 223, 224. See also Pregnancy

Oath, 163, 202, 248. See also Jephthah: vow; Nazarite: vow
Owen, Emily, Anglican author and composer, 132: on Jael, 115–16, 132–35, 142, 148

Patriarchal: bias, 12; context, 204; patriarchy, 198, 226, 228
Patriotism, 30, 95–97, 102, 104, 134, 162, 175–76, 197
Paul, Saint, 8, 27, 33, 111, 144, 146, 149
Piety, 7, 13, 88, 90, 97, 100, 125, 128, 207. See Cult of domesticity
Pilgrim's Progress, 37, 48. See also Bunyan, John
Poetry: Hebrew: 77, 80–81, 85–86, 104–5, 11
Prayer, 50, 56–57, 67, 74, 192, 205, 207, 212, 215, 219–24, 234, 240
Pregnancy, 203, 204, 212, 226. See also Nursing/lactation

Pride, 39, 60, 106, 128, 145, 151, 176, 180, 192, 194
Priestley, Joseph, 164
Presbyterian, 21, 93, 121, 129
Progressive history, 120, 136. See Evolutionary
Progressive revelation, 13, 102. See Evolutionary
Property rights. See Achsah: property rights
Prostitute, 7–8, 17, 20, 26, 54, 155, 231, 233, 242, 248–49. See also Rahab: identity as zonah or prostitute
Prostitution, 6, 242, 243, 249, 253. See also Rahab; Levite's concubine
Purity, 7, 13, 22, 98, 103, 151, 187, 237, 243. See also Cult of domesticity

Quaker, 5, 9, 91, 105, 164, 211. See Society of Friends

Rahab, 19–54; Book of Hebrews, 20, 27, 32–34, 43–44, 51; conversion, 20, 31–32, 41–44; deception/liar, 6, 12; example of faith and good works, 27; identity as zonah or prostitute, 20, 26, 31–32, 54; proselyte, 22, 24; widow, 25, 27; wife of Salmon, 22, 24, 27, 32, 39, 51. For Rahab and justification by faith, see Hebrews 11:31 (Scripture Index); by works, see James 2:25
Rahab's character: bad, 34; charity, 34, 49; discretion, 31, 33; hospitality, 38; loyalty to God, 21, 26, 30; lying, 25- 26, 41; mercy, 38–39, 46, 50; resolute, 46; smart, 46; treason, 20
Rape (or ravish), 244–46, 248–49, 256
Reception history, 1–2, 5, 76, 155
Rights. See Women's rights
Rizpah, 221
Roman Catholic, 69, 141, 164, 224. See Catholic
Rossetti, Christina Anglo-Catholic poet, 15, 194
Rothschild, Annie de and Constance de Rothschild, Jewish educators, 4, 16, 135–36: on Jael, 115, 136–38.
Rowson, Susanna Haswell, British-

American author and educator, 16, 25, 166: on Jephthah's daughter, 166–68; on Rahab, 20, 25–30, 37, 41

Sacrifice: See Jephthah: sacrifice of his daughter; Jephthah's daughter: sacrifice of
Samson: 12, 203–4, 212–13, 217, 220–22, 226–29, 231–40, 243. See also Milton, John; Samson Agonistes
Samson Agonistes, 234–35. See also Milton, John
Schimmelpenninck, Mary Anne, Moravian, well-educated author, 164: on Jephthah's daughter, 157, 162, 164–65
Self-development, 198, 200
Self-sacrifice, 7, 95, 96, 157, 175, 176, 194, 198–200
Sermons, 9, 41, 89, 116, 141, 149, 212, 216, 220, 249
Sex, sexuality, 4, 5, 7, 8, 16, 20, 78, 79, 90, 98, 100–101, 111–13, 119, 132, 133, 139, 200–202, 208, 231, 242–44, 248. See also Gender
Sin, 6, 15, 19, 24, 41–45, 50, 53, 101, 103, 107, 115, 117, 123, 126, 130–31, 144–46, 149, 151–53, 166–67, 175, 180–81, 197, 206, 212–13, 215, 222, 227, 233, 241, 246, 249–50, 257
Sisera, 11, 13, 15, 75, 80–81, 87–88, 90, 92–93, 95–97, 107, 110, 114–22, 126, 129–32, 134, 136–45, 148, 150–54
Sisera's mother, 75, 110, 114, 115
Slenker, Elmina (American atheist), 115, 141–42
Smith, Eliza, "A Clergyman's Daughter," Presbyterian author, educator, 129–30: on Jael, 115, 130–31, 133, 136, 148, 154; on Jephthah's daughter, 166
Southworth, Louisa, Post-Christian suffragist, contributor to The Woman's Bible, 200: on Jephthah's daughter, 162, 200–202
Society of Friends, 211. See Quaker
Spiritual, 18, 57, 68, 69, 81–83, 85, 88–89, 91, 100, 113, 145, 175, 217, 220–21, 229, 234–35, 242–43, 253, spiritual lesson, 10, 34, 37, 56–57, 74, 79, 138, 150, spiritual sense/meaning, 5, 15, 34, 56, 59, 115, 144, 149, 194. See also Hermeneutics; Woman's nature
Stanton, Elizabeth Cady, social activist and commentator, 12, 13, 16, 51–52, 68, 111, 152, 198, 226, 228; on Achsah, 56, 68–70, 74; on Jael, 115, 152–53; on Jephthah's daughter, 198–200; on Manoah's wife, 204, 217, 228–29; on Rahab, 20–21, 52–54.
Steele, Eliza R. Stansbury, Presbyterian writer of fictionalized biography, 121–22, 168: on Jael, 13–14, 115, 122–29, 138; on Jephthah's daughter, 168–74
Stowe, Harriet Beecher: activist who preached with her pen, 9, 10, 11, 17–18, 77, 101–2, 138, 236: on Deborah, 102–5; on Delilah, 231–32, 236–39; on Jael, 138–40; on Jephthah's daughter, 157, 162
Submission, 13, 158, 162–63, 186, 198, 199, 202. See Cult of domesticity
Suffrage, 7, 8, 52, 111, 192, 200, 225, 226

Temperance movement. See Balfour, Clara; Beck, Mary Elizabeth; Woosnam, Etty; Wright, Julia McNair. See also Alcohol
Ten Commandments, 15, 46, 116, 224
Tennyson, Alfred, 6, 7, 96
Tonna, Charlotte Elizabeth, British author, advocate of the study of Greek and Hebrew, 12, 57
Treachery, 117, 118, 120, 134–35, 139, 141, 233. See also Violence
Trimmer, Sarah, Anglican educator and commentator, 9, on the Levite's concubine, 245–46
Tucker, Charlotte Maria, Anglican author, educator, missionary, 17, 36–37, 67; on Achsah, 56, 67–69; on Rahab, 15, 19, 37–40. See A.L.O.E.
Typology, 15, 18, 37. See also Hermeneutics: allegory; spiritual sense

Unitarians, 224
Ussher, Bishop James, 11, 31, 204, 248

Index of Names and Subjects

Veil of silence, 82
Victimization of women, 14, 18, 114, 117, 122, 124, 163, 170, 196, 201, 234–35, 243, 246, 250, 253–54
Victorian: concerns, 204, 246; era, 4, 9; Jews, 13; society 14, 20; women, 8
Violence, 2, 4–5, 16, 18, 117, 118, 132, 147, 258
Violence against women, 115, 134, 245, 256–57. See also Rape
Virginity. See Womanhood: virginity
Vivian (tales of King Arthur), 232, 243

Whately, Elizabeth Jane, evangelical Anglican apologist, 20, 141; on Jael, 115–16, 141–43
Wilcox, Ella Wheeler, American New Thought poet, 240: on Delilah, 232, 240–41
Woman question, 7, 76, 85–86, 94, 99, 103, 158, 192
Womanhood: emotional part of, 256; ideal of, 201; pictures of, 237; sacrifice of womanhood to egotism of man, 254; traditionally portrayed, 201; type of, 199; virginity, 157, 175, 178, 187, 193–95, 201, 202
Woman's beauty, 232
Woman's differences with man, 7, 76, 94, 101, 106, 204, 232
Woman's education, 7–8, 17, 21, 48, 77, 85, 94, 98, 117, 119, 174, 212–13, 248
Woman's equality with men, 62, 66, 68–69, 77–78, 83, 94, 100–103, 201, 210–11
Woman's freedom: of action, 83; and Deborah, 13; free agency, 199, 227; and Jephthah's daughter, 174; of position, 83
Woman's nature, 6–8, 13, 30, 41, 57, 76, 82, 85–86, 91, 94, 99, 105–6, 117, 132–34, 148, 158, 210, 232, 235, 242–43, 255
Woman's responsibilities, roles, and duties: companion, 250, 254–55; conjugal, 79, 83, 210; domestic 84, 94–95, 99, 106, 110, 210, 228; economic 7–8, 55, 70; guardian of the household, 83–84; helpmeet, 91–93, 106, 110; mother, 17, 43, 86, 89, 94, 97, 103, 112, 143, 168, 199, 221, 227; professional, 8; prophet, 75, 101–2, 104–8, 249; traditional role, 7, 57, 76, 78, 106, 204, 212, 220; use of natural gifts, 79, 82, 211, 243
Woman's sensuality, 103, 232
Woman's spiritual nature, 234–35, 242
Woman's superiority, 79, 87, 205, 211
Woman's traits: benevolence, 87–88; feminine character, 85, 87–88, 90, 176; gentleness, 87; intuitive, 94; modesty, 87; as moral beacons, 7; natural reserve, 88; passive in politics and war, 114; peacemakers, 114; timidity, 148; trustworthy, 114. See also Angel; Cult of domesticity; Humility; Piety; Purity; Submission
Women and war: fighting in war ill becomes them, 95, 100; passive in war, 114
Women as priests, 7
Women preaching, 9, 91, 149. See Mothers' meetings; Sermons
Women's rights, 7, 48, 52, 55, 64, 70, 73, 152, 192, 198, 228, 248
Women's sphere: distinct from men, 6–7, 78, 82, 84; domestic or private sphere, 7, 14, 70, 94, 99, 106, 112; higher sphere, 100; natural sphere, 10; public/private distinction 76–77, 119; public sphere, 8, 13–14, 85
Women's suffrage, 7–8, 52, 111, 192, 200, 225–26
Woosnam, Etty, British Anglican educator, 10, 15, 27, 41, 143; on Jael, 115, 143–47, 149; on Rahab, 41–44
Wordsworth, Elizabeth, anti-suffrage women's educator, founder of Lady Margaret Hall, Oxford, 8
Wright, Julia McNair, Presbyterian educator, social justice advocate, 16, 76–77, 93–94: on Deborah, 94–101

Yonge, Juliana, eighteenth-century commentator, 9

Index of Scripture

Genesis	
2	94
2:18	91, 254
3:15	172
6–8	42
12:3	43
12:11	59
19	245, 246, 258
19:15–25	43
22:1–19	202
25:27	58
28:14	43
49:26	61

Exodus	
9:16	142
12:1–24	42
14	42
24:10–11	209
33:18	208
33:20	208

Leviticus	
1–7	42
18:21	251
19:3	103
26:11–17	107
27:1–5	171
27:5	167, 169

Numbers	
13:30	72
14:30	59
22–24	134
27:1–11	64, 68, 69, 73
35:9–34	42
36:1–9	64, 69, 73

Deuteronomy	
1:34	72
5:9–10	175
20	29
21:10–14	139
22:8	23
31:6	71
34:9	71

Joshua	
2	19
5:12	27
6	19
14:9	60
14:12	61
15:13–19	55
15:19	60
23:13	126
24:15	216
24:20	126

Judges	
1:11–15	55
1:15	71
2:11–22	75
3:2–25	235
4–5	78, 115, 120, 138, 142
4:1–4	107
4:1–16	75
4:4	86, 92
4:6	92
4:6–7	107
4:6–9	80
4:9	107
4:17–22	114
4:17–24	75
4:21	116
4	117, 145
5	75, 118, 128
5:1–31	75
5:2–5	89
5:7	108
5:21	136
5:24–27	114
5:30	122
5:31	152
10:6–12:7	155
11	155, 162, 175
11:30	202
11:30–31	122

Index of Scripture

11:30–40	165
11:31	164
11:37	193
11:38	195
13–17	236
13–16	231
13	203, 217, 220, 221
13:1–24	212
16:4–22	231
18	246
19–21	245
19	247, 249
19:2	244
19:24	255
20–21	246, 253
20:16	256

Ruth
2:1	43

1 Samuel
1–3	107
11:7	247
14:24–30	202
14:43–45	202

2 Samuel
21:8–12	221
24:14	44

1 Kings
11:26–14:20	142
19:18	78

2 Kings
4:1–37	50
5:1–14	42
9:25–10:17	142

1 Chronicles
4:15	65, 73

Job
14:7–9	73

Psalms
16:6	60
25:12–14	219
25:14	217
51:6	135
54:14	59
76:10	142
81:10	61
83:9	136
89:9	136
107:6, 13, 19, 28	107
120	215
127	206
128	206

Proverbs
6:1	169
7	232, 236
7:26–27	239
7:27	240
22:6	216
23:7	146
31:10–31	73

Ecclesiastes
8:17	135

Song of Songs
5:2	252

Isaiah
9:6	218
12:3	62
24:20	40
25:8	257
26:19	257
44:3	61
46:7	123

Jeremiah
31:1	48, 49

Ezekiel
38:20	40

Micah
7:19	44

Matthew
1:5	20, 26, 39, 54
1:5–6	24
5:3	252
5:16	44
7:11	61
10:34	147
13:17	62
13:23	252
20:27	110
25:5	251
27:3	134
28:3, 4	218

Mark
10:13–15	252

Luke
1:42	114
7:36–50	249, 258
7:37	257
7:40–50	252
7:45	251
8:40–48	249, 258
8:44–45	252
10:20	217
10:24	62
10:37	252
11:13	61
16:10	110

John
1:14	218
4:10	61
21:12	218

Acts
1:9	217, 218
17:10–12	15

Romans
8:37	147
13:12	251

15:4	57, 58	**1 Thessalonians**		**1 Peter**	
		1:9	59	1:11	62
1 Corinthians		4:16	40	3:5	58
7:6	149			3:6	59, 250
7:34–35	194	**1 Timothy**		3:15	224
10	144	2:13	107		
10:4–5	146	2:14	59	**2 Peter**	
10:11	59, 145	4:2	257	3:10	40
11:3	91				
12:31	61	**2 Timothy**		**Revelation**	
15:33	169	2:19	217	7	37
				1:16–17	218
2 Corinthians		**Hebrews**		3:20	249, 252, 258
6:17, 18	219	6:10	225	22:17	62
8:8	149	10:17	44		
10:4–5	146	11:11	59	**Judith**	
10:12	61	11:31	20, 27, 33, 34, 43, 47, 51, 54	13:16	133
				13:17	114
Galatians		11:32	156		
5:22–23	147			**Wisdom of Solomon**	
		James		5:15	225
Philippians		2:25–26	43		
3:13–14	61	2:25	20, 27, 38, 40, 54	**2 Maccabees**	
		2:26	46	7:1–29	225

www.ingramcontent.com/pod-product-compliance
Lightning Source LLC
Chambersburg PA
CBHW032002220426
43664CB00005B/114